T0229699

Social Media for Government

Social media are playing growing roles within public administration, and with it, there is an increasing need to understand the connection between social media research and what actually takes place in government and nonprofit agencies. Most of the existing books on the topic are scholarly in nature, ignoring the vital theory-practice connection. This book bridges that gap, explaining how the effectiveness of social media can be maximized in the public sector. With chapters written by leading scholars and practitioners, this book provides practical, hands-on advice on how to: manage employee use of social media sites, most effectively reach the public during a crisis, apply public record management methods to social media efforts, create a social media brand, and provide government transparency while respecting privacy laws. For each topic, a collection of practitioner best practices and tools are included. *Social Media for Government* responds to calls within the greater public administration discipline to enhance the theory-practice connection, giving practitioners space to tell academics what is happening in the field and encourage further meaningful research into social media use within government.

Staci M. Zavattaro is an Assistant Professor of Public Administration at the University of Central Florida, USA.

Thomas A. Bryer is Associate Professor and Director of the Center for Public and Nonprofit Management at the University of Central Florida, USA. He is also Fulbright Core Scholar from 2015–2017 at Kaunas University of Technology, Lithuania.

Social media has, without a doubt, a great potential to transform government and the way government agencies interact with citizens and other stakeholders. This book takes a theory-practice approach and is able to produce powerful insights from government managers to academics and to other government managers. *Social Media for Government* starts building a necessary bridge between social media practice and research and, therefore, I highly recommend it.

Ramon Gil-Garcia, *State University of New York at Albany, USA*

This book will be truly appreciated by both scholars and agency staff alike. As someone who has been immersed in public sector social media for nearly a decade, both as a practitioner and advisor, I deeply relate to this insider's view of managing the opportunities and risks of social technologies in bringing value to our public.

Kristy Dalton, *CEO of Government Social Media LLC, USA and "GovGirl.com"*
Internet personality

Social Media for Government offers terrific advice for government social media coordinators. The real world examples from fellow "govies" is invaluable and serves as a great resource for those just starting out or looking to enhance their social media engagement.

Luke Stowe, *City of Evanston Digital Services Coordinator, USA*

Social Media for Government

Theory and Practice

Edited by Staci M. Zavattaro and Thomas A. Bryer

NEW YORK AND LONDON

First published 2016
by Routledge
711 Third Avenue, New York, NY 10017

and by Routledge
2 Park Square, Milton Park, Abingdon, Oxon OX14 4RN

Routledge is an imprint of the Taylor & Francis Group, an informa business

Library of Congress Cataloging-in-Publication Data
Names: Zavattaro, Staci M., 1983–, editor. | Bryer, Thomas A., 1978–, editor.
Title: Social media for government : theory and practice / edited by Staci M.
Zavattaro and Thomas A. Bryer.
Description: New York : Routledge is an imprint of the Taylor & Francis
Group, an Informa Business, [2016] | Includes bibliographical references
and index.
Identifiers: LCCN 2015030887 | ISBN 9781498704564 (cloth : alk. paper) |
ISBN 9781315643564 (ebook)
Subjects: LCSH: Public administration–Technological innovations–United
States. | Administrative agencies–Information technology–United States.
| Administrative agencies–United States–Management–Technological
innovations. | Electronic government information–United
States–Management. | Social media–Political aspects.
Classification: LCC JK468.A8 S65 2016 | DDC 352.3/802854678–dc23
LC record available at http://lccn.loc.gov/2015030887

ISBN: 978-1-4987-0456-4 (hbk)
ISBN: 978-1-315-64356-4 (ebk)

Typeset in Goudy
by Wearset Ltd, Boldon, Tyne and Wear

Contents

Figures

Tables

Acknowledgments

We are both proud of this book and the contents herein. Our journey toward exploring social media in public administration began in 2010 during the Public Administration Theory Network conference in Lexington, Kentucky. We realized we shared a mutual interest in this emerging technology, so came together to produce a groundbreaking symposium in *Administrative Theory & Praxis* in 2011 about the subject. We thank then-editor Thomas Catlaw for his support of that project.

From that conversation, we have continued our research into social media—both together and independently—that led to this volume. We know such an endeavor would not be possible without the participation of excellent thought leaders and cutting-edge practitioners exploring the ins and outs of social media use in the public and nonprofit sectors.

We wish to thank all of the contributors to this volume who dedicated time, energy, and passion to their chapters. The authors are the real stars of this project.

We also want to thank the entire editorial team at Routledge for their efforts toward making this volume a success. We thank everyone in acquisitions, production, editing, and marketing for their hard work and care.

Part I
Social Media in Government

An Introduction

Introduction and Overview

Staci M. Zavattaro

Warren Kagarise had a daunting task when he began his job as a Communications Coordinator for the City of Issaquah: launch a strategic social media presence. Kagarise, who was formerly a reporter for the Seattle suburb's local newspaper, crossed over into the city government to start this digital communications strategy. Truly, that was the only direction he had when starting this journey toward social media development. Kagarise spent months researching the city's demographics, speaking with other social media managers in the area, and developing policies and practices for operating the social platforms. Finally, he and the communications staff made public presences on Facebook, Twitter, Instagram, and YouTube. Eventually, that arsenal grew to include Vine, Pinterest, Foursquare, and Google+. Viewing the City's website (www.ci.issaquah.wa. us) reveals links to the social sites and a video explaining the city's goals and objectives with the platforms.

Today, Kagarise and the communications team are trying to stay up to date with the latest information communication technology developments. Recently, Kagarise discussed with us how city officials might capitalize on Meerkat or Periscope, which are live-streaming applications that work in conjunction with Twitter feeds. Possibilities included live streaming events such as the local farmer's market, city meetings, or even daily glimpses into what city employees do each day. Some concerns regarding the technology remained, such as privacy and even the necessity of the tool. That is a question many social media coordinators face: why do this? Kagarise details his journey within the pages of this edited volume, illustrating how Issaquah began its social media journey and how the city continues to grow through these various media.

Social media are understood here as "technologies that facilitate social interaction, make possible collaboration, and enable deliberation across stakeholders" (Bryer & Zavattaro, 2011, p. 328). Social media platforms include, but certainly are not limited to, Facebook, Twitter, Instagram, YouTube, Vine, Pinterest, blogs, wikis and more. Criado, Sandoval-Alazman, and Gil-Garcia (2013) define several functions of the social media sites:

> social networking (e.g., Facebook), microblogging (e.g., Twitter), multimedia sharing (e.g., YouTube), virtual worlds (e.g., Second Life), mashups and open data (e.g., Data.gov), questioning tools (e.g., Quora),

crowdsourcing (e.g., Mechanical Turk), collaboration tools (e.g., Peer-to-Patent and Wiki Government), tagging (e.g., Digg), and content syndication (e.g., RSS).

(Criado et al., 2013, p. 320)

The authors go on to note that government agencies should set clear goals when it comes to deploying a social media strategy, lest administrators get caught engaging with trendy technology without purpose.

Social media tools are not inherently social. Designers of the platforms can decide how much—or how little—interaction to build in (Bryer & Zavattaro, 2011; DeSanctis & Poole, 1994). For many government agencies, this interactivity continues to be a constant debate about power sharing and power preserving (Bryer, 2013; Hand & Ching, 2011; Mergel, 2013a, 2013b). Public administrators often view social media as panaceas to increase citizen engagement and participation given that people can use tools 24 hours a day, seven days a week (Meijer, 2015). Additionally, most people can access social media via cellphones, but this accessibility does not cover the entire population (Smith, 2015). Seemingly, social media managers in the public, private, and nonprofit sectors might be using the adage, "if you build it they will come." Questions, however, remain about this normative assumption: Is it correct? Do people want to engage with government and nonprofit agencies via social media? If so, how? If not, why not?

This edited volume tackles these questions in a variety of ways. The book is unique in that it brings together scholar and practitioner voices to explore the growing trend of social media use in the public and nonprofit sectors. Focusing on these two sectors (public and nonprofit) is important given the explosion of agencies deploying the social sites. At the federal government level in the United States, President Obama began his time in office by issuing a memorandum calling for open government, transparency, and citizen participation (Orszag, 2009). Since then, the White House has capitalized upon the social technologies available by trying Google Hangouts, Twitter Town Halls, and We the People, an online petition site that allows citizens to post ideas that, if given enough support, are taken to the president for potential action. Local governments, too, are adopting and adapting various social media technologies with mixed success (Bonsón, Torres, Royo, Flores, 2012; Hand & Ching, 2011; Mossberger, Wu, & Crawford, 2013; Oliveira & Welch, 2013; Zavattaro, French, & Mohanty, 2015).

At the nonprofit level, organizations are also beginning to harness the power of social media for charitable purposes or to increase awareness of issues (Waters, Burnett, Lamm, & Lucas, 2009). During 2014, the Ice Bucket Challenge went viral, with people from across the world pouring buckets of cold water over their heads to raise awareness for ALS, commonly called Lou Gehrig's Disease. Not only did the challenge go viral, the organization also raised $220 million from the campaign (ALS Association, 2015), which an individual with ALS began to raise awareness of the disease and raise funds for a cure. The trend of nonprofit organizations using social media continues to grow. As an example,

Briones, Kuch, Liu, & Jin (2011) describe how the American Red Cross builds relationships with its audiences via social media. Interactivity and dialogue are used, the authors find, to connect with younger donors and volunteers. The challenge remains, however, not alienating older audiences and developing the technical know-how to execute social media properly (Briones et al., 2011).

Given the growth in social media use within the public and nonprofit sectors, this book is a timely exploration into both opportunities and challenges associated with the tools.

Contributions to the Volume

We have organized the volume into two major parts, on the themes of internal organizational social media use and external social media use. By internal organizational use, we mean the way in which organizations in the public and nonprofit sectors are using social media tools to conduct their affairs. External social media use means the ways in which organizations can use the social media platforms to communicate organizational messages to various publics. It is within this part that practitioner voices really shine to give context to the academic writings.

Internal Organizational Social Media Use

In Part II, "Social Media: Internal Management and Issues," we include chapters from Martinella Dryburgh and Karabi Bezboruah; Cayce Myers; Patricia Franks; Staci Zavattaro; Warren Kagarise; Lindsay Crudele; Nicole Elias and Peter Federman; and Ray Parr.

We begin with Dryburgh and Bezboruah's chapter, which provides a broad and important overview of social media policies and practices related to employees' participation in the digital commons. They explore the idea of a digital commons as a space where people can come together to embody de Tocqueville's notion of civil society. Digital commons are spaces where technology allows for the sharing of information and knowledge in a continuous fashion. Using the example of Dallas, Texas, Dryburgh and Bezboruah explain how city officials there are creating a digital commons through various social media offerings. They conclude with an important discussion regarding how the digital commons blurs lines between public and private lives and the influence this has especially on government employees.

Chapter 2 comes from Myers, a public relations scholar, to explain the relationship between Federal Trade Commission (FTC) policies and social media content. He details how digital technologies often confound the differences between public relations and advertising, making it difficult to tell where one ends and the other begins. Within social media, Myers points out how this process often is more confusing when it is unclear if, for example, tweets are promoted advertisements for a particular company or product. While the FTC is chiefly concerned with private business, regulations still apply to nonprofit organizations. Myers explains how nonprofit organizations' social media coordinators can better understand the regulations to avoid potential pitfalls and legal trouble.

In Chapter 3, we continue with important internal organizational policies regarding social media and records management. Franks, a leading expert on records management, details how social media changed the records management landscape by adding another layer of required maintenance. Franks details the rules and regulations that govern public sector records management related to social media. Practitioners will find particularly helpful her checklist for managing social media-related records. Her tips include developing a strategic plan related to records management, identifying records and non-records, outlining a maintenance schedule, and evaluating the entire process to know when corrections are needed.

Chapter 4 from Zavattaro concerns how organizations can develop and maintain a brand identity via social media. Essentially, this is important for public and nonprofit organizations alike to maintain continuity and trustworthiness. If someone comes across a social media site and they are unsure of its origins, they are likely to click elsewhere for the information. Tools from both corporate and place branding can help maintain this continuity across platforms, as well as ensure messaging matches up. This match comes from internal understanding of social media's role within the organization.

Chapters 5 and 6 are our first practitioner chapters. The first is by Kagarise, the City of Issaquah communications coordinator mentioned at the outset of this chapter. While Kagarise mostly details external communications, he also sheds light on the logic behind decisions to use social media platforms in specific, strategic ways. In the next chapter, Crudele tells the story of how the City of Boston launched and used social media.

Chapters 7 and 8 work together to explain the growing use of dashboards in the U.S. federal government. Elias and Federman undertake a detailed analysis of how the Office of Personnel Management (OPM) uses dashboards to aggregate, understand, explain, and share data with internal and external audiences alike. Parr, a personnel psychologist with OPM, gives a practitioner perspective on these useful new tools.

External Social Media Use

Chapters in the next part, "Social Media: External Relations," come from Lori Brainard; Stephanie Slater; Clayton Wukich and Alan Steinberg; Suzanne Frew and Alisha Griswold; Rowena Briones, Melissa Janoske, and Stephanie Madden; Greg Higgerson, Melissa Kear, Maria Shanley, and Dave Krepcho; Arthur Sementelli; and Thomas Bryer. As readers will see, each chapter deals with a specific aspect of public administration and nonprofit management such as emergency management, law enforcement, and nonprofit outreach. Chapters from Bryer and Sementelli take a critical look at social media use in government, painting a picture of sometimes problematic uses of the tools. We felt chapters such as these were important to include to ensure scholars and practitioners alike have a full picture regarding not only the benefits of social media but some of the pitfalls as well.

Chapter 9 details how police departments in the Washington, DC, area deploy various social media tools to engage residents in policing decisions and activities. Brainard uses this chapter to build upon her previous work in the subject, detailing here how the D.C. police precincts have either expanded or shrunk their social media offerings throughout the past decade. Brainard's chapter is particularly valuable given the longitudinal nature of the study, allowing readers to understand how and why the department has changed its social media strategies through time. She finds that police departments might be missing a crucial opportunity to engage residents by controlling most of the conversation. (The #MyNYPD campaign on Twitter, though, serves as a counterbalance to this important point. When the police Twitter account asked people to share stories of their interactions with police officers using the #MyNYPD hashtag, many respondents posted pictures of police using force, thus removing control from the department and placing it with the people.) As Brainard points out, social media are becoming crucial tools for police departments to repair shattered perceptions throughout the country in light of increased police violence.

Chapter 10 presents a grounded practitioner view of how a specific police department has used Twitter and other social media tools to build relations with community and enhance trust in the police. Slater discusses the Boynton Beach (Florida) Police Department's innovative strategies when it comes to engaging with the public via social media.

Chapter 11, from Wukich and Steinberg, describes ways in which emergency managers are using social media tools to communicate with relevant publics before, during, and after emergency situations. They find that most information about emergency management on social media relates to disaster prevention rather than mitigation. Within the chapter, Wukich and Steinberg detail three strategies that emergency management organizations are using social media to communicate with external publics: information dissemination, situational awareness via social media monitoring, and interaction with users to generate real-time information. They detail how each strategy manifests within emergency management, prevention, mitigation, preparedness, response, and recovery.

In Chapter 12, Frew and Griswold provide the emergency management practitioner perspective. They detail fundamental shifts in communication strategies, noting how social media plays a continuous role in this communications movement. They detail several benefits of using social media during emergency situations: relationship building, communication improvement, research expansion, and situational awareness. Practitioners from all kinds of organizations can find useful tips and tricks in this chapter, especially considering that all emergencies are not natural or man-made disasters. Organizations going through a leadership crisis, for example, can take hints from Frew and Griswold when it comes to correcting potentially negative images.

In Chapter 13, Briones, Janoske, and Madden employ a case study approach to understand the success and failure of nonprofit social media campaigns. They compare and contrast the aforementioned ALS Ice Bucket Challenge and Invisible Children's Kony 2012 campaign. Using the concept of hashtag activism, Briones and her colleagues offer nonprofit scholars and practitioners alike tips for creating successful online campaigns, including gaining influencer support (such as a celebrity endorsement), developing realist calls-to-action messages, and responding to potential public challenges in a timely manner. Not only can nonprofit organizations learn from this chapter, practitioners in the public sector can take the tips and apply them within those particular organizations.

Chapter 14 remains focused on nonprofit organizations, with Higgerson, Kear, Shanley, and Krepcho's explanation of how the Second Harvest Food Bank of Central Florida uses social media to engage supporters. They offer several tips for nonprofit organizations embarking on a social media campaign: be strategic with messaging, know your audience, and keep engaging. Readers will be particularly keen on their real-life examples, which others can use as possible templates for their organization's social media outreach.

Chapters 15 and 16, from Sementelli and Bryer respectively, turn a critical eye toward social media use within public and nonprofit organizations. Sementelli takes a critical theoretical approach to explore how social media creates what he calls "branded man." For Sementelli, the branded man (or, of course, woman) is defined as someone who identifies with symbols and trappings. This is not surprising—people have always wanted to "keep up with the Joneses" by driving a nice car or carrying a nice purse. The digital threats to privacy, however, are creating a branded man in online spaces. Facebook algorithms, for example, can track your online searches and then populate advertisements on your personal timeline that echo the web hunt. Sementelli argues that people are inadvertently and willingly giving up privacy for this convenience, and the world can identify them as "branded people" through their online behavior.

Finally, Bryer draws on popular culture to make the point that the "reality" disseminated through social media may be quite damaging to government operations. He challenges policies that promote both full transparency and limited transparency, ultimately arguing for an social media approach that embeds citizen education within it.

The concluding chapter outlines avenues for future research and questions that still linger when it comes to understanding the potentials and pitfalls of social media use in the public and nonprofit sectors.

Conclusion

We hope readers appreciate delving into the book as much as we enjoyed working with all the wonderful contributors. We anticipate chapters in this book will provoke discussion and thought, as well as open up possible avenues for future research and practical applications. Social media technologies continue to change constantly, and it can be daunting for public servants to keep up, especially in the face of limited time and resources. Criado et al. (2013) detail some continuing and emerging challenges related to social media use in the public sector: ability to innovate, effective outcome measurement, user needs (what do citizens or stakeholders want from government social media?), citizen engagement and co-production, and finally open government/big data challenges.

Various relationships exist when it comes to social media use in the public sector: citizens to government, government to citizen, and citizen to citizen (Linders, 2012; see also Bryer & Zavattaro, 2011). Each style requires different capabilities on the part of citizens and public administrators to achieve efficacy. Bryer (2013) elucidates several ways to design social media for civic engagement, ideally leading to empowered citizens who can engage in meaningful co-production with government and nonprofit agencies. The chapters in this volume offer some insights for achieving meaningful relationships via social media platforms, but work remains when it comes to achieving mutual use (Mergel, 2013a, 2013b). Possibilities abound, and we hope readers enjoy the varying perspectives offered herein.

References

ALS Association. (2015). Impact of the Ice Bucket Challenge. Retrieved from: www.alsa.org/news/archive/impact-of-ice-bucket-challenge.html.

Bonsón, E., Torres, L., Royo, S., & Flores, F. (2012). Local e-government 2.0: Social media and corporate transparency in municipalities. *Government Information Quarterly*, 29(2), 123–132.

Briones, R. L., Kuch, B., Liu, B. F., & Jin, Y. (2011). Keeping up with the digital age: How the American Red Cross uses social media to build relationships. *Public Relations Review*, 37(1), 37–43.

Bryer, T. A. (2013). Designing social media strategies for effective citizen engagement: A case example and model. *National Civic Review*, 102(1), 43–50.

Bryer, T. A., & Zavattaro, S. M. (2011). Social media and public administration. *Administrative Theory & Praxis*, 33(3), 325–340.

Criado, J. I., Sandoval-Alazman, R., & Gil-Garcia, J. R. (2013). Government innovation through social media. *Government Information Quarterly*, 30(4), 319–326.

DeSanctis, G., & Poole, M. (1994). Capturing the complexity of advanced technology use: Adaptive structuration theory. *Organization Science*, 5(2), 121–147.

Hand, L. C., & Ching, B. D. (2011). You have one friend request: An exploration of power and citizen engagement in local governments' use of social media. *Administrative Theory & Praxis*, 33(3), 362–382.

Linders, D. (2012). From e-government to we-government: Defining a typology for citizen coproduction in the age of social media. *Government Information Quarterly*, 29(4), 446–454.

Meijer, A. (2015). E-governance innovation: Barriers and strategies. *Government Information Quarterly*, 32(2), 198–206.

Mergel, I. (2013a). Social media adoption and resulting tactics in the U.S. federal government. *Government Information Quarterly*, 30(2), 123–130.

Mergel, I. (2013b). A framework for interpreting social media interactions in the public sector. *Government Information Quarterly*, 30(4), 327–334.

Mossberger, K., Wu, Y., & Crawford, J. (2013). Connecting citizens and local governments? Social media and interactivity in major U.S. cities. *Government Information Quarterly*, 30(4), 351–358.

Oliveira, G. H. M., & Welch, E. W. (2013). Social media use in local government: Linkage of technology, task, and organizational context. *Government Information Quarterly*, 397–405.

Orszag, P. (2009). Open government directive. Retrieved from: www.whitehouse.gov/sites/default/files/omb/assets/memoranda_2010/m10-06.pdf.

Smith, A. (2015). U.S. smartphone use in 2015. Retrieved from: www.pewinternet.org/2015/04/01/us-smartphone-use-in-2015.

Waters, R. D., Burnett, E., Lamm, A., & Lucas, J. (2009). Engaging stakeholders through social networking: How nonprofit organizations are using Facebook. *Public Relations Review*, 35(2), 102–106.

Zavattaro, S. M., French, P. E., & Mohanty, S. (2015). A sentiment analysis of U.S. local government tweets: The connection between tone and citizen involvement. *Government Information Quarterly*. 32(3), 333–341.

Part II

Social Media

Internal Management and Issues

1 The Impact of the Public Commons on Public Sector Organizations

Martinella M. Dryburgh and Karabi C. Bezboruah

In today's highly connected, cyber-networked world, many individuals and organizations routinely engage in online activities using social media sites. Websites such as Twitter, YouTube, Facebook, Vimeo, and Instagram, as well as their accompanying smartphone applications, have the power to "significantly alter citizen engagement, to change the rules of the game" (Hand & Ching, 2011, p. 363) by allowing citizens to engage with public servants at various levels of government. Similarly, social media sites have been immensely helpful for nonprofit organizations as they also seek a higher level of engagement with the public.

As both government and nonprofit agencies are making routine use of the Internet and social media sites, researchers have begun to study the best ways to effectively incorporate online sites into their daily operations. For example, in government organizations, Hrdinova, Helbig, and Peters' (2010) research led to guidelines on how to engage citizens while using these social media tools in a responsible manner. In the nonprofit world, a survey by Steele, McLetchie, and Lindquist (2010) of the Bridgespan Group helps agencies use social media in a way that can create real value for them. Both these lines of research help public organizations develop and achieve tangible goals by incorporating social media into their standard operations.

However, there is limited research on the impact of personal usage of social media sites and its effect on the accountability of public sector organizations. By including both governmental and nonprofit organizations within the public sector realm, we ask the following questions: What is the online "public sphere" or "digital commons" that is defined by the Internet and the public sector? How does participation in the online public sphere affect the players (individuals, communities, and organizations)? Are there costs to any of these parties for their participation in the digital commons?

This chapter is organized as follows: First, we discuss the terminology used in reference to the World Wide Web that connects individuals and creates another level of boundary-less virtual information sharing space. Second, we examine how participation in the online public sphere affects individuals, organizations, and communities. Third, we explore the costs and challenges of participation in the online public sphere. Finally, we make recommendations based on our review of literature and case examples from public and nonprofit sector organizations found in the media.

The Online Public Sphere or Digital Commons

The Internet has been labeled an online "public sphere" or new "digital commons" where individuals can come together to create what Alexis de Tocqueville referred to as a "civil society" that is important to a functional democracy. In a civil society, people from all walks of life come together with the express purpose of improving life for everyone in the community (MacKinnon, 2012). This includes improving life through government organizations and non-profit agencies. The digital commons is a virtual civil society where citizens come together to express opinions, organize over shared interests, and protect their rights (MacKinnon, 2012). To understand how the Internet became the home of a new public sphere and its importance to enhancing democracy, it is critical to understand how this online space and its components were created.

This new online public sphere was the outgrowth of coders and engineers working together to create free and open-source software as well as technical standards that were freely available to anyone at any time. The lack of copyright on these materials enabled the creation and development of software and technology that still remain part of the digital commons (MacKinnon, 2012). When individuals participate in the digital commons they are known as "netizens" and become a part of the global conversations happening in this space.

Beyond the technical standards and open-source software, information and communications technologies, networking technologies, blogs, social software, and globalization all played a part in developing the new public sphere (Kahn, Gilani, & Nawaz, 2012). Information and communications technologies refer to items such as computers and cellphones that allow individuals to "access, analyze, create, exchange and use data, information and knowledge" (Kahn et al., 2012, p. 45). When information and communication technologies combine with the Internet, citizens have the necessary access to information and connectivity that allows them a higher level of participation in the digital commons (Kahn et al., 2012).

The physical infrastructure that powers the Internet includes telephone lines, cables, and satellites. This is also known as the networking technologies that drive the public sphere (Kahn et al., 2012). Social media software such as wikis, Facebook, and Twitter allow individuals to use the digital commons to establish social relationships and share information (Kahn et al., 2012). This includes establishing relationships and sharing information between individuals, various levels of government, and nonprofit agencies that are associated with issues that are important to each person. Information can be shared further across the digital commons with the use of blogs, or online journals. Additionally, globalization is a key factor in the growth of the digital commons. The new public sphere allows political action and activism to grow from the small local stage to large national and global stages precisely because there are no national boundaries that constrain the digital commons (Kahn et al., 2012). In the words of MacKinnon (2012, p. 17), "the digital commons is a vast and growing universe of engineering inventions, software, and digital media content, created by people who have chosen to share their creations freely."

Indeed, one can think of the digital commons as the new public sphere because its audience and resources are not limited to a few select individuals. People from very different backgrounds have access to the Internet and to the information available there (Brin, 1998). Moreover, advancements in information and communication technologies removed the limits of time and geography, which allows more people to participate in the digital commons. The digital commons is a place where people can come together to form relationships even if they are not in the same place at the same time (Kahn et al., 2012). The removal of temporal and geographic barriers is critical to the rise of the digital commons since the new public sphere exists in virtual and public spaces (Kahn et al., 2012). In other words, while individuals can participate in the digital commons across time and space, they "remain at core flesh-and-blood people with physical and often very local needs" (MacKinnon, 2012, p. 27).

According to Brin (1998, p. 150), "the Internet seems to run on an ad hoc basis" where one group cannot claim to have control over the structure because of its diversity. Indeed, MacKinnon (2012) states that corporate entities as well as public organizations can participate in the digital commons in a positive manner. However, if public agencies or corporations behave in an unethical manner, the digital commons is where citizens can come together to organize and speak out against wrongdoing.

As the digital commons becomes more established and part of everyday life for many individuals, many government actions are taking place in this virtual public sphere. E-government, where organizations use the Internet to provide government services, has become one way that individuals conduct business. People can log on to government websites and pay fines, renew licenses, pay bills, or apply for permits, as well as getting general information by using Frequently Asked Question sites (D'Agostino, Schwester, Carrizales, & Melitski, 2011). On the other hand, e-governance focuses on using the digital commons as a way to encourage dynamic relationships between government and citizens where both sides interact with each other. This interactive dynamic enhances and supports democracy by encouraging transparency and accountability in government organizations and reducing the possibility of corruption (D'Agostino et al., 2011). Moreover, participation in the digital commons by governments and citizens helps to mediate the relationships between the two parties, much like laws, constitutions, and other political processes (MacKinnon, 2012). In other words, e-government focuses on the administrative business of government, while e-governance is focused on the political aspects of government and democracy (Calista & Melitski, 2007).

Although there are many positive outcomes to the growth of the digital commons, there are still some negative aspects to this new public sphere. As Kahn et al. (2012) point out, providing access to the digital commons may not result in the public's participation. Furthermore, even when people use the digital commons for political action, they may not resolve issues due to a lack of civil discourse (Kahn et al., 2012).

While it may be tempting to equate the digital commons as a new wave of democratic polity, MacKinnon (2012) points out a few problems with this logic.

First, she observes that the leading change agents of the digital commons, digital-savvy programmers and early adopters of technology who represent a wide range of political viewpoints, may not necessarily look out for the rights of the commons' global participants. Second, out of all the players in the digital commons, whose ideas of right and wrong behavior will become the standard and how will they be enforced? Indeed, "it seems inconceivable that the world's 'netizens' will naturally act, in aggregate, in a way that serves the common good and respects the rights of vulnerable minorities and people with peaceful but unpopular views" (MacKinnon, 2012, p. 26). Therefore, protecting minorities and individuals who are not tech-savvy should be one of the goals of the digital commons. Similarly, it is up to netizens to preserve the rights and interests of individuals against corporations and government entities that seek to exploit them (MacKinnon, 2012).

The new online public sphere is a digital space where people can use the Internet and communications technologies to create communities around their shared interests. This includes government issues as well as nonprofit endeavors. Overall, the digital commons is a place where support, dissent, and radical conversations can take place in a welcoming environment.

Social Media Participation and Its Effect on Individuals, Organizations, and Communities

One way for individuals and organizations to come together to create vibrant communities in the online public commons is through the use of social media software. For this chapter, social media (also known as social network sites or social network applications) is defined as Internet software technology that individuals or organizations can use to share information with others (Dryburgh, 2010). Popular social media applications include Facebook, Twitter, Instagram, YouTube, and Vimeo. The applications can be used on computers or on smartphones, meaning that individuals who use the applications can share information and communicate quickly and easily. The applications allow individuals with shared interests, which include common political or charitable interests, to come together. People can share news and information as well as have discussions on issues they find important by using social media applications.

Effect on Individuals

As the use of social media becomes a part of everyday life for many individuals, the frequent use of social networking sites work to increase a person's social capital (Gil de Zuniga, Jung, & Valenzuela, 2012). Social capital is defined as the resources an individual can access through their network of personal contacts. Social capital and the use of social media can help individuals become more involved in political or government organizations as well as nonprofit groups (Gil de Zuniga et al., 2012). By increasing social capital and becoming more informed regarding the civics and politics in their social networks, individuals can increase their sense of democratic citizenship. Democratic citizenship is enhanced when citizens are informed and knowledgeable about the issues that are affecting the society around them and can become more informed voters (McGregor & Sundeen, 1984). Using social media to increase knowledge of the issues affecting their communities has the potential to increase social capital and enhance democratic citizenship.

Effect on Public Sector Organizations

Public sector organizations are making use of social media to reach their e-governance and e-government goals. For instance, sharing information regarding the activities of public sector organizations may help make agencies and public servants accountable to their constituents because they are sharing information about their activities in a potentially timely and efficient manner. This feeds into the idea of "government in the sunshine" or the idea that government activities should be open to scrutiny and not hidden behind a veil of secrecy.

Effect on Communities

As individuals and public organizations make use of more social media tools, there are opportunities for both to engage in public speech (Shirky, 2011). Furthermore, Gil de Zuniga et al.'s (2012) research has found that use of social media to learn about community-affecting issues and engage public organizations results in greater civic engagement as well as online and offline political participation where people in the community seek to influence government or public policy (Gil de Zuniga et al., 2012).

According to the Pew Research Center's report on civic engagement, individuals connected to the Internet are using the digital commons to connect to politicians and public organizations in various ways. Some 18% of American adults have used online methods such as email or text messages to contact a government official regarding an issue that is personally important (Smith, 2013). Another 20% use Facebook or Twitter to follow political candidates, public figures, and other elected officials. According to Smith (2013), social media has increased civic engagement for the 60% of American adults who use sites such as Twitter or Facebook. Of those using social media, civic engagement was displayed in the following manner:

1   35% of social media users encourage others to vote;
2   34% of social media users share their personal thoughts or comments regarding political issues;
3   33% of social media users re-post information related to political issues;
4   21% of social media users are members of a group that focuses on political issues.

Overall, social media use brings together individuals and public organizations so that both benefit through these interactions and build stronger, more connected communities. As previously stated, people may increase their social capital by connecting with others who care about similar issues. Individuals also potentially benefit from the advantages gained by making use of e-government and e-governance initiatives found in government organizations. Finally, by connecting people with public organizations via social media, individuals can be more involved and knowledgeable about issues affecting their communities, thereby increasing their level of democratic citizenship.

Example: Dallas, Texas

Dallas, Texas is a large metropolitan city that exemplifies how social media can be used and its effects on individuals, public organizations, and a large metropolitan community as they come together in the new digital commons. First, individuals can use any of the Dallas City Hall online resources to enhance their social capital. For instance, Dallas residents can connect with others who care about similar issues by posting to the City of Dallas Facebook page. From this initial Facebook page, individuals can also make connections through the city's Instagram, Vimeo, and Twitter feeds. The use of social media allows individuals to increase their level of democratic citizenship by linking to networks and public organizations where they can make their voices heard.

Second, Dallas City Hall has an extensive online presence that is an example of how the digital commons is used for e-government purposes. For instance, the Dallas City Hall's main web page has links for users to pay traffic or parking tickets, get information on arrest warrants, pay water bills, or look for city employment. The page also has links to additional resident information such as requesting birth or death certificates, public transportation information, and getting garage sale permits. Furthermore, there are links to public hearing notices where residents can gather additional information on city council decisions. Beyond the main Dallas City Hall web page, the city has social media links to Twitter, Facebook, Instagram, YouTube, LinkedIn, Vimeo, and Pinterest (Dallas City Newsroom, 2014).

Before the online public sphere was firmly established, tracking down information regarding government services and activities, even at the local level, was a daunting task. Paying bills, renewing licenses, and getting permits were done in person or over the phone and might involve long and frustrating waits. Now that many major cities have taken steps to establish themselves in the online public sphere, information can be found fairly easily by just connecting to the Internet. Individuals no longer need to be in physical proximity to buildings where they can get city services. People are no longer bound to time constraints where they must conduct business between 8:00 a.m. and 5:00 p.m. They are free to conduct e-government transactions at any time they want, anywhere they want.

Third, the Dallas City Hall's online presence also supports e-governance activities. For example, Mayor Mike Rawlings, as well as all city council members, the city manager, and other city officials, have city-supported websites that provide extensive information on each person's position and how they support the city (Dallas City Hall, 2014). Mayor Rawlings' Facebook, Twitter, Instagram, and Pinterest accounts also share information on how the mayor is working to improve residents' lives in the city of Dallas. Moreover, these social media sites invite feedback from residents regarding what they approve or do not approve about Mayor Rawlings' work for the city.

Fourth, communities in the Dallas metropolitan area are affected when individuals and organizations interact in the digital commons. Online political participation is encouraged when residents are able to comment on the work that agencies and politicians are conducting. Offline participation is also encouraged: for example, residents are encouraged to interact with public officials and learn about community initiatives and participate in events such as Operation Blue Shield (which builds partnerships between individuals, communities, and law enforcement agencies) or Operation Beautification (where the goal is to clean up the city through the combined efforts of residents and public organizations). This online and offline political participation is what Shirky (2011) and Gil de Zuniga et al. (2012) point to as the effect on communities when individuals become informed citizens and support issues about which they care.

Additionally, officials such as the Dallas mayor and city manager are not the only politicians that are putting social media to work on their behalves. As of 2015, Governor of Texas Greg Abbott, as well as Texas State Representative Ron Simmons, are using social media sites such as Facebook to promote their work, connect with their current supporters, and recruit new supporters. These social media sites are helping to connect officials at all levels of government with people who can provide feedback and opinions on their work and encourage a two-way dynamic between the officials and citizens.

Effect on Nonprofit Organizations

Nonprofit organizations have been at the forefront in using social media to engage with their donors and other stakeholders, gain visibility, and promote their causes. A survey of about 500 nonprofits by the Case Foundation finds that 97% have a Facebook page, and 88% stated that email and websites were their most important communication tools (Sharma, 2014). Indeed, a major share of the social media usage among nonprofit organizations is for generating funds (Sharma, 2014).

Consider the immense success of the "Ice Bucket Challenge" of the ALS Association, initiated in summer 2014, that resulted in $115 million in donations. The ALS Association is the only nonprofit conducting research toward finding a cure for and supporting treatment of patients with Lou Gehrig's disease, a progressive neurodegenerative disease. The Ice Bucket Challenge proved to be popular among celebrities as well as regular citizens, where each individual poured a bucket of ice water over his or her head and challenged others to do the same or make a donation to ALS within a day.

This challenge on social media had two important goals—first, it raised awareness of a health issue that affects about 30,000 Americans, and second, it raised millions of dollars to support treatment for affected individuals and conduct research toward finding a cure. The monetary aspect, of course, received more media coverage. This initiative spurred other similar initiatives such as the "Rice Bucket Challenge" in India and other South Asian nations to address the problem of hunger, where an individual would donate a bucket of rice to a poor person or a charitable organization, and then challenge others in their social network to do the same by posting photos and videos. Due to its fragmented nature, any official number of rice donated does not exist. However, social media, especially Twitter (#ricebucketchallenge), is full of examples of rice donations made by individuals and organizations.

The Costs of Online Participation for Individuals, Organizations, and Communities

As individuals, organizations, and communities come together in the digital commons through the use of social media, there are costs that come along with such activities. For individuals, the greatest cost of engagement in the digital commons is the blurred boundaries between public and private behavior when the person acts as a citizen versus a government employee (Bezboruah & Dryburgh, 2012). For organizations and communities, there may be a level of shame and embarrassment that comes from social media campaigns that go terribly wrong.

The concept of privacy is difficult to define because it is highly dependent on the wants of the individual as well as community and social standards. However, Dobel (1999) stated that privacy is the ability a person has to protect certain areas of his or her life from examination by others. In the digital age, privacy has become fluid because when information is placed on the Internet, it may be viewed as private by some and public by others. Sharing information using social media sites, social media applications, blogs, etc., has made sharing once private information deceptively easy. For many individuals, sharing private information online may not have career- or life-altering consequences; for citizens who are also public organization employees, the costs of sharing private information online may be high.

Public administrators may choose to share all kinds of personal information during their off-work time. As they do so, they can take advantage of privacy settings and protect their social media accounts with passwords (Bussing, 2011). However, they may also choose to allow all their social media accounts to be publicly viewed by anyone with an Internet connection. Online privacy may be conceptualized in terms of accessibility, that is, tools such as passwords are the only protection between making social media private versus publicly available (Moshirnia, 2009). Without privacy protections, individuals who are government employees open themselves to scrutiny that could result in serious ramifications for their careers.

Consider the situations of two schoolteachers, Vinita Hegwood and Angela Box. Vinita Hegwood was an English teacher at Duncanville High School until one tweet from her personal Twitter account brought her an avalanche of unwanted attention (WFAA-TV, 2014). The explicit tweet read "Who the f– made you dumb a– crackers think I give a squat f– about your opinion on my opinions RE: #Ferguson. Kill yourselves!" which referenced the shooting of an unarmed African American teenager by a white police officer in Ferguson, Missouri (WFAA-TV, 2014). The profanity-laden tweet went viral, Hegwood was labeled a racist, and the Board of Trustees of the Duncanville school district fired her within days of her sharing the tweet. Although Hegwood stated that the tweet was in response to other tweets she received regarding her thoughts on the Ferguson shooting, the damage was done and she had lost her job due to a personal tweet.

Contrast Hegwood's situation with that of Angela Box, a third grade teacher in Houston. Box regularly appeared on an online conservative talk show where she is accused of calling Muslims "bacon haters" and using racial slurs against President Barack Obama. While Box has gained attention from national media outlets for her remarks, parents in the Houston school district are concerned that her conservative beliefs will affect the way she teaches her students. However, unlike Hegwood's swift firing by the Duncanville school district, the Houston school district where Box is employed has chosen to not fire her. From their standpoint, Box can exercise her First Amendment rights and express her opinions when she's away from work and during her personal time (Gillespie, 2014). In fact, Angela Box has a Facebook page dedicated to her (We Stand With Angela Box), which has over 2,000 likes, and a personal website where other supporters can contact her (www.angelassoapbox.com). This is an example of increasing social capital: Box's supporters are using social media to connect and support an issue they deem important and are making their voices heard through online participation.

These two situations show the difficulty of protecting privacy when people participate in the digital commons. Moreover, they show two different reactions to two similar problems: what is to be done when government employees express personal opinions on the Internet and those opinions may contradict the values of their hiring organizations? The cost to Vinita Hegwood was high, as the Duncanville school district fired her almost immediately after learning about her tweets. The cost to Angela Box was less than Hegwood's; however, her actions have created a conflict dynamic between her and the Houston school district that acts as her employer.

Additionally, this situation between two teachers, school districts, and their communities show how organizations and communities are affected by the ever-changing boundaries of personal and public information. Both women's professional lives were affected when they shared personal information using social media. Organizationally, both school districts were forced to make decisions regarding how they were going to deal with these situations when they came to the attention of administrators. Communities were also affected by the online discussions regarding both situations, in which residents openly discussed whether these teachers' controversial views would affect the children with whom they came into contact.

While online scrutiny by community members can hold public organizations to a high level of accountability, participation in the digital commons can open the door to an unwanted level of scrutiny. Since part of organizational accountability now includes publicly sharing information on the Internet for constituents to see, this means that organizations face favorable and unfavorable feedback. While unfavorable feedback can help to keep government agencies behaving in a socially just manner, it may also be a potential source of embarrassment for the organization and the community it represents.

For example, the New York Police Department attempted to use Twitter as a community-building tool by asking citizens to share any photos they have where a member of the NYPD is featured using the #MyNYPD tag. As they made this request, the department shared a photo of two smiling officers with their arms around a man who was also smiling. Obviously, NYPD expected to see photos of officers being helpful and friendly with people in the community.

What actually happened when #MyNYPD started trending? Twitter users shared less than flattering photos involving NYPD officers. A message offering "free massages from the #NYPD" shared a photo of officers forcibly restraining an African American man against a squad car during the Occupy Wall Street protests (Oh, 2014). Another photo of an officer roughly pulling a woman's hair states that the NYPD will detangle your hair. Finally, a photo with no message depicts an NYPD officer holding a gun and getting ready to shoot a dog (Oh, 2014). Obviously, this is not the reaction that the NYPD intended. However, this is another example of how members of the community use online participation in social media to provide valuable feedback to a public agency of how they are viewed by the public.

There are some considerable costs to using social media in the digital commons. For individuals who hold positions as public employees, their private information can become public and affect their professional lives. For organizations and communities, social media can shed light on issues that may bring a high level of embarrassment to everyone involved.

The Challenges to Participation in the Public Commons

Most public sector agencies actively use social media tools to communicate information, engage citizens, and for outreach purposes (NASCIO, 2010). Similarly, other research (Mergel, 2012) suggests that besides information dissemination, public sector organizations generate information from citizens through social media in order to increase citizen participation and discourse. The challenge is to find ways to encourage two-way communication between the entities that is both relevant and constructive. Although social media adoption by the public sector has been touted as furthering decision-making and collaboration (Mergel, 2013), and organizations often encourage officials to be active and engaged with citizenry in the public commons, there exists potential risks too. As in the aforementioned cases of the NYPD and the teachers, the boundaries between public and private opinions get blurry and can lead to serious issues for both the individual and the organization.

Nonprofit organizations generally promote their causes and solicit support through social media. Employees often are very passionate about the causes and tend to be very vocal on social media through posts, blogs, and Twitter feeds.

Some even have the logo of their organization in their personal social media sites, which has the potential for misuse. A challenge, then, is the overlapping of the personal and organizational opinions and how to differentiate between an individual and organizational position statement. Another challenge for non-profits is violating the prohibition of support of a political campaign or candidate for elected office. If nonprofit employees post about their support or lack thereof for a particular candidate, it can have negative implications for the organization as charitable organizations are restricted from political activity. Similarly, posting or blogging in a personal forum about donors or stakeholders that are easily identifiable and linked to the employer can lead to defamation and loss of support for the organization.

The Challenge of Sustainability

Social media has increased access to government information, long considered significant in the democratic process for enhanced transparency, trust, and decision-making (Jaeger & Bertot, 2010). Such information needs to be stored and archived for it to be retrieved later. However, with rapid changes in technology, governmental organizations have a tough time storing and retrieving files archived in various formats. Similarly, changes in social media formats have also challenged government officials in keeping up with the change. Research (Jaeger & Bertot, 2010; Mulgan, 2007) suggests that most social media adoptions by government were done without any in-depth analysis of their uses and effectiveness. Adoptions are primarily media-driven rather than based on study. As a result, most of the information disseminated through social media has a short-term life, and technology officers within government departments have to continuously train themselves in the latest social media tool in order to engage in bi-directional conversation with citizens. Recent research by Mergel (2013) states that social media adoption decisions are based on information about best practices in their peer network, observations of perceived best practices in the public and private sector, and "market-driven" citizen behavior, which suggest a mix of informal study and popular acceptance.

In the nonprofit sector organization, social media is primarily used as a marketing and communications tool, but this often has potential legal risks. Most nonprofits use social media to generate donations, and 39 states in the United States require some type of registration for soliciting funds within their jurisdiction. Therefore, the simple inclusion of a "Donate Now" button on a social media page can lead to registration for solicitation and resulting legal implications.

The Challenge of First Amendment Rights

The popularity of social media for public information dissemination is evident from the Facebook pages and Twitter feeds, among other formats, of most governmental agencies. This has, however, placed immense challenge on public employees' First Amendment rights. Although public sector employees do not forfeit their First Amendment rights due to their employment, they are more scrutinized for their behavior and are regulated to a greater extent than the general population. Specifically, their freedom of speech may be regulated to protect legitimate government interests. Consider the case of the New York Police Department, which issued policies in 2013 for formally governing the use of social media by its employees, following the resignation of one of its officers for a series of racially inflammatory Twitter posts. Such policies regulate the online behavior of public employees, but simultaneously pose significant restrictions on a public employee's expressive rights. Public employees' and administrators' views on current events posted on social media networks are hardly private, and any instances of bias and discriminatory behavior can significantly affect the organization they represent. Consequently, irresponsible behavior online can lead to termination from employment and other forms of punishment.

This discussion warrants the understanding of public employees' protected speech in cyberspace and the legal limits of organizational social media policies. Herbert's (2013) comparative analysis of public and private sector employee legal cases regarding social media finds that labor laws must be restructured to address the current needs through initiatives such as: state laws restricting employer access to social media accounts; carefully drafted organizational social media policies; training that allows individuals to understand the impact of posts on self and organization; and the importance of legal checks to ensure that the principles of free speech, freedom of association, and due process are preserved as well as providing a balance between employer and employee rights.

The Challenge of Transparency

Transparency is a key goal for many public organizations as they make use of social media in the digital commons. However, using social media to get a two-way communications dynamic between citizens and public agencies requires organizational policies that can help guide communication so that it is productive. Furthermore, social media policies are necessary so they can help protect community members, public employees, and the organization as a whole from negative consequences of participation in the digital commons. Research by Hrdinova et al. (2010) focuses on how to create effective social media policies so government organizations can institute some control over their social media sites to encourage productive civic engagement and mitigate potential negative consequences. Their research found eight elements that are essential for an effective government social media policy:

1   Employee Access—A focus on employees and how they access social media sites. There may be limits on the sites an employee can access during work hours.
2   Employee Conduct—This regulates employee behavior with respect to communicating professionally on social media sites. Policies may provide specific examples of unprofessional conduct or refer the employee to an existing ethical or other professional code of conduct.

3 Social Media Content—This area specifies how the content of social media sites will be created as well as how content is managed.

4 Security of Social Media Sites—Security concerns for public organizations focus on both technological (securing passwords and ensuring the security of websites) and behavioral security (online harassment, bullying).

5 Legal Issues—Social media policies often include language that reminds employees of their legal duties, such as copyright and privacy laws, and records management when engaged on social media sites.

6 Citizen Conduct on Social Media Sites—This section reminds citizens that there are rules of conduct pertaining to offensive language or the promotion of illegal activities when they participate in government media sites.

7 Account Management—This part of the policy allows government agencies to control the message they are sending to others by clearly defining how social media accounts are created, maintained, and destroyed.

8 Acceptable Use of Social Media—Acceptable use wording explains an agency's position on how its resources will be used when accessing social media.

These elements are limited to social media policies at the organizational level, but do not address social media usage by public employees in their personal time using their personal computers and mobile devices. Bezboruah and Dryburgh (2012) found that 20 city governments had distinct social media policies online. Now, most governmental agencies have such policies to address the growing issue of cyber behavior. These policies are put in place to help everyone who participates in the digital commons be transparent on how behavior is regulated on organizational social media sites.

Recommendations

The use of social media by individuals, organizations, and communities in the digital commons is increasing at a rapid pace. This use can bring about positive benefits such as increases in social capital and civic engagement, and higher rates of participation in online and offline political activities. However, challenges do exist such as how to foster positive engagement, protecting the First Amendment rights of public employees, how to properly sustain information when technology changes at a rapid pace, and how to ensure transparency between stakeholders when they engage each other using social media. The costs related to improper use of social media can be high, such as when online activities affect the real lives of individuals and bring embarrassment to organizations and communities. Therefore, the following recommendations are suggested.

Public and Private Conduct Are Synonymous

Public and nonprofit sector employees must maintain professionalism while using employer social media (Hrdinova et al., 2010). Additionally, while using private social media during personal time, such employees must behave in a manner appropriate for public scrutiny. With most agencies implementing social media policies that encourage transparency, honesty, privacy, security, and professionalism, employees need to be mindful of such policies while posting or blogging about issues. Some organizational social media policies ask that public employees add disclaimers to their personal web pages to reiterate that the opinions expressed are their own. In spite of the presence of disclaimers, it is easy to relate content to the organization, which could lead to defamation and sometime litigation. It is therefore suggested that public employees must be aware that the boundary between public and private is very negligible and take appropriate measures to maintain professional integrity in both the public and personal online realm.

High Ethical Standards

Public and nonprofit sector employees, due to the nature of their employment, are held to higher ethical standards than the private sector. Such employees must be prudent in their use of language in both public and private spheres. As Hrdinova et al. (2010) asserted, account management is also an important element in a social media policy. It is crucial to define who can create, maintain, and destroy employees' social media sites.

For example, after a tweet regarding drinking beer was accidently posted on the Red Cross account, the nonprofit had to get involved in damage control. The learning point in this case is that the Red Cross responded to this negative post with a humorous one, but did admit that the original post was supposed to be for a personal tweet. Later, media coverage of this accident caused a pledge campaign from the beer-making company, bars, and private donors, and #gettingslizzard, a reference to drinking too much, trended on Twitter and resulted in donations. In the same vein, policies must clearly explain the expectations regarding employee conduct during their professional and personal lives using professional or personal equipment. The accessibility of social media sites in smartphones and hand-held gadgets results in more impulsive posts on social media. Organizations can benefit from encouraging employees to exercise good judgment and common sense when using social media sites during their personal time.

Evolving Policies

Organizational policies must be aligned to the evolving trends in social media tools and usage. As Hrdinova et al. (2010) found, employee access is one of the crucial parts of an effective social media policy. An organizational social policy may choose to limit or prohibit usage of social media during work hours using employer technologies, as well as limit their access to social media during work hours even when they are using their personal technologies. With rapid evolution of social media tools' access and usage, organizational policies may need to be rewritten to address the needs and clearly transmit the expectations to the employees. In the case of the Red Cross's fiasco with the rogue tweet from an employee, the organization responded in a timely manner within about an hour. Yet, this accident was retweeted and covered in the media well enough to bring dishonor to the reputable organization. The timely apology and admittance of mistake by the social media director of the Red Cross as well as the use of humor helped reduce embarrassment and solidify leadership in the online sphere.

Communication and Training

A crucial part of social media policy dissemination within the organization is the communication and training of employees regarding the use of social media. Reminding employees of their legal duties is another necessary social media policy element (Hrdinova et al., 2010). When employees participate in professional social networking sites, they are required to follow the laws, especially laws that deal with software and copyright as well as rights to speech and expression. In this information age, public and nonprofit employers must remind their employees to judiciously post content regarding their involvement in activities on personal social media sites that can negatively impact their organizations. Additionally, training on acceptable social media usage must be provided to communicate the expectations of model behavior in online forums.

Conclusion

Social media has been adopted and used by a vast number of public and non-profit organizations. As evidenced from the way public organizations disseminate information, update citizens regarding emergencies, and use it as an outreach tool, social media can be immensely effective if implemented in a prudent manner. Similarly, nonprofit organizations use social media to connect with stakeholders, collaborate with other organizations and citizens, advocate for their causes, and generate funds. While the adoption of social media tools can benefit the organizations, it can be risky too. This chapter details some of the costs to public and nonprofit sector organizations and their employees as a consequence of unprofessional and negligent behavior while participating in electronic social media. We recommend that public and nonprofit sector organizations and their workers employ good judgment and professional behavior when participating in social media regardless of work or personal time. This is because public and nonprofit sector employees are held to a higher standard due to the nature of their employment—they work for the benefit of the public, and are held accountable as such. Therefore, despite having freedom of speech and expression, these individuals might best demonstrate unbiased attitudes and strive for excellence in their personal and professional lives.

References

Bezboruah, K., & Dryburgh, M. (2012). Popularity of social media sites and its impact on administrative accountability: An exploration of theory and practice. *International Journal of Organizational Theory and Behavior, 15*(4), 469–495.

Brin, D. (1998). *The transparent society.* New York: Basic Books.

Bussing, H. (2011). Employee privacy 3: Social media. *HR Examiner* (Online). Retrieved December 1, 2014, from www.hrexaminer.com/employee-privacy-3%E2%80%94social-media.

Calista, D. J., & Melitski, J. (2007). E-government and e-governance: Converging constructs of public sector information and communications technologies. *Public Administration Quarterly, 31*(1/2), 97–120.

D'Agostino, M. J., Schwester, R., Carrizales, T., & Melitski, J. (2011). A study of e-government and e-governance: An empirical examination of municipal websites. *Public Administration Quarterly, 35*(1), 3–25.

Dallas City Hall. (2014). City of Dallas. Retrieved January 29, 2015, from www.dallascityhall.com.

Dallas City Newsroom. (2014). Civic media feed: To engage, enlighten, and empower you to become connected with your city. Retrieved January 30, 2015, from www.dallascitynewsroom.com.

Dobel, J. P. (1999). *Public integrity.* Baltimore, MD: Johns Hopkins University Press.

Dryburgh, M. (2010). *Public virtue, cyber vice: Rethinking public service ethics in the age of the internet.* Doctoral dissertation, University of Texas.

Gil de Zuniga, H., Jung, N., & Valenzuela, S. (2012). Social media use for news and individuals' social capital, civic engagement and political participation. *Journal of Computer-Mediated Communication, 17*(3), 319–336.

Gillespie, L. (2014). HISD teacher under scrutiny for comments. *Houston Chronicle Online.* Retrieved on January 29, 2015, from www.chron.com/news/houston-texas/houston/article/HISD-teacher-under-scrutiny-for-comments-5894201.php.

Hand, L. C., & Ching, B. D. (2011). You have one friend request: An exploration of power and citizen engagement in local governments' use of social media. *Administrative Theory and Praxis, 33*(3), 362–382.

Herbert, W. A. (2013). Can't escape from the memory: Social media and public sector labor law. Retrieved December 29, 2014, from www.americanbar.org/content/dam/aba/events/labor_law/2013/04/aba_national_symposiumontechnologyinlaboremployment law/12_herbertpanel.authcheckdam.pdf.

Hrdinova, J., Helbig, N., & Peters, C. S. (2010). Designing social media policy for government: Eight essential elements. Albany, NY Center for Technology in Government, University of Albany. Retrieved October 3, 2011, from www.ctg.albany.edu/publications/guides/social_meda_policy/social_media_policy.pdf.

Jaeger, P. T., & Bertot, J. C. (2010). Transparency and technological change: Ensuring equal and sustained public access to government information. *Government Information Quarterly, 27,* 371–376.

Kahn, M. Z., Gilani, I. S., & Nawaz, A. (2012). From Habermas model to the new public sphere: A paradigm shift. *Global Journal of Human Social Science, 12*(5), 43–51.

MacKinnon, R. (2012). *Consent of the networked: The worldwide struggle for internet freedom.* New York: Basic Books.

McGregor, E. B., & Sundeen, R. (1984). The great paradox of democratic citizenship and public personnel administration. *Public Administration Review, 44* (Special Issue), 126–135.

Mergel, I. (2012). The social media innovation challenge in the public sector. *Information Polity: The International Journal of Government & Democracy in the Information Age*, 17, 281–292.

Mergel, I. (2013). Social medial adoption and resulting tactics in the U.S. federal government. *Government Information Quarterly*, 30(2), 123–130.

Moshirnia, A. (2009). Employee privacy and social networks: The case for a new don't ask don't tell. Retrieved December 1, 2014, from www.citmedialaw.org/blog/2009/employee-privacy-and-social-networks-case-new-don%E2%80%99t-ask-don%E2%80%99t-tell.

Mulgan, R. (2007). Truth in government and the politicization of public service advice. *Public Administration*, 85, 569–586.

NASCIO. (2010). A national survey of social media in state government. Retrieved December 16, 2014, from www.nascio.org/publications/documents/nascio-socialmedia.pdf.

Oh, I. (2014). This NYPD idea backfired horribly on Twitter. *Huffington Post*. Retrieved November 30, 2014, from www.huffingtonpost.com/2014/04/22/mynypd-nypd-twitter_n_5193523.html.

Sharma, R. (2014). How nonprofits use social media to engage with their communities. *Nonprofit Quarterly*. Retrieved December 16, 2014, from https://nonprofitquarterly.org/management/23837-how-nonprofits-use-social-media-to-engage-with-their-communities.html.

Shirky, C. (2011). The political power of social media: Technology, the public sphere, and political change. *Foreign Affairs*, 90(1), 28–41.

Smith, A. (2013). *Civic engagement in the digital age: Online and offline political engagement*. Pew Research Center. Retrieved November 30, 2014, from www.pewinternet.org/2013/04/25/civic-engagement-in-the-digital-age.

Solomon, D. (2014). A Houston third grade teacher is in trouble for making racial slurs on a public access show. *Texas Monthly* Online. Retrieved December 1, 2014, from www.texasmonthly.com/daily-post/houston-third-grade-teacher-trouble-making-racial-slurs-public-access-show.

Steele, R., McLetchie, S., & Lindquist, C. (2010). *Getting social media right: A short guide for nonprofit organizations*. New York: The Bridgespan Group.

WFAA-TV. (2014). School board fires Texas teacher over Ferguson tweet. *USA Today* Online. Retrieved December 1, 2014, from www.usatoday.com/story/news/nation/2014/11/14/texas-teacher-fired-ferguson-tweet/19020821.

2 Disclosure in Online Promotions

The Effect of FTC Guidelines on Digital Public Relations and Advertising

Cayce Myers

Producing online content that can appeal directly to consumers and cut through digital clutter is a difficult task. There is the issue of having to compete with too much information as well as the issue of choosing the right platform to disseminate content. Social media, portable devices, and sophisticated website creation have been a blessing and curse to online content production. The benefit of these changes is that web content is now more sophisticated than ever. The downside is that this sophisticated content may get organizations in legal trouble with the Federal Trade Commission (FTC). This chapter examines the legal downside of online promotional content and how the FTC is attempting to regulate public relations, marketing, and advertising online.

One of the most important aspects of today's new digital reality is that old definitions of marketing, public relations, and advertising that focus on product awareness, persuasion, and brand management are largely irrelevant because they do not specifically focus on the newness of social media as a communication medium. The introduction of social media into public relations practice has changed the historical distinctions between advertising and PR. In the past the most obvious difference between the two communication forms was paid versus unpaid promotions. Social media has rendered this distinction between the two forms of communication arbitrary because social media accounts are typically free to set up and maintain. In fact, the blurring of public relations and advertising is reflected in new all-compassing language of strategic communications. Both fields now use social media as a method to reach out to publics or customers to maintain brands' or organizations' digital image.

All of the change in the field of communication has not occurred within a vacuum. Aside from the changes that have occurred in professional identities within communications practice, social media has caused a change in the legal world. As it has in previous decades, the law has developed in reaction to technological advancement. Because of this, law is frequently in the position of catching up to the technological realities of our time. Laws affecting social media are no different. Since the introduction of social media in the 2000s, laws ranging from employee speech to political communication have been created in reaction to widespread social media use. For instance, the National Labor Relations Board began providing limits on how employees could be reprimanded for social media workplace complaints (*Hispanics United of Buffalo v. Carlos Ortiz,*

2012). At the state level there have been new laws protecting employees' right to maintain social media privacy in job interviews (Utah Stat. Ann. §38-48-202). Both U.S. federal and state jurisdictions began to determine when social media accounts created by workers become the legal property of their employers (*Eagle v. Morgan et al.*, 2011, 2013; *PhoneDog v. Kravitz*, 2011, 2012).

Because of these legal changes it is important for public relations practitioners, or workers in any communications practice, to stay abreast of current legal developments. Additionally, it is equally important for the creators of laws, whether it be legislatures, courts, or agencies, to understand how new technologies work so laws can be properly tailored to the technological realities they attempt to regulate (Myers, 2014; Myers & Lariscy, 2013).

This chapter addresses this new legal and technological reality that has occurred in light of new FTC regulations concerning social media promotions. In 2000 and 2013 the FTC issued guidelines concerning how and when social media can be used for promotional purposes. While these new guidelines are general suggestions for practice and not laws, they provide an insight into how the FTC may regulate social media in the future. This chapter begins by explaining the role the FTC plays in developing laws that affect commercial content. Next, the FTC guidelines published in 2000 and 2013 concerning online promotions, specifically social media promotion, are examined. This chapter concludes by providing normative suggestions for public relations practitioners, lawmakers, nonprofits, and public sector organizations on how these new guidelines will affect online content as well as regulate social media promotions. This chapter not only intends for practitioners to be aware of the current realities of FTC social media regulation, but also presents practitioners and lawmakers with predictions in how future laws concerning social media promotions may develop.

The Powers and Function of the Federal Trade Commission

Created during the first term of Woodrow Wilson's administration, the Federal Trade Commission was established to protect consumers from unfair commercial speech. Today, the FTC is an independent agency within the U.S. government with a complex system of management that includes investigation and adjudicative functions. To understand the FTC it is necessary to understand how it functions as an agency, as well as how the agency interprets its own role in the U.S. economy.

The structure of the FTC is similar to other large federal agencies. At the head of the agency is a five-member board that is appointed by the President of the United States. From this board a Chairman is chosen to lead the commission. The board consists of members of both political parties and at no time can it consist of more than three members of the same party (15 U.S.C. §41). There are also three bureaus within the FTC that have different functions. The Bureau of Economics examines FTC rules and regulations. The Bureau of Competition examines mergers and acquisitions to see if such conglomerations violate antitrust laws. Most important to advertising and public relations is the Bureau of

Consumer Affairs, which investigates promotional materials and determines how these promotional materials may affect consumers. The power of the FTC stems from its investigation and adjudication powers. FTC power is expansive and when an investigation is commenced against an organization the FTC has subpoena power to force organizations to turn over information.

The FTC both investigates and regulates "unfair and deceptive acts or practices in an affecting commerce" that affect consumers in all areas of commerce except in financial institutions, credit unions, and common carriers (15 U.S.C. §45(a)(1)). When a claim is made that an organization or person is engaging in "unfair acts and practices," particularly unfair advertising and promotion, the FTC investigates this claim (15 U.S.C. §45(a)(1)). After the investigation the agency may have a hearing on the matter where an Administrative Law Judge (ALJ) will hear the matter and make a decision. If the party accused of violating these laws is unhappy with the ALJ's decision, the party can appeal the decision to the FTC Commission. Finally, a Commission decision can be appealed through the federal district and appellate courts only after all appeals within the FTC have been exhausted. If the FTC finds any misconduct the organization found liable can be subject to civil penalties of up to $10,000 per violation and up to one year in prison (15 U.S.C. §54). This means that taking a case through the entire appeals process is a lengthy and expensive process (15 U.S.C. §45).

The FTC's ability to regulate promotional materials is broad. Under 15 U.S.C. §55 "false advertisement" has a broad definition. The federal code states:

> The term "false advertisement" means an advertisement, other than labeling, which is misleading in a material respect; and in determining whether any advertisement is misleading, there shall be taken into account (among other things) not only representations made or suggested by statement, word, design, device, sound, or any combination thereof, but also the extent to which the advertisement fails to reveal facts material in the light of such representations of material with respect to consequences which may result from the use of the commodity to which the advertisement relates under the condition prescribed in said advertisement, or under such conditions as are customary or usual.
>
> (15 U.S.C. §55(a))

This means that false advertisement includes both what is said in a promotional statement and what is omitted. This regulation also determines what is "misleading" by looking at how a consumer might interpret the message. This vague standard has no real objective factors and places the fact-finder in the position of making a personal determination of what consumers may or may not think (Moore, Maye, & Collins, 2011).

Claims made in promotional materials must also have prior substantiation (FTC, 1983). This means that material claims of fact, such as an advertisement stating that a car can get certain miles per gallon, must be determined through legitimate tests or investigations prior to the creation of the promotional content. These claims cannot be supported by evidence obtained after the creation of the promotional material. However, the FTC recognizes that promotional materials will contain "puffery" or statements that promote the product based on un-provable statements, such as "Brand X is the best washing powder," that are meant to only persuade consumers to purchase the product (Moore et al., 2011, p. 249).

It is important to note that this "false advertisement" definition goes beyond academic and industry definitions of advertising (15 U.S.C. §55(a)). It includes communication practices associated with advertising, public relations, marketing, and general business communications. This means that advertisements, press releases, press kits, pitch letters, and any other promotional communications can be regulated by the FTC (*Smith-Victor Corp. v. Sylvania Electric Products*, 1965; *Nike Inc. v. Kasky*, 2003). Crafting a legally defensible promotion is difficult because of the changing expectations of the FTC, the blurred lines between puffery and provable statements, and changing consumer expectations. The digital age further complicates matters because both technology and Internet platforms are rapidly changing. Old FTC laws are now being applied to a new commercial world. Recognizing this problem, the FTC began issuing guidelines about online promotions and how the FTC will continue its protection of consumers on the web.

FTC Guidelines on Online Promotions in a Pre-Social Media Age

It is commonplace for federal and state agencies to superimpose older requirements on new technologies. The FTC recognized in the early 2000s that the Internet would change the way organizations did promotional communications. Because of this they issued specific guidelines in May 2000 in a document called *Dot Com Disclosures*. Under 15 U.S.C. 57(a) the FTC has the authority to create rules that regulate deceptive advertising and may require disclosures for certain promotional communication regardless of the way the promotion is delivered to the public. In fact, the FTC has issued specific agency laws, referred to as the Code of Federal Regulations (CFR), that specifically address certain types of disclosures required in individual industries such as automotive parts, jewelry, or wool (16 C.F.R. §§20, 23, 300). The FTC also has specific CFRs that address how products can be described, specifically how warranties, which are statements made about the quality and function of a product, can be delivered to online consumers (16 C.F.R. §702.3).

In *Dot Com Disclosures* (FTC, 2000), the FTC wanted to supplement these federal statutes and CFRs with a set of guidelines for how disclosures could be best made in online promotions. These guidelines are not laws. Instead they are suggestions written by FTC officials to help organizations navigate the expectations of the agency. By issuing these guidelines the FTC is in effect telling those regulated by the agency what the agency's expectations are and how the agency will evaluate organizations' online promotional materials. It could be argued these guidelines are somewhat more useful than laws. They provide organizations an insight into the interpretive and analytical approach of the FTC.

By adhering to the guidelines an organization can be more confident that their online promotions would survive FTC scrutiny if an investigation were to take place (FTC, 2000).

Disclosures can take many forms depending on the product. The FTC is concerned with organizations presenting promotional material that may confuse or mislead the public (15 U.S.C. §55). Primary among these concerns is a fear that organizations will promote themselves in a manner that causes financial or physical harm to consumers (FTC, 1983, 2000). Disclosures are important to promotional content. The FTC states that advertisements (1) must be "truthful and not misleading," (2) have "substantiation" or "evidence" to support the underlying claims, and (3) must not be "unfair" (FTC, 2013, p. 4). The idea behind disclosures is that they protect consumers who may rely on promotional materials to make consumer choices. Disclosures serve an important function of supplementing a promotional message; however, it is relevant to note the disclosure cannot save a false ad by providing a disclaimer. Rather, a disclosure is like an additional explanation that supplements and clarifies the message's claims (16 C.F.R. §§255.2, 702.3).

In *Dot Com Disclosures* (FTC, 2000), the FTC gave an overview of how it thought organizations could use online promotions. This analysis included guidelines for organizations that were cross-tabbed with specific hypothetical examples of how promotional materials, including the sale of goods, could be used. The FTC was particularly concerned with how consumers bought items online. It was concerned that online consumers would not receive the proper disclosures on products because of the multi-clicking pay process for online purchases. It was also concerned about how online retailers used rave customer reviews of products without disclosing these reviews were not typical consumer experiences. It is important to note that this early attempt at regulating Internet promotions was done in a pre-social media environment. At the time of these guidelines, the FTC thought of online promotion as occurring mainly on organizational websites, not third party websites such as Facebook. Because of this, FTC regulations and suggestions were written with the idea that organizations had complete control over content and website interface (FTC, 2000). *Dot Com Disclosures* was also written at a time when buying items from a website was a fairly new practice, so the FTC wanted consumers to enjoy the same protections in purchasing as they would receive in a physical store.

The essence of *Dot Com Disclosures* was twofold. First, the FTC wanted online advertisers to know that older regulations by the FTC would apply to digital information. This included rules about emails. Specifically the FTC wanted organizations to know that laws that allowed for notice to customers, monthly charges for subscriptions, warranties, and direct solicitations of customers were applied to email the same way they were applied to traditional mail. Second, and more importantly, *Dot Com Disclosures* wanted the producers of online promotions to know that the FTC recognized that the Internet had changed the nature of promotional materials. The way websites were structured, how users read online content, and the growth of online sales changed the way promotions worked. The FTC stated that the Internet had changed the way content, particularly disclosures, were disseminated and read. The FTC's *Dot Com Disclosures* (2000) set out to give practical advice to organizations on how they could comply with the FTC's expectations while engaging in the growing digital marketplace.

The primary concern of the FTC's 2000 guidelines was the placement of disclosures. According to *Dot Com Disclosures*, a disclosure must be displayed in a "clear and conspicuous" location on the website (FTC, 2000, p. 5). The FTC gave six non-dispositive factors that determined the "clear and conspicuous" requirement of online promotions. These six factors are: "proximity and placement" of the disclosure, the disclosure's "prominence," the number and quality of "distracting factors in ads," "repetition" of the disclosure, "multimedia messages" that match both the underlying promotion and the disclosure, and the use of "understandable language" in the disclosure (FTC, 2000, pp. 6, 12, 13, 14). The most detailed, and perhaps most important, of the six factors was the "placement" of the disclosure within the website and the "proximity" of the disclosure in relation to the promotional message (FTC, 2000, p. 5). Both of these terms mean essentially the same thing in the FTC report. The FTC considers a successful disclosure to be one that is obvious to the consumer and can be found and understood easily by an online customer. However, the FTC recognized that the old rules concerning the location of a disclosure in print media could not be easily applied to online content.

One of the first issues about online disclosures was the length of the message and its relation to scrolling. The FTC found that scrolling was acceptable if the online user was aware scrolling was required to obtain the message. Making a user aware of scrolling requirement was important to the FTC. They stated that "text prompts," "scroll bar," and "virtual design" were tools an online content creator could use to ensure that disclosures were read by consumers (FTC, 2000, p. 7). The length of these disclosures also meant that content creators had to be sensitive to the limitations of the technology they were using.

The role of disclosures via hyperlinks was particularly concerning to the FTC. In the 2000 guidelines, the FTC acknowledged that certain promotional information about safety, health, and cost required extensive disclosures. Hyperlinks allowed for this type of disclosure without compromising the necessary content. Like scrolling, the FTC said hyperlinks needed to be obvious to the online readers. The guidelines stated that the link needed to be "obvious" to users as well as properly identified so consumers would recognize its function and importance on the web page (FTC, 2000, p. 8). The FTC warned against those content creators who would be "coy" in their creation of hyperlinked disclosures (FTC, 2000, p. 8). The guidelines specifically mentioned that using single words or special symbols, such as asterisks, as cues for hyperlinks were too inconspicuous for consumers. Clear, easily found hyperlinks that only required users to click once was the preference of the FTC.

The construction of disclosures in online promotions also applied to various types of online content. The FTC was cognizant, even in 2000, that users look at online content non-chronologically. Because users did not necessarily visit a homepage first, the FTC wanted disclosures to be made throughout a website.

They also wanted content producers and web designers to use graphic design elements to set-off disclosures within a website or promotional message. They even commented that the graphics used in online promotions could not overpower the disclosure message. Disclosures also needed to match the structure of the promotional material. For instance, an audio-visual promotion online could not contain a hyperlink text-only disclosure (FTC, 2000).

Foreshadowing the issue of social media promotions, the FTC warned that their guidelines and expectations may shift as a result of new technologies. The guidelines suggested that content creators recognize the limitations of new technologies and their disclosure abilities. They also suggested that new technologies or user norms did not negate FTC guidelines on disclosures. The *Dot Com Disclosures* guidelines (FTC, 2000) were written when the Internet was in a major state of flux. Social media had not yet become popular with online users and online purchasing was still in its infancy. The writers of *Dot Com Disclosures* (2000) did well to create a flexible guide that could be incorporated with new technology. However, what the FTC did not anticipate in 2000 was the potential emergence of hand-held computers and other mobile technologies. These guidelines also did not anticipate online networks that had limited and restricted space of content. Because of this the FTC needed to update its guidelines for this new digital reality.

New FTC Regulations on Social Media Promotions

The one thing the FTC did anticipate in 2000 was that Internet technology was changing rapidly. In 2000, the FTC said that content creators needed to use mass communication research on user trends and technological development to tweak existing disclosure content (FTC, 2000). Beginning in the mid-2000s, social media became widely used and became a major tool for online image management and promotional materials. Public relations practitioners and advertising executives began using social media as a method of interacting with customers and publics in a new way. By late 2000s the use of social media in public relations, advertising, and marketing became commonplace. Even academic institutions picked up on the trend of social media and began teaching courses on how to use this new tool of communication (Li & Bernoff, 2008; Scott, 2013).

In response to this growth of social media promotions the FTC issued new guidelines, *.com Disclosures* (2013), concerning social media disclosures. These new guidelines were designed as a supplement and update of the older *Dot Com Disclosures* (2000). These new disclosure guidelines for online promotions reiterated many of the guidelines given by the FTC in 2000. The FTC specifically stated that these new guidelines are to directly apply to advertising and marketing materials published online. What is significant about these new FTC guidelines is the statement that certain types of platforms could be eliminated altogether from promotional use if the space on these platforms did not allow proper disclosure. The means that social media such as Twitter, which has a 140 character limit on tweets, could be eliminated from promotional use.

Compounding this issue on space limitation is the rather vague FTC standard for proper disclosure. In the Introduction of *.com Disclosures* (2013), the FTC states: "The ultimate test is not the size of the font or the location of the disclosure, although they are important considerations; the ultimate test is whether the information intended to be disclosed is actually conveyed to consumers" (FTC, 2013, p. 1). The concern over consumer confidence in online commerce and promotions has been an issue for the FTC since 2000. However, like the guidelines given in 2000, the FTC does not give a rubric for proper disclosure. Instead the FTC said:

> There is no litmus test for determining whether a disclosure is clear and conspicuous, and in some instances, there may be more than one method that seems reasonable. In such cases, the best practice would be to select the method more likely to effectively communicate the information in question.
>
> (FTC, 2013, p. 2)

The mechanics for disclosures in social media is the same standards articulated by the FTC in 2000. The FTC wants disclosures to be close to the "triggering claim" (FTC, 2013, p. 8). Scrolling is allowed for disclosures so long as it is not hidden or difficult for users to manage. Similar to *Dot Com Disclosures* (2000), the FTC allows hyperlinks to make disclosures in social media so long as the disclosure given is not an "integral part of a claim" (FTC, 2013, p. 10). For instance, the FTC said that a promotion for a portable cooler that claimed to keep food cold could not use a hyperlink disclosure that said the cooler may not keep food cold enough to eliminate bacteria in temperatures above 80 degrees. This hyperlink is still determined to be unacceptable to the FTC even when the link is labeled "Important Health Information" (FTC, 2013, p. A-6). This illustrates the long-standing FTC concern that when content producers promote items or services that may create significant health risks, those disclosures must be prominently displayed. However, this rule comes with a caveat. The FTC also states that claims that are "too complex to describe next to the basic price information" may be disclosed through a hyperlink even though this disclosure directly relates to important claims made in the promotion itself (FTC, 2013 p. 10).

The guiding principle behind disclosure requirements in the *.com Disclosure* (2013) guidelines is that content producers should be as conspicuous as possible with disclosure information. Space limitations or technological limitations of computers, cellphones, and other portable technologies are not going to excuse a FTC violation. The 2013 guidelines take into account the limitation of portable devices. Particularly concerning to the FTC is how the technological structure of cellphones may inhibit users from obtaining important disclosure information. For instance, the FTC said that a disclosure that was not easily read on a smartphone may not meet FTC standards if a user would have to zoom in on the disclosure. This issue with smartphone technology also affects content production on traditional websites. The FTC warns that websites creators should consider not only how their disclosure content appears on a home computer but also how it would appear on a mobile device. They suggest the best way to avoid potential disclosure noncompliance is for web creators to create mobile-friendly sites in addition to their regular websites (FTC, 2013).

Content producers may be tempted to parse words or use abbreviations to save space in social media outlets with space limitations. However, the FTC states that acronyms and other shorthand references may be confusing to consumers. This is particularly important in customer endorsements. The FTC gives one example in .com Disclosures (2013) of a customer endorsement placed in a sidebar of a website. The customer endorsement was the result of a free sample of the product. Under FTC guidelines, endorsements that are solicited by free samples must be disclosed. However, in this example the disclosure was made by placing the letters "FS," meaning free sample, by the endorsement (FTC, 2013, p. A-12). The FTC states this use of "FS" is deceptive because it is not intuitive to online readers that this means free sample (FTC, 2013, p. A-12). Disclosing the status of a paid endorser is no different for personal web pages. Influential bloggers may receive free samples from an organization in hopes of receiving a positive review. However, the FTC requires these bloggers to disclose their relationship with the organization. Although a blogger may do this in the blog or on their web page there is still potential for legal trouble. The FTC states that long blog posts should make required disclosures at multiple points in case readers leave the page or follow an embedded link. This is a particularly problematic issue for promotional material because organizations do not necessarily have control over how bloggers write. However, even though a blogger is autonomous over his or her blog, the organization seeking an endorsement may be legally held responsible for a blogger's decision to disclosure information improperly.

The use of space-limited social media, such as Twitter, also presents challenges to endorsements. Twitter, which limits posts to 140 characters, cannot contain lengthy content. The FTC provided an example of a diet pill promotion that was tweeted. The tweet read "Shooting movie beach scene. Had to lose 30 lbs in 6 wks. Thanks Fat-away Pills for making it easy. bit.ly/f56" (FTC, 2013, p. A-17). The link at the end of the promotion is a disclosure about actual results of the pill. The content produced was a paid-for promotion that requires disclosure (16 C.F.R. §255). The FTC states that a correct way to do this promotion is to write "Ad: Shooting movie beach scene. Had to lose 30 lbs in 6 wks. Thanks Fat-away Pills for making it easy. Typical loss lb/wk" (FTC, 2013, p. A-18). In this example, the promotion began with "Ad:" indicating this was a paid endorsement (FTC, 2013, p. A-18). The hyperlink provided was acceptable to the FTC even though it dealt with health issues. However, it is important to note the hyperlink had a description "Typical loss" (FTC, 2013, p. A-18). This use of a prefix before the hyperlink is important, according to the FTC. The FTC made a point of saying that an initial disclosure on Twitter that the writer is a paid spokesperson does not satisfy FTC guidelines because subsequent tweets may bury the initial disclosure. Additionally, the FTC argues that links without any descriptors may be ignored by consumers. Other use of hashtags to indicate paid promotions, such as "#spon" which means "sponsored by an advertiser," does not meet FTC guidelines because users may not know what these hashtags mean (FTC, 2013, p. A-20).

These new guidelines signal a change in online promotion. Previously the FTC was preoccupied with how consumers understand disclosures in the purchasing or subscription process. Now it seems that the FTC is concerned with how users understand disclosures within formats that are more restricted. As portable devices and social media outlets become smaller and more restricted in space, promotions will have to change. This may be better for consumers but may signal a halt to the growth of digital PR and advertising.

Suggestions for Practitioners and Lawmakers about FTC Regulation

These new social media regulations set new parameters for digital promotions. In the past, social media has been very appealing to PR practitioners and advertisers because the medium presumably had no boundaries beyond the technological apparatus in which it works. However, new FTC guidelines concerning social media promotion illustrate that government agencies are aware of and concerned with how promotions are being done online. Because of this communication professionals should expect the fluid boundaries of social media promotions to become more rigid in the future.

In light of these new FTC guidelines there are four key things PR practitioners and advertisers should do in their online promotions. First, they should think how a disclosure could be made in a particular social media platform. In the past, broadcast and print disclosures could be created as "one size fits all" because print and broadcast presented only a few options for disclosure. Social media presents many different platforms that change as the technology develops. Facebook disclosures would work differently than Twitter disclosures because of space limitations. Similarly, new social media platforms emerge constantly. At the time of writing Facebook, Twitter, and YouTube are well-established social media sites, and for new social media users these platforms may seem like old social media. Newer platforms such as Flickr, Meetup, Vine, and Tagged are taking users away from older social media sites by targeting niche groups. Content creators need to explore how disclosures would work in these types of platforms and how users would obtain this disclosure information.

Second, the advertising and public relations industry needs to think not only of how disclosures would work in social media platforms but also of how disclosures would work on certain portable devices. Social media platforms have changed in response to technological changes in portable devices. Smartphones allow users of social media to use these sites in a way that is different from home computers. Because of this the social media interface is different in some versions of social media that are viewed on portable devices. In designing a disclosure for social media on portable devices the practitioner needs to consider important technological issues such as download time, whether the disclosure requires sound, and if the disclosure requires the user to go to a different web page. All of these issues involve accessibility, which is an essential component to the FTC social media disclosure guidelines.

Third, content producers need to think about how to design digestible disclosure information. It is tempting to create an information overload when writing a disclosure because the organization can have peace of mind that every possible scenario is covered. However, in light of recent FTC regulations, disclosures that are merely an information dump are considered improper. That means that disclosures that link to large PDF files or long audio files may be determined improper even if they include all the pertinent information. This creates a new opportunity for practitioners to work with legal counsel in organizations to craft disclosure language that is both legally sound while also easily digestible for users. Disclosures are no different from any other communication. They must reach the intended public and inform them. Crafting a disclosure that is easily digestible for the user while providing the legally required information is no small task. Using user-generated communication norms, such as hashtags, may not be enough for a legally sound disclosure. However, practitioners who write legally sound disclosure may create new managerial possibilities for the field.

Finally, and perhaps most importantly, these new social media disclosure requirements may require advertising and PR professionals to rethink social media use for some platforms. This may be a difficult proposition for some practitioners because it involves not using certain media that could convey a promotional message effectively to targeted publics. However, if a platform does not allow for the proper disclosure needed then that platform cannot be used by the organization. The most obvious platforms this may affect are those outlets such as Twitter that have severe limitations on the amount of content that can be posted at one time. This does not mean that all platforms with space limitations are off-limits for promotional purposes. However, it does mean that certain types of organizations and products may require longer, more detailed disclosures.

While this list of suggestions is not exhaustive, it does represent major components of these new FTC guidelines. Communication practice changes with changing times and technology. Similarly lawyers know that legal guidelines are not static. The FTC is a federal agency that has evolved over the past 8 decades of its existence. Administrations, bureaucrats, and objectives change. With those changes come new policies and procedures. The most recent FTC guidelines may not be the guidelines 10 years from now. However, what is almost certain is that monitoring and regulating social media content is not going to go away. It will become more clear-cut and regulated as agencies gain more insight into how social media is used and misused by organizations. For advertising executives and PR practitioners it is important to keep current with the regulations and to use and respect the guidelines currently in place.

The FTC has done a good job in providing guidelines for digital promotions. However, in crafting these guidelines the FTC still has the opportunity to further refine their expectations. The FTC has shifted their focus from one concerned with online commerce in 2000 to one concerned with how users understand promotional materials in a smaller, rapidly paced digital sphere. In the future the FTC needs to remember that with changes in digital technology and formats comes changing consumer expectations. As consumers increasingly use smaller hand-held devices and more complex social media communication, their proficiency in Internet norms and structures improves. While it is understandable that the FTC is concerned with deception in promotional materials, it is also evident that Internet literacy is on the rise. Because of this the restrictive disclosure requirements given by the FTC should change to reflect a different generation of Internet users.

It seems that digital technology has become faster, more personalized, and more portable. It is also clear that these new technologies are rapidly taking the place of older media. In fact, within broadcast media it seems that older technologies, such as television, are being subsumed by portable digital devices linked to the Internet. Because of this the novelty of Internet purchasing has waned. U.S. e-commerce is expected to be $414 billion by 2018 (Mulpuru, 2014). This means consumers are more exposed on to online promotional messages and arguably are better equipped to process, understand, and act accordingly in light of this promotional content. This means that regulations by the FTC should reflect these social changes and consumer expectations. Perhaps in the future digital promotions will not have the same disclosure requirements in 2018 as they had in 2014.

Implications for Nonprofits and Public Sector Promotions

While the FTC is most often associated with the regulation of for-profit businesses, it can also regulate nonprofit entities under 15 U.S.C. §§44, 45. In 15 U.S.C. §45(a)(2) the FTC is given jurisdiction over "persons, partnerships, or corporations." Specific entities not regulated by the FTC are banks, federal credit unions, common carriers, and "persons, partnerships, or corporations" regulated by the Packers and Stockyards Act (15 U.S.C. §45(a)(2)). A reading of this implies that nonprofit entities would be included in the jurisdiction of the FTC because nonprofits do engage in commerce.

In 1999 the United States Supreme Court confirmed this reading of the statute in *California Dental Association [CDA] v. FTC* (1999). In that case the United States Supreme Court held that the FTC had jurisdiction to regulate nonprofit organizations because nonprofits provide monetary rewards for members as described in 15 U.S.C. §44. In *CDA v. FTC* (1999) the FTC challenged the CDA's use of a screening process that evaluated and restricted advertisements that included pricing and quality statements about dental services. The CDA was a nonprofit entity that was tax-exempt under 26 U.S.C. §501(c)(6) but contained components that provided members with certain benefits including insurance and financing. These benefits to members fell under the definition of a corporation under 15 U.S.C. §44. Today many nonprofits have the same function as the CDA in which members benefit from the organization's ancillary services. In *CDA v. FTC* (1999) Justice David Souter held there was no threshold test for when a nonprofit could be considered to be engaged in member benefits as defined under 15 U.S.C. §44. That means that potentially all nonprofit organizations are subject to the same type of FTC regulations as a for-profit business.

This decision has a major impact for large nonprofit entities that provide member benefits. It is important to note these member benefits need not be required or even used by members. The CDA provided financing and insurance to its members, much like many nonprofit organizations today. This makes the FTC regulations on social media disclosures as applicable to nonprofits as it is for for-profit corporations. With the increased use of social media for fundraising it is easy to see how disclosure information is pertinent to nonprofits. To avoid a potential investigation or sanction by the FTC, content producers in nonprofit organizations need to ensure that the promotional materials and the method of contribution adheres to the FTC disclosure requirements found in both *Dot Com Disclosures* (2000) and *.com Disclosures* (2013).

In the past, the public sector was not affected by FTC regulations on promotions because public sector organizations typically do not provide paid-for services or goods. However, with the recent passing of the Patient Protection and Affordable Care Act and Health Care and Education Reconciliation Act (Pub. L. No. 111-148, 2010; Pub. L. No. 111-152, 2010; 26 U.S.C. 5000A) FTC regulations may now apply to public sector organizations, specifically health exchanges. Under these new laws federal and state governments established health exchanges, also known as health insurance marketplaces, that assist consumers in purchasing health insurance. Government-run exchanges are not selling insurance directly to consumers, but serve as a type of middleman for the process. However, their role in insurance purchasing is similar to other third-party facilitators of online commerce, such as Internet clearing houses eBay or Amazon. Because of the new role state and federal governments play in insurance purchasing it is conceivable that FTC regulations on online promotions and disclosures could affect health exchange content.

While there has yet to be an issue with FTC regulations on health care exchanges directly, there is a growing concern by the FTC that health exchanges are subject to misrepresentations by outside groups posing as government actors. While private health exchanges do exist, there are some groups presenting themselves as government-backed health exchanges to defraud potential consumers (FTC, 2012). This entry into monitoring health care exchanges is part of a larger trend for the FTC, which increasingly has become more involved in monitoring and regulating the health care industry, especially health care data. In the current health care system health exchanges are working with for-profit insurance companies to sell insurance to uninsured Americans. This hybrid relationship is similar to the CDA which, despite its nonprofit status, worked with for-profit companies to give member benefits. It is important to note that if the FTC attempted to take a role in regulating the health exchanges they would probably trigger interagency wrangling over who controls the implementation of the Affordable Care Act, especially since health exchanges are governed by the Department of Health and Human Services. Likewise, health exchanges are subject to change in structure depending upon the U.S. Supreme Court's decision in *King v. Burwell* (2015).

All of this is important for public sector organizations because it signals new possibilities for regulation by the FTC. This is particularly important for quasi-public sector organizations that are private organizations providing governmental services, such as health exchanges. Because of government privatization and the larger role the U.S. government has in health care, content production and the public sector's presence on the Internet and social media will increase dramatically. This, coupled with the rise of fraudulent organizations representing themselves as government entities, signals that the FTC may become more involved in regulating content of all types. All of this means that it is important for public sector workers in all areas, especially those engaged with content production, to be aware of the contours of FTC laws concerning disclosures.

Conclusion and Implications for Communication Practice

Public relations practitioners, advertisers, lawmakers, nonprofits, and public sector organizations should take note that new laws are emerging in response to the growth of new digital platforms and technologies. The success of e-commerce has led to greater regulations on content and its means of conveyance. Because of this anyone engaged in online promotions should take note of these changes. While the general rule that old laws still apply to new technologies is still true, it is also true that new legal expectations are emerging for the digital age. While U.S. federal agencies want to regulate this growing market, they do not have policies that are unrealistic. All for-profit, nonprofit, and public sector entities engaged in online promotion should take note that new technology does not exist in a lawless state.

Perhaps the most powerful tool in any professional's arsenal is media research. Content producers are experts in spotting trends in communication. As the FTC suggests, using research on user trends and norms allows organizations to anticipate how disclosures can be effectively made (FTC, 2000, 2013). By using this knowledge, those engaged in online promotions can not only make great strides in promotional communication, but can do so within the legal boundaries of the digital age.

References

Additional definitions, 15 U.S.C. §55.
Definitions, 15 U.S.C. §44.
Eagle v. Morgan et al., 2011 U.S. Dist. LEXIS 147247. Retrieved from Lexis database.
Eagle v. Morgan et al., 2013 U.S. Dist. LEXIS 34220. Retrieved from Lexis database.
False advertisements; penalties, 15 U.S.C. §54.
Federal Trade Commission established; membership; vacancies; seal, 15 U.S.C. §41.
Federal Trade Commission. (1983, March). FTC policy statement regarding advertising substantiation. Retrieved from www.ftc.gov/public-statements/1983/03/ftc-policy-statement-regarding-advertising-substantiation.
Federal Trade Commission. (2000, May). *Dot com disclosures: Information about online advertising.* Retrieved September 14, 2014, from www.ftc.gov/sites/default/files/

attachments/press-releases/ftc-staff-issues-guidelines-internet-advertising/0005dotcom staffreport.pdf.

Federal Trade Commission. (2012, July 13). FTC alert: Scammers out to trick consumers using the Supreme Court's Affordable Care Act ruling. Retrieved March 17, 2015, from www.ftc.gov/news-events/press-releases/2012/07/ftc-alert-scammers-out-trick-consumers-using-supreme-courts.

Federal Trade Commission. (2013, March). .com Disclosures: How to make effective disclosures in digital advertising. Retrieved September 14, 2014, from www.ftc.gov/sites/default/files/attachments/press-releases/ftc-staff-revises-online-advertising-disclosure-guidelines/130312dotcomdisclosures.pdf.

Guides concerning use of endorsements and testimonials in advertising, 16 C.F.R. §255 (2009).

Guides for the jewelry, precious metals, and pewter industry, 16 C.F.R. §23 (2010).

Guides for the rebuilt, reconditioned and other used parts in the automobile industry, 16 C.F.R. §20 (2002).

Health Care and Education Reconciliation Act, Pub. L. No. 111-152 (2010).

Hispanics United of Buffalo, Inc. v. Carlos Ortiz, Case 03-CA-027872.

King v. Burwell, U.S. Supreme Court, No. 14-144 (2015).

Li, C., & Bernoff, J. (2008). Groundswell: Winning in a world transformed by social technologies. Boston, MA: Harvard Business Press.

Moore, R., Maye, C., & Collins, E. (2011). Advertising and public relations law. New York: Routledge.

Mulpuru, S. (2014, May 12). US ecommerce grows, reaching $414B by 2018, but physical stores will live on. Forbes.

Myers, C. (2014). "Social media as the new water cooler": Implications for PR practitioners concerning the NLRB's stance on social media and workers' rights. Public Relations Review, 40(3), 547–555.

Myers, M., & Lariscy, R. (2013). Commercial speech, protected speech, and political public relations. Public Relations Review, 332–336.

Nike Inc. v. Kasky, 539 U.S. 654 (2003).

Patient Protection and Affordable Care Act, Pub. L. No. 111-148 (2010).

PhoneDog v. Kravitz, 2011 U.S. Dist. LEXIS 129229. Retrieved from Lexis database.

PhoneDog v. Kravitz, 2012 U.S. Dist LEXIS 10561. Retrieved from Lexis database.

Pre-sale availability of written warranty terms, 16 C.F.R. §702 (1987).

Requirement to maintain minimum essential coverage, 26 U.S.C. 5000A.

Rules and Regulations Under the Wool Products Labeling Act of 1939, 16 C.F.R. §300 (2000).

Scott, D. (2013). The new rules of marketing & PR: How to use social media, online video, mobile applications, blogs, news releases, & viral marketing to reach buyers directly (4th ed.). Hoboken, NJ: John Wiley & Sons.

Smith-Victor Corp. v. Sylvania Electric Products, Inc., 242 F. Supp. 302 (N.D. Ill. 1965).

Unfair methods of competition unlawful; prevention by commission, 15 U.S.C. §45.

Unfair or deceptive acts or practices rulemaking proceedings, 15 U.S.C. §57(a).

Utah Stat. Ann. §38-48-202.

3 Applying Records Management Principles to Managing Public Government Social Media Records

Patricia C. Franks

The use of public social media tools by federal, state, and local government agencies has evolved from novelty to commonplace. Citizens, comfortable using social media in their personal lives, expect to be able to interact with government officials in a similar manner. Government agencies, eager to be viewed as open and transparent, embrace the ease with which they can use social media to share information with the public. Public administrators and IT professionals at all levels of government use these technologies to deliver services, communicate information, respond to emergencies, and facilitate interactions between the government and the community.

The Federal Government Social Media Wiki lists 123 government entities, and all but one employ at least one official public social media tool (GovSM, 2014). The one entity, the Occupational Safety and Health Administration (OSHA), does have a presence in social media, however, through the Department of Labor's Twitter account. A 2012 study conducted by the National Association of State Chief Information Officers (representing state chief information officers and information technology executives and managers from U.S. state governments) revealed that 100% of respondents reported that their states use social media in some manner. A study conducted by the International City/County Management Association (ICMA) revealed that 84% of responding local governments maintain a social media presence (NASCIO, 2013, p. 1).

The Federal Records Act (44 U.S.C. 3301) defines federal records as any material that is recorded, made, or received in the course of federal business, regardless of its form or characteristics, and is worthy of preservation (NARA, 2013). State and local governments employ similar definitions when identifying records for which they are responsible. Some social media content is likely to meet the definition of a record in use by the government entity and must be managed according to applicable laws, regulations and agency policies. "The backbone of a transparent and accountable government is good records management. To put it simply, the Government cannot be accountable if it does not preserve—and cannot find—its records" (NARA, 2014, 29).

Those responsible for records management face numerous challenges, including identifying social media records, capturing records in a manner that ensures authenticity, disposing of records that no longer have value, and ensuring access by preserving records of value and making them available to the public.

In addition, consideration must be given to non-records, which present their own, unique challenges.

Challenges of Applying Records Management Principles to Social Media Records

Records and information residing in official social media accounts present two distinct categories of challenge: intellectual and functional. The intellectual challenges include identifying social media records, analyzing governing laws and regulations including Public Records and Freedom of Information laws, negotiating terms of service agreements when possible, conducting a risk assessment that addresses terms that cannot be negotiated, developing social media/ records management policies, and training and monitoring employees. The U.S. government has been successful in negotiating General Services Administration (GSA) Terms of Service Agreements on behalf of federal agencies with social media providers, including Cooliris, CrowdHall, Facebook, Flickr, Foursquare, Google+, Hackpad, Hulu, IdeaScale, Instagram, LinkedIn, Pinterest, Slide-Share, Storify, Tumblr, Twitter, Vine, and YouTube.

Each agency is advised to check the GSA negotiated Terms of Service Agreement to see if it meets their needs. If not, they may seek further modification. The National Archives and Records Administration (NARA, 2013) developed a general clause to use in standard GSA Terms of Service agreements that states both the agency and the contractor must manage federal records in accordance with all applicable records management laws and regulations, including but not limited to the Federal Records Act (44 U.S.C. Chs. 21, 29, 31, 33) and NARA regulations at 36 C.F.R. Chapter XII, Subchapter B. Managing the records includes, but is not limited to, secure storage, retrievability, and proper disposition of all federal records including transfer of permanently valuable records to NARA in a format and manner acceptable to NARA at the time of transfer.

State and local governments are not in as strong a bargaining position as the federal government. However, NASCIO and the National Association of Attorneys General have collaborated on Terms of Service negotiations with social media providers on behalf of state governments. To date,

> Facebook has made changes to its standard terms that apply to state and local governments. Twitter incorporated revisions in Section 12B of its most recent general TOS update. YouTube terms are available to state government agencies that request them through their State CIOs. Negotiations with additional providers are ongoing.
>
> (DigitalGov, n.d.)

The functional challenges include: designing and developing methods and acquiring technology or services to capture and manage social media records; carrying out retention and disposition actions—including legal holds; providing access to current information to employees and the public—including

Freedom of Information Act (FOIA) requests; appraising social media content; and preserving and providing access to records with historical and research value.

While federal government agencies launched social media initiatives shortly after President Obama began his first term, most of them did so without considering records management requirements. However, today agencies realize that social media content may very well be public records. Before a social media initiative is launched, those following best practice adopt a social media policy, identify records that will be created by or posted to official accounts, and determine how the records will be captured and managed.

Social Media Policies

Although social media may be equated with electronic correspondence for scheduling purposes, social media is different from email and instant messaging in a number of ways.

> With social media, new features are being, standards are non-existent, privacy settings change overnight, and the legalese in terms of service agreements is continually modified to include new features and settings, which means that your social media policy must be more closely monitored and frequently fine-tuned.
>
> (Franks & Smallwood, 2014, p. 257)

In addition to social media policies, government agencies have multiple policies in place, such as Internet policies, electronic communications policies, privacy policies, and records management policies. When implementing or modifying social media policies, all existing policies should be evaluated to identify gaps and harmonized to ensure there are no conflicting or inconsistent guidelines. A comprehensive social media policy will address roles and responsibilities, communications and training, and metrics and monitoring. It should also acknowledge records management considerations and refer to the agency's records management responsibilities.

For example, the U.S. Coast Guard's *Social Media Handbook* (n.d.) advises that records of official sites be kept in accordance with records management schedules. The U.S. Coast Guard's *Social Media Field Guide* (2013) complements the policy and provides information, including records management guidance, specific to Facebook, WordPress, Twitter, YouTube, and Flickr. For example, Twitter account managers are advised to establish a separate, non-personal Backupify account to maintain archived data of the official Twitter account. Backupify is a company that provides data storage in the digital cloud, as well as offers data backup and recovery services.

In another example, the *Guidelines and Best Practices for Social Media Use in Washington State* recognizes that all content published and received by the agency using social media in connection with the transaction of the agency's public business are public records for the purposes of Chapter 40.14 RCW

(Preservation and Destruction of Public Records). The agency retains social media public records and disposes (destroys or transfers to Washington State Archives) of social media public records only in accordance with records retention schedules approved by the State Records Committee under RCW 40.14.050. The State Records Committee applies records retention schedules to social media public records consistent with the application to non-social-media public records, based on the function and content of the public record. For example, comments received via social media are retained for the same period as they would have been if they had been received by the agency via email or non-electronic means.

In a local-level example, the Social Media Policy of the City of Cambridge, MA, specifies that city social media sites are subject to Massachusetts public records and records retention laws, rules, regulations, and policies. Any content maintained in a social media format that is related to city business, including a list of subscribers, posted communication, and communication submitted for posting, may be a public record subject to public disclosure. The department site administrator must maintain records in accordance with Massachusetts public records and record retention laws, rules, regulations, and policies.

Identifying Social Media Records

A strategic approach to implementing any social media initiative requires that the proposal for approval include the identification of any social media records likely to be created as a result and a plan for managing those records according to the agency's records retention schedule.

Federal Records and Social Media Content

The Federal Records Act (44 U.S.C. 3301) considers "any material that is recorded, made or received in the course of Federal business, regardless of its form or characteristics, and is worthy of preservation" a public record. Social media content that meets this definition must be managed according to the laws and regulations that govern public records. The statute and the regulations guiding its implementation require each agency to determine what federal records they create or receive. Guidance is provided in 36 C.F.R. Chapter XII, Subchapter B.

NARA provides practical advice to federal agencies in NARA Bulletin 2014-02, which suggests that answering "yes" to any one of the following questions implies that the social media content under examination is likely to be a Federal record:

- Does it contain evidence of an agency's policies, business, or mission?
- Is the information only available on the social media site?
- Does the agency use the tool to convey official agency information?
- Is there a business need for the information?

(NARA, 2013)

NARA Bulletin 2014-02 further states: "A complete Federal record must have content, context, and structure along with associated metadata (e.g., author, date of creation). The complete record must be maintained to ensure reliability and authenticity."

State Records Laws and Social Media

States are subject to their own public records laws. The State of Texas, Department of Information Resources (DIR), for example, collaborated with 34 state agencies to develop the *Social Media Resource Guide* regarding the use of social media tools for official state business (Texas, 2013). The DIR states that all content posted by the agency or the public on an agency's social media website is considered a state record (Government Code, §441.180(11)) and is subject to State Records Retention requirements specified in Government Code Chapter 441, Subchapter L, 441.180–205, with two exceptions: duplicate content and transitory information.

Examples of social media records that are considered public records and subject to Texas State retention requirements include communications (e.g., messages, posts, photographs, and videos) and records, regardless of classification, that are the subject of legal hold (suspension of records disposition) due to any litigation, claim, negotiation, audit, open records request, administrative review, or other action involving the record initiated before the expiration of the records' retention period (Texas Government Code (TGC), 441.187).

In another example, *Guidelines for Electronic Records Management* developed by the Ohio Electronic Records Committee identifies a challenge: that of managing and disposing of the considerable amount of non-record content transmitted via social media that is not considered a record under state and federal law (Ohio, 2012). Failure to manage non-records content will result in difficulty in retrieving information, wasted records storage resources, and additional e-discovery costs in the event of lawsuits, FOIA requests, and other legitimate requests for information.

Local Government Records and Social Media Content

Local government agencies take their records management guidance from that provided by the state. New York State guidelines for local government agencies managing social media records include the following recommendations:

- Determine whether content is substantial enough to constitute a record, especially if the site relates to a finite project or has not been maintained.
- Treat a site that functions as a form of content management (as in a blog that unites related information from diverse sources) as one discrete record, because extricating information based on the creator will destroy the integrity of the record.

[...]

- Manage emails and other communications sent or received via social media sites according to existing policies (if any) on email management. You may possibly equate email with correspondence for scheduling purposes.

(New York State Archives, 2010)

Capturing Social Media Records

Another challenge to managing social media records stems from the nature of public sites themselves—they are owned and controlled by third-party providers. Social media content is ephemeral. Tweets, posts, and comments can easily be deleted. Social media providers may cease to exist or change their terms of service making it difficult or impossible to locate and download content when needed. For legal protection, a way to make social media conversations more persistent is required.

The New York State Archives guidance reflects on the challenges posed by loss of control of social media records and the necessity of capturing social media content in this manner:

> By law, you must ensure that records are accessible and are retained for the duration of their retention periods. This means you will usually need to manage most records—except for records with very short retention periods—in your own technical environment.

(New York State Archives, 2010)

NARA Bulletin 2014-02 (NARA, 2013) suggests the following options to capture social media content:

- Using web crawling or other software to create local versions of sites;
- Using web capture tools to capture social media;
- Using platform specific application programming interfaces (APIs) to pull content;
- Using RSS Feeds, aggregators, or manual methods to capture content; and
- Using tools built into some social media platforms to export content.

To this list should be added using social media archiving and compliance services to capture and archive social media content for you.

Social Media Capture Methods, Tools and Technologies

The methods, tools, and technologies employed to capture social media depend upon the social sites used by the government, the extent of the use of social media, and the resources available. In some instances, such as when uploading images to Flickr, videos to YouTube, or profiles to Facebook, content considered records can be captured into a records management system before uploading. In other cases, when content is posted directly to the social media site, such as comments from citizens, capture must take place after posting. One way to accomplish this is through RSS feeds of comments posted to the site.

Native Archiving Tools

Another option is to use native archiving tools offered by the social media site. This can become complicated for agencies, since most employ more than one social media service. Among the top five most popular social media networks based on monthly activity since 2010 are Facebook, Twitter, and LinkedIn. In 2014, Pinterest and Google+ ranked numbers four and five (eBIZ/MBA, 2015). Each of these social media networking sites can contain records; however, what can be downloaded and how that can be accomplished using the tools provided differs from one social media network to the next.

Facebook provides users with an option that enables content download in the form of a zip file containing one HTML page named index.htm and two folders, one for images and one for additional HTML files. The index.htm page links to content found in the images and HTML folders including contact info, wall, photos, synced photos, videos, friends, messages, pokes, events, settings, security, ads, private notes, mobile devices, places, and survey responses.

As with Facebook, Twitter allows the account owner to request their Twitter archive, which starts with their first tweet. It contains an index page that serves as the home from which all other files downloaded can be accessed. Any links included within the tweet will be preserved; however, the link leads to a live site and the content related to that link may be changed or removed over time. Because tweets are continually added, a decision will need to be made as to how often to request download of the Twitter archive.

It is possible to delete specific posts as well as your entire account. When posts are deleted, they are removed from the owner's account, the timeline of any accounts followed, and Twitter search results. Retweets of the deleted tweet will also be deleted. However, if other users have quoted your tweet or retweeted your tweet with comments of their own, their tweets will not be removed. Tweets cannot be removed from third-party websites, applications, or search engines. Accounts can be deleted by requesting "deactivation," which should occur within a few minutes. The content will be retained for 30 days from date of deactivation. During that time, it can be reactivated. After 30 days, it will be permanently deleted.

LinkedIn allows the owner to download data from the Privacy & Settings page. Similar to Facebook and Twitter, a data archive is prepared and an email message is sent when it is ready. Among the data in the archive are registration information, login history, email address history, account history, a list of first-degree connections, photos, endorsements, recommendations given and received, ads clicked on, and the targeting criteria LinkedIn uses to show you ads. LinkedIn's data-retention policy states that data will be removed from

LinkedIn's production system within 24 hours of the time an account is closed. Closed account information is deleted and logs or other backup information is de-identified within 30 days of account closure.

The steps taken to use native archival tools for Facebook, Twitter, and LinkedIn may change over time. They are provided as an illustration of how time-consuming this approach will be. Many government agencies employ more than just these three social media networks. For example, White House official social media accounts include Facebook, Twitter, YouTube, Vimeo, Pinterest, Google+, LinkedIn, Flickr, Foursquare, Storify, Digg, and Myspace. Ideally, an automated approach is needed.

Web Crawlers and Web Harvesting Tools

Agencies can automate the capture process through the use of web crawlers and web harvesting tools. Archive-It is a web archiving service offered by the Internet Archive for collecting and accessing cultural heritage on the web. The Maryland State Archives uses the services of Archive-It for web pages, blogs, and social media. Notice the information at the top of Figure 3.1 about the collection process (Archive-It, 2014).

The content collected through Archive-It is hosted on the Internet Archive data center, but those using the service can collect, catalog, and manage their collections with 24/7 access and full text search available for their use as well as the use of their patrons.

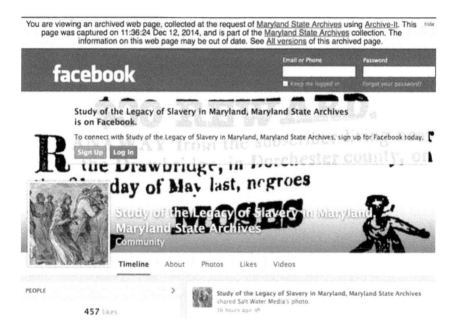

Figure 3.1 Facebook Page Captured Using Archive-It and Made Accessible Through the Internet Archive.

Heritrix (DCC, 2013) powers the Internet Archives and is provided free for download as an open source, extensible, archival-quality web crawler. Heritrix support is provided only for the Linux environment. Users include the British Library, the United States Library of Congress, and the French National Library. This option is for advanced users who have the resources to devote to setting up and managing the web crawler.

Social Media Archiving Services

To the archivist, the term "archive" is defined as "to transfer records from the individual or office of creation to a repository authorized to appraise, preserve, and provide access to those records" (Pearce-Moses, 2005). But in this context, the term means capturing and storing content in a digital repository according to the rules established by the owner of that content and the capabilities provided by the service provider.

The advantage of entering into an agreement with a social media archiving service is that they communicate directly with each social network on behalf of the agency through the use of an application programming interface (API) in order to capture complete records in their raw, native format. The content is stored in the vendor's repository but the agency is provided administrative access through a dashboard that allows the administrator to search, filter, and produce content for e-discovery.

Although the terms "compliance" and "e-discovery" are used most often to market these services, several make a point to explain how they can help the government agency with their records management obligations. One vendor, ArchiveSocial, states its services comply with state and federal records management laws as well as SEC and FINRA requirements. ArchiveSocial offers social media archiving solutions for public records found in Facebook, Twitter, YouTube, LinkedIn, and Instagram. With the help of ArchiveSocial, the City of Austin was the first city to launch an open archive of social media content for citizens to search and access records (see Figure 3.2).

A second social media archive vendor, Smarsh, explains that its government services assist the agency with records retention, FOIA, compliance and litigation through archiving and policy enforcement of social networking websites, audit trails, and reporting. Smarsh archives content from both public and enterprise social media, including Facebook, Twitter, YouTube, LinkedIn, and Instagram, SlideShare, Flickr, Google+, Microsoft Yammer, IBM Connections, Jive, Pinterest, and Salesforce Chatter. In addition, this service supports capture and management of websites, blogs, RSS feeds, text messages, instant messages, and email messages.

The Lee County (Florida) Visitor and Convention Bureau uses Smarsh to archive content from Pinterest in order to comply with the Florida Sunshine Law, which requires government agencies to make official business records, including social media posts, made or received by the government available for public inspection to anyone who asks for it. According to Laura Chmielewski, Director of Marketing and Communications, they first entered into the agreement with Smarsh and only then launched Pinterest (Smarsh, 2014).

Figure 3.2 Screen Capture of Result of Query on City of Austin's Social Media Archive (powered by ArchiveSocial).

Understanding and Meeting Retention Requirements

Retention schedules include the mandatory period for which a record should "be kept in a certain location or form for administrative, legal, fiscal, historical, or other purposes" (Pearce-Moses, 2005, p. 346).

The term "social media record" does not refer to a classification of record but rather to any records posted to or residing in social media technologies. In spite of the fact that social media content may be in the possession and control of a third party, the government agency has the ultimate responsibility to ensure compliance with all governing laws, regulations, and policies. In order to do that all records, regardless of physical form or characteristics, must be analyzed to see if they are covered by an existing records retention schedule.

A Social Media/Records Classification Crosswalk is provided in Figure 3.3 as a model for understanding how records created by new media could relate to current retention classifications.

The content in the left column of Figure 3.3 will come from your own entity's social media initiatives. Those in the right column will come from your entity's records retention schedule. "If [any of] the content represents a new record series, the records retention schedule must be updated" (Franks, 2013).

For example, the Arizona State Library published the *General Retention Schedule for All Public Bodies on Electronic Communications, Social Networking and Website Records* (2012). The general advice is to retain all social networking/Web 2.0 records (including blogs, wikis, Twitter, Facebook, and related applications) for the same period as required for other formats of the same records

Social media/records classification crosswalk
Forms of communication

Social media content (examples for discussion only)		Existing records schedule (possible existing categories)
Focus group in webinar (PRA)	⬌	Information gathering (survey)
Blogs with comments disabled	⬌	Journal; press releases; advertising
Blogs with comment enabled	⬌	Electronic forum; publc appearance
Wiki	⬌	Project file; data collection tool,
Profile, pictures, banner ads	⬌	Advertisement
Tweet	⬌	Public appearance; advertisement
Retweet	⬌	Public appearance; endorsement
Social networking sites	⬌	Interactive, electronic forums
Announcement on Facebook wall	⬌	Public appearance; press release
Reply to post (social networking site)	⬌	Correspondence
YouTube video	⬌	Personal appearance
Email within social networking sites	⬌	Correspondence; other email
Chat room discussions (Linkedin Q&A)	⬌	Public appearance

Figure 3.3 Example of a Social Media/Records Classification Crosswalk (source: www.archives.gov/records-mgmt/training/raco/2011/raco11-franks.pdf).

Note
Adapted from presentation at RACO 2011.

series. Additional guidance recommends transitory records (e.g., general comments, feedback on Facebook walls) be retained only until there is no longer a need for administrative or reference purposes and records with historical value be preserved permanently. Arizona's guidance also cautions that requests for public comment on policies, procedures, or topics that may come up for possible consideration at future board/council meetings may make such communications "executive correspondence" that sets or discusses policy and therefore requires permanent retention on microfilm (Arizona State Library, n.d.).

Disposition Requirements

A retention schedule also provides instructions for the disposition of records throughout their lifecycle. Disposition is not the same thing as destruction or deletion. Rather, an appraisal of records can result in a decision to transfer records to an archive for long-term or permanent storage.

Deletion/Destruction

The viral nature of social media makes deleting all copies of content virtually impossible. However, the agency can mitigate risk posed by social media by ensuring that only information intended for the public is posted on public sites.

Care must be taken to ensure that information containing personally identifiable information (PII), information that is not yet publicly released elsewhere, or information that is sensitive, classified, or for "Official Use Only" is not available to the public.

Risk can also be mitigated through the implementation of a "defensible deletion" strategy. Defensible deletion is a comprehensive approach agencies can take to reduce storage costs and legal risks associated with electronically stored information (ESI). Defensible deletion depends upon a well-established records retention policy based on the operational needs of the agency as well as legal and regulatory requirements.

In the event of litigation, requesting parties may obtain social media content along with other ESI through traditional discovery. Interrogatories will ask the respondent to identify all websites, including social media sites, used to communicate with the public; the custodian of the account; the user name associated with that website; the names of all individuals who have access to that account; the last time the account was accessed; and the contact information and other information associated with the account (Roffman & Freskos, 2013). If content is deleted in a consistent manner according to the agency's retention and disposition schedule, the agency can defend its destruction/deletion actions in court.

Transfer to an Archives

Only about 2–5% of all federal government records created by the federal government in any given year are judged to have continuing value. A growing portion is created electronically, including those generated through the use of social media. Government entities, including the White House, producing such records must transfer them to NARA for safekeeping and to provide access to the public. State and local governments must adhere to similar long-term records requirements.

The ability to transfer records relies in part upon the ability of the transferring agency to present them in a format acceptable to the archives. NARA accepted only six different file formats in 2004; today it accepts 54 file formats organized into 10 categories: computer aided design (CAD), digital audio, digital moving images (digital cinema, digital video), digital still images (digital photographs, scanned text, digital posters), geospatial formats, presentation formats, textual data, structured data formats, email, and web records (NARA, 2014, March 3).

As disposition of the data is performed, whether deletion or transfer to an archives, logs must be maintained that detail the date and disposition of the document, including the user who executed the disposition.

Best Practices

Best practices are continually emerging, but social media is mature enough to enable the development of specific guidance related to social media records management. A number of considerations that must be made have not been

Table 3.1 Social Media Records Management Checklist

Basic Considerations
✓ Become familiar with social media in use within the agency.
✓ Develop a strategic plan to handle social media records—both static and dynamic, including people, objectives, strategies, and technologies.
✓ Examine the terms of service agreements in place with each social media provider, identify risks, and negotiate more favorable terms if necessary/possible.
✓ Ensure that the agency has unrestricted access to the content and tools/services required to manage social media records throughout its lifecycle.

Policy Considerations
✓ Develop or revise the agency's social media policy to include a reference to records management requirements and records management policy.
✓ Be sure the existing records management policy includes a reference to social media records.
✓ Identify and harmonize all related policies (e.g., electronic communications policy, privacy policy).
✓ Publicly state you will be capturing and keeping social media information to comply with existing laws and regulations as well as to support your business operations.

Retention Considerations
✓ Identify records and non-records content created through the use of social media that must be managed.
✓ Develop a process to capture and manage social media records and non-records.
✓ Determine retention requirements by creating a crosswalk between social media records included in the current retention schedule.
✓ If new records categories are created, add the new records series to the existing records retention schedule.

Disposition Considerations
✓ Determine the disposition (deletion/destruction or transfer to an archive) of social media records.
✓ Periodically delete social media content (from all storage locations, including the social media site) according to your formal records retention policy.
✓ Establish a method to retrieve the social media content so that it is available in a non-proprietary format (or that the agency has access to the vendor's software or source code).
✓ Transfer social media records with enduring value to an archive and provide access for historical or research purposes where possible.

Ongoing Considerations
✓ Evaluate the results of the processes employed.
✓ Keep abreast of changes to social media terms and conditions and new social media technologies employed.
✓ Enforce, evaluate, and update your Social Media and Records Management policies and practices.
✓ Scan the horizon for the next new technology that results in records that must also be captured and managed—it's sure to come.

addressed in this chapter, because they apply equally to content residing in the cloud or in other repositories provided by third parties: for example, encryption of data in transit and at rest and legal jurisdiction in which content resides on servers and backup servers.

The choice to use social media will rest with business units that identify a purpose (e.g., public relations, emergency management) and the decision-makers that sanction the use based on a cost/risk–benefit analysis. Records management considerations come into play once a decision to use social media has been made but before it has been implemented. The Social Media Records Management Checklist in Table 3.1 is not exhaustive, but it provides recommendations that will aid those responsible for ensuring the agency is in compliance with external laws and regulations, as well as internal policies to perform their duties.

Conclusion

Government agencies on all levels are increasing their use of social media in order to engage with the public, and it is likely that some of the social media content meets the definition of a public record. If so, the agency has an obligation to capture, manage, preserve, and provide access to the records throughout their useful life based on governing laws, regulations, and policies.

Because of the variety of social media platforms and the fact that new vendors will enter the market, it is not possible to provide specific guidance for all types of social media technologies. However, designing a social media strategy comprising three elements (policies, controls, and operational guidelines) will ensure that the agency has a framework in place that can be adapted to existing and emerging social media technologies and applications.

References

Archive-It. (2014, December 12). *Maryland state archives collection*. Retrieved from https:// wayback.archive-it.org/2504/20141212113624/www.facebook.com/pages/Study-of-the-Legacy-of-Slavery-in-Maryland-Maryland-State-Archives/381817628501007.

Arizona State Library. (2012, January 19). *General retention schedule for all public bodies on electronic communications, social networking and website records* (pp. 20–22). Retrieved from www.azlibrary.gov/sites/azlibrary.gov/files/arm-all-general-schedules-10-09-2014. pdf.

Arizona State Library. (n.d.). *Guidance on social networking* (p. 2). Retrieved from www. azlibrary.gov/sites/azlibrary.gov/files/arm-guidance-on-social-networking.pdf.

Austin, City of. (n.d.). *Social media archive*. Retrieved from www.austintexas.gov/page/ social-media-archive.

Cambridge, City of. (2013, May 2). *City of Cambridge social media policy*. Retrieved from www.cambridgema.gov/~/media/Files/publicinformationoffice/Social-Media-Policy-05-02-13.ashx.

DCC. (2013, June 5). *Heritrix*. Retrieved from www.dcc.ac.uk/resources/external/ heritrix.

DigitalGov. (n.d.). *Federal-compatible terms of service agreements*. Retrieved from www. digitalgov.gov/resources/federal-compatible-terms-of-service-agreements.

eBIZ/MBA. (2015, February). Top 15 most popular social networking sites. Retrieved from www.ebizmba.com/articles/social-networking-websites.

Franks, Patricia C. (2013). *Records & information management*. Chicago, IL: Neal-Schuman.

Franks, P. C., & Smallwood, R. F. (2014). Information governance for social media. In R. F. Smallwood (Ed.), *Information governance concepts, strategies, and best practices* (p. 257). Hoboken, NJ: John Wiley & Sons.

GovSM. (2014, May 23). Federal agencies. Retrieved from http://govsm.com/w/Federal_ Agencies.

NARA. (2013). NARA bulletin 2014-02. Retrieved from www.archives.gov/records-mgmt/bulletins/2014/2014-02.html.

NARA. (2014, March 3). NARA bulletin 2014-04. Retrieved from www.archives.gov/records-mgmt/policy/transfer-guidance-tables.html.

NARA. (2014). *Open government plan: National Archives and Records Administration, 2014–2016* (p. 29). Retrieved from www.archives.gov/open/open-government-plan-3.0.pdf.

NASCIO. (2013, June). Examining state social media policies: Closing the gaps. *NASCIO Issue Brief*, p. 1. Retrieved from www.nascio.org/publications/documents/NASCIO_2013SocialMediaIssueBrief.pdf.

New York State Archives. (2010, May 24). Records advisory: Preliminary guidance on social media. Retrieved from www.archives.nysed.gov/records/mr_social_media.shtml.

Ohio Electronic Records Committee. (2012, July 11). *Social media: The records management challenge*. Retrieved from www.walterhav.com/pubs/OhioERC-Guideline-Social-Media.pdf.

Pearce-Moses, R. (2005). *A glossary of archival and records terminology* (pp. 29, 346). Chicago, IL: Society of American Archivists.

Roffman, D., & Freskos, D. (2013, October 25). Five tips for managing social media and e-discovery collections. *KMWorld*. Retrieved from www.kmworld.com/Articles/Editorial/ViewPoints/Five-Tips-for-Managing-Social-Media-and-E-Discovery-Collections-92863.aspx.

Smarsh, Inc. (2014). Case study: Permission to Pinterest. Retrieved from www.smarsh.com.

Texas Department of Information Resources. (2013, February). *Social media resource guide*. Retrieved from www.dir.texas.gov/management/socialMedia/Pages/resourceguide.aspx.

U.S. Coast Guard. (2013, June). *Social media field guide*. Retrieved from https://drive.google.com/file/d/0B1NpsZVxKxbDSWx3Z3g4Z2NyR3c/edit.

U.S. Coast Guard. (n.d.). *Social media handbook*. Retrieved from www.auxpa.org/resources/Social_Media_Handbook_Attachment_14.pdf.

Washington State, Office of the Governor. (2010, November). *Guidelines and best practices for social media use in Washington State*. Retrieved from www.governor.wa.gov/news/media/guidelines.pdf.

4   Some Ideas for Branding via Social Media

Staci M. Zavattaro

The Greater Starkville Development Partnership (GSDP) has a presence on various social media platforms. The Partnership, a nonprofit organization that serves as Starkville, Mississippi's economic development arm as well as the convention and visitors bureau, has a Facebook page, Twitter feed, YouTube channel, blog, and Pinterest page, to name a few. Each is tailored to different audiences. For example, the Partnership hosts an event called Unwine Downtown several times a year, whereby ticketholders can shop in downtown retailers while sipping wine and enjoying discounts. On its Pinterest page, Partnership employees post photos of the wines available, as well as offerings from the stores, as a means of enticing people to participate. The Facebook and Twitter pages offer information on Partnership events (including, of course, Unwine Downtown), new business openings, and support of the local university, Mississippi State University. After all, the Partnership's slogan and overall brand identity is: Starkville: Mississippi's College Town. No matter which social networking site someone visits, it is clear that each page is part of the Partnership's official communication channels through consistent colors, font, slogan, logo, and tone.

This chapter brings together some of the best practices I have found through my research of both local city governments and local-level destination marketing organizations (DMOs) regarding how to build an interactive, meaningful social media presence. After all, the idea behind the digital tools is to be *social*, but those features are not inherently built in (Bryer & Zavattaro, 2011). Government users can make the tools as interactive or as static as they see fit, and gaining the level of interactivity required for meaningful dialogue is no easy task (Mergel, 2013a). In her study of U.S. federal government agencies on social media, Mergel (2013a) found that administrators "do not desire to create a direct, reciprocated relationship with citizens by following citizens back and having creative conversations online" (p. 331). While dialogue might not be the ultimate end for governments of all levels on social media, there are still tips and tricks public administrators can use to move toward making the platforms meaningful for citizen engagement if not full collaboration. A first, critical step toward that is to ensure page visitors know the social site is official, and a consistent brand identity and tone goes toward achieving that end.

As noted above, these recommendations come from two main sources of my research. In the first set of research, colleagues at Mississippi State University

(MSU) and I conducted semi-structured interviews with DMO managers in a Southern U.S. state, asking about everything from place brand development and communication to evaluation and success measures. We did not ask a question about social media, but eight of 12 interviewees indicated the tools' importance to their jobs. Interviews yielded interesting information about social media as it relates to brand awareness, interactivity, and evaluation. The second study from which these recommendations draw examined more than 4,700 tweets from various local government agencies throughout the United States. Local governments were picked using systematic random sampling, and tweets were collected for six weeks during September and October 2013 using MSU's Social Media Tracking and Analysis System housed in the Social Science Research Center. In that research, my colleagues and I looked expressly at sentiment, asking if tone on social platforms matters for interaction. The answer is yes, and how that happens is detailed below.

First, the chapter begins with an overview of branding in an online context, especially how it relates to decision-making and interaction with agencies. Next, the best practices are offered before concluding with avenues for future research.

Branding and Social Media: An Important Intersection

According to the American Marketing Association, the leading U.S. group specializing in all aspects of marketing, a brand is defined as a "name, term, design, symbol or any other feature that identifies one seller's good or service as distinct from those of other sellers" (Marketing Dictionary, 2014, p. 1). Branding is the act of developing, communicating, and evaluating these unique markers (Anholt, 2007). Put simply, brand is the noun, branding is the verb—the action of translating the brand into a known association with the organization. Within a corporate context, brands and branding are not new ideas. Indeed, brands are viewed as vital strategic management tools that aid with overall organizational success and culture building (de Chernatony, 2010; Hatch & Schultz, 2001). An important shift, as Hatch and Schultz (2001) detail, is moving from product brands to organizational brands, bringing attention to the whole rather than a small part. This becomes particularly important in the context of public sector agencies as they begin to mirror in policies and practices public relations and marketing firms (Zavattaro, 2010, 2013). The key to success is support throughout the entire organization, as everything about an organization can communicate (Kotler & Levy, 1969).

For purposes of this chapter, social media are understood as "technologies that facilitate social interaction, make possible collaboration, and enable deliberation across stakeholders" (Bryer & Zavattaro, 2011, p. 327). Examples include, but certainly are not limited to, Facebook, Twitter, YouTube, Vine, Pinterest, blogs, and wikis. According to findings from the Pew Research Internet Project, 74% of online adults used some type of social networking site (Pew Research, 2014). The cellphone evolution toward "smart phones" with internet connectivity means that social media sites are accessible right in someone's pocket. Indeed, Pew researchers found that 40% of cellphone owners access a social networking site through those mobile devices. Increasingly, the tools are being used not only for friendship connections but also for political and social activism (or, some would argue, "slacktivism") as well (Pew Research, 2014). Relatedly, Mergel (2013a) found that, as of May 2012, "the 698 departments, agencies, and initiatives of the U.S. federal government have created 2,956 Facebook pages, 1,016 Twitter accounts, 695 YouTube channels, and 498 Flickr pages to promote their online content and connect to their stakeholders and audiences" (pp. 327–328). As such, the social networking sites are becoming tools for at least sharing information with digital users. Ideally, social media tools can foster real-time information sharing and knowledge co-creation. Specifically, though, the focus of this chapter is on how public and nonprofit agencies alike can tailor their social media sites to embody the organization's brand identity and values.

Yan (2011) offers nine tips for social media branding. The first four center on the need for organizations to build dialogue and community with followers by developing a sense of community and shortening the gap between "us" and "them." He then argues that doing this initial groundwork of community building will increase trust from the users and allow the organization to build and maintain a competitive advantage while also using the social media followers as an integral source of knowledge to help the organization grow. Taken together, Yan notes, the steps toward community building and knowledge sharing should allow the organization to increase brand awareness, associations, and perceived quality—all key components of brand equity, defined as the price premium someone is willing to pay for a branded product versus a similar non-branded alternative (Aaker, 1991; Keller, 1993). One barrier to evaluating steps toward building place brand equity is public sector brand managers not having enough resources or training to properly evaluate these critical components of awareness, associations, and quality (Zavattaro, Daspit, & Adams, 2015).

Recommendations in this chapter come with a caveat for scholars and practitioners alike. Scholars can work toward developing better measures of success for place branding management, including a social media component that managers can use within existing organizational capabilities. For practitioners, they can focus on measuring a few things well to figure how marketing and branding efforts are influencing those outcomes. As such, readers can implement recommendations in part or whole as they see most appropriate.

Considering the recommendations in this chapter come from two studies, one related to DMOs and the other to local governments in the U.S., both literatures will be briefly engaged here to give readers a foundation of both. It is fully acknowledged that this is not a comprehensive review of either literature, but trends from both are highlighted to give context to the chapter.

Social Media Use in Government Agencies

To begin, U.S. government agencies at all levels are turning toward branding and marketing strategies as key governance strategies to improve and/or strengthen an organization–public relationship (Eshuis, Braun, & Klijn, 2013). Social media sites are one component of this shift and not panaceas to increase citizen engagement (Bryer & Zavattaro, 2011). Research into early adopters within various government agencies has found that ideals of citizen access to government 24/7, as well as an improvement in citizen collaboration, have not panned out as planned (Brainard & Derrick-Mills, 2011; Brainard & McNutt, 2010; Hand & Ching, 2011; Mergel, 2013a, 2013b; Rishel, 2011). One reason is what Bryer (2011) calls the costs of democratization, meaning that there are costs to participation coming from both the government agencies and citizens alike. For example, government agencies must dedicate financial and personnel resources to developing a solid social media program, while citizen users must themselves find time to access the social sites (see also Vicente & Novo, 2014, who found that users' digital skills were critical for online engagement via social media). Indeed, government agencies then might be opening up the capacity for engagement rather than active collaboration if social media sites are not developed with connectivity and interactivity in mind (Zavattaro & Sementelli, 2014).

Mergel (2013b) elucidates three ways U.S. federal government social media managers are deploying social networking tools: representation, engagement, and networking. Representation means that the agency wants a presence on the social sites because of their popularity, usually creating pages and profiles on some of the most popular social sites (Facebook, Twitter, and YouTube, based on her findings). Agencies using this style, Mergel found, are likely to repurpose older content that has already appeared in other official agency communications. This commonly is called a "push" communication strategy whereby the agency simply pushes information out to its publics without really wanting to generate dialogue or knowledge sharing. Second, engagement tactics appreciate conversation and interactivity, though "there are very little role models within government to mirror an interactive approach" (ibid., p. 128). Ideally, the engagement tactic includes conversations between the agency and users, moving beyond pushing information in a one-way manner. Finally, a networking strategy "allows government to absorb comments, gain valuable insights about the sentiments around mission-relevant issues or emergent topics their perceived online audiences talk about across social media channels" (ibid., p. 128). Here, government agencies remain neutral and do not try to actively drive dialogue, instead letting ideas and co-production emerge naturally. Again, Mergel found that agencies adopting a networking strategy are the exception rather than the rule. Indeed, my own research, as well as that of other scholars in public administration studying social media, confirms the high presence of push strategies rather than engagement (Brainard & Derrick-Mills, 2011; Brainard & McNutt, 2010; Hand & Ching, 2011; Rishel, 2011).

Social Media Use in Destination Marketing

The second kind of organizations from which the recommendations in this chapter come is DMOs, nonprofit organizations responsible for creating brand identity strategies for legislatively designated geographical areas. Put simply, DMOs usually are the chief branding and marketing organization for a locale and come in many forms, including local governments, convention and visitors bureaus (CVBs), economic development partnerships, visitors' centers, and chambers of commerce, for example. DMOs do not work alone; instead, they usually are responsible for coordinating stakeholder networks that include, but certainly are not limited to, local residents, business owners, tourists, hospitality professionals, state government officials, and more (Munar, 2012). Coordinating and informing all of these stakeholder groups can sometimes pull DMO managers away from marketing communications and sound performance measures toward stakeholder education (Zavattaro et al., 2015).

Undoubtedly, the Internet is a vital vehicle through which potential tourists, residents, and business owners find out information about a place, and social media are becoming part of that information-gathering process related to tourism ventures (Xiang & Gretzel, 2010). The expansion of social media, however, has highlighted a similar challenge for government agencies and DMOs (and other public, private, and nonprofit organizations): controlling the message (Munar, 2012). Similar to Mergel's findings (2013b), Munar (2012) found that DMOs tend to push information out to social networking site users rather than engaging in interactivity and dynamic participation. Again, in another parallel with Mergel, managers in Munar's study (2012) indicated that using social media to gather and analyze information from users was an important function but one deployed not nearly enough because of resource constraints. Based on my research of DMOs in a Southern U.S. state, when social media metrics are analyzed, they are rather simplistic (for example, number of followers indicates more people are aware of the organization or destination, but managers reported using no evaluations to see how a social media "like" translates to actual visitation) (Zavattaro et al., 2015).

Considering public and nonprofit organizations still struggle with engaging via social media, this chapter pulls together some of the recommendations and findings through my previous research. The chapter addresses a point brought up during a panel at the 2014 meeting of the American Political Science Association conference in Washington, DC. During the panel, an audience member noted that the research from public administration scholars into social media often finds what *does not* work instead of offering what *does or could*. The recommendations offered are moving toward means through which public administrators of all stripes can work to reach Mergel's (2013b) engagement strategy and eventually on to networking, should those agencies desire this kind of collaboration and dialogue.

Branding on Social Media: Some Recommendations

The following list comes from selecting some of the top-cited information from studies I have conducted into place branding practices in DMOs and local governments alike. Each will be discussed further herein but include: maintain a consistent identity and voice, adopt a positive tone to increase engagement, strategically deploy social media platforms, and evaluate social media metrics. This last suggestion includes a vital knowledge management component that could push us closer to Mergel's (2013b) suggestion for collaboration and networking to delve into the full co-creative power of the tools.

Maintain a Consistent Identity and Voice

Truly, this recommendation applies to all media communications coming from an organization and not only social media. Sometimes, however, social media get left out of this process, so practitioners are encouraged to include a coherent brand identity on all the social sites the organization uses. Put simply, a brand identity is what the organization attempts to create and relates closely to brand image, which is what appears in a consumer's mind (Anholt, 2007). Public administrators can try to control the brand identity, but ultimately the place brand's success is up to the consumers who either visit or not, open a business or not, relocate or not. Despite this inherent challenge, administrators can still work toward developing a strategic, coherent brand identity that is communicated succinctly through various channels to allow administration and site users alike to tell a brand story together.

One can think of this as the brand personality of the organization. Oftentimes, we attribute human personalities to product and place brands (Brown & Campelo, 2014), so that personality should be reflected consistently within a social space through brand interactions. Study findings confirm that brand personality in online spaces influence a consumer's interaction with the brand (Chung & Ahn, 2013), so public social media managers can capitalize on this by showcasing interactivity through a positive brand personality. An important part of this is a consistent presentation of tone, wording, colors, and language. For example, the GSDP has its slogan and logo on all the social platforms so visitors know this is official information. Tamarac, Florida, a city in Broward County, also maintains a consistent brand identity on its social media platforms. Its Facebook and Twitter pages, for example, both feature the city logo, but the Facebook page does not contain the slogan (The City for Your Life), which features prominently on the Twitter feed. Coordinating the two is a simple way to begin building a consistent brand identity. With Tamarac, however, there is little interaction and conversation between the city and its residents/commenters. Brand personality alone is not enough to encourage dialogue—but it is a good start.

Developing a Positive Tone

The second recommendation comes from my research into local government use of Twitter. Results from that study, originally presented at the 2014 meeting of the American Political Science Association, indicated that social media managers throughout U.S. local governments who adopted an overall positive tone were more likely to see engagement than administrators who maintained a neutral tone. In that data set, collected with Mississippi State University's

SMTAS system, included tweets to and from 125 cities throughout the U.S. The SMTAS software collected tweets for that project based on Twitter handles collected from a database of 750 cities randomly selected from the ICMA Yearbook. Of those 750, 125 had active Twitter feeds during the time of the data collection, which lasted from September until October 2013. SMTAS pulled more than 17,000 tweets, and we deemed 4,779 usable for the project. Removed were handles that appeared to be from non-public organizations (a ski lodge, for example), as well as public safety agencies, as the focus of the project was on local governments rather than specific departments.

SMTAS included software that analyzed sentiment, the positive or negative tone of the tweets collected. Computer-based sentiment analysis tools examine topics using positive or negative emotions rather than more nuanced language (Bae & Lee, 2012; Stieglitz & Dang-Xuan, 2013). Put simply, the software looks through pre-determined word banks for positive and negative poles. So, for example, the system would have a hard time analyzing a tweet such as "I love rain, but hate snow" because of "love" and "hate" included in one chunk of text. As such, the SMTAS sentiment analysis tool has an 80% accuracy rate, meaning that 80% of text analyzed is coded correctly. Overall, our data set of 4,779 tweets had a neutral tone, meaning that government agencies in our sample (which ranged from small townships to big cities throughout all four Census regions of the U.S.) adopt a neutral, authoritative, expert tone. Digging deeper, however, revealed that cities that adopted a more positive tone, shared more information (retweets), and included photos in tweets were more likely to encourage engagement with followers.

To show an example of this occurrence, Blue Springs, Missouri (population approximately 53,000) communicates directly with followers on its Twitter page *because it set the tone for open communication.* To wit, the "about us" descriptor on the Twitter page mentions a focus on community cooperation. If someone retweets a city post, the social media manager is sure to thank the person for sharing the information. In another recent instance (November 2013), a citizen tweeted at the city about a neighbor blowing leaves into the street. The city responded by saying they will share the information with the Code Enforcement division who can then inspect the situation. Another resident tweeted to ask about a police department presence on Twitter. The city responded that the police department is on Facebook, not Twitter, and the resident replied with a happy, "Thanks!" The city's social media coordinator is sure to share information, include photographs, and embrace an overall positive tone that encourages engagement.

The next step would be for cities and public organizations of all kinds to move toward a networking use of social media for increased collaboration and knowledge sharing, but that still eludes many government agencies (Mergel, 2013b). No matter the path chosen, public administrators should work to ensure that social media tools are part of a strategic, consistent communications plan and not deployed for the sake of having a presence.

Strategic Use of the Platforms

It often proves tempting for individuals to create a presence on the latest social networking site without understanding quite yet how the tool works, why, and for what purpose. Public administrators also might fall into this same spiral, which means there might not be enough time, money, or personnel to operate all the sites well (Bryer, 2011; Mergel & Greeves, 2012). Each platform attracts certain kinds of audiences and serves different purposes. It might be difficult, but social media managers should work to understand the purpose of the popular social networking sites to determine how they fit in with a strategic communication plan that reaches target audiences. I should caution that public agencies also should focus on their websites, as these portals still remain vital components of information gathering. Managers in my study of DMOs in the Southern U.S. states indicated the importance of strategic communications to attract target audiences, and social media are critical components of that strategy.

Jennifer Gregory, the chief executive officer of the GSDP, described how her agency uses social media as such:

> We try to always have a strategic purpose for our decision-making whether it is to enhance the quality of life or to produce economic impact through tourism events or things like that. So we're constantly trying to use newest and best practices especially through social media and online marketing, I think that one way we are being innovative is that compared to other community development organizations, we've kind of emerged as a leader in marketing ourselves but specifically through social and digital media.

When I asked her to give an example of the strategic use of social media, she talked about a popular event in Starkville called PumpkinPalooza, an outdoor festival celebrating the Halloween/fall season that coincides with a home football game to increase attendance. She detailed how the Partnership might send out a tweet telling people to mark their calendars for the event, and then take to their blog the next day to share additional information about the event in more detail. The Facebook page will contain some of the same information, she said, but also feature a link to the Partnership's Pinterest page that features fall fashions available from local retailers that might be appropriate for the event and beyond. As she explained,

> We want to keep connected, keep people interested, and change it up a little bit, so while a Pinterest page might not provide economic impact, if we can show some of the great styles of what our retailers sell, that might encourage someone to attend the event, go shopping with one of our stores, eat dinner. And that does have an economic impact, so that's kind of how we might connect all of our different social media outlets for one common purpose.

Platforms, in other words, create spaces to increase organizational capacity for collaboration rather than actual collaboration when not updated regularly or used only to push information (Mergel, 2013a, 2013b; Zavattaro & Sementelli, 2014). Knowing more about which audiences gravitate toward which platforms can guide administrators. According to findings from the Pew Research Center, Facebook remains the most popular social networking site with 71% of online adults using the platform as of 2013 (Duggan & Smith, 2013). Facebook users are demographically diverse, yet trending a bit older. Pew statistics reveal, however, more segmented demographics on the other platforms. Pinterest, for example, and perhaps not surprisingly, attracts more female users, while Twitter and Instagram (a popular photo-sharing site) appeal to young, non-white urbanites (Duggan & Smith, 2013). Facebook and Twitter are the most popular for gathering news and information (Holcomb, Gottfried, & Mitchell, 2013), so administrators should keep that in mind when deciding what content to publish on those sites.

A consistent strategy, though, is one that is measured and evaluated against overall organizational and branding goals. This leads to the final topic mentioned frequently in my previous research into social media.

Evaluate Social Media Metrics

It was interesting to me and my colleagues that we never asked DMO managers in the Southern states about social media, yet the topic came up frequently in our interviews without prompting. When social media were discussed, the managers noted the importance of analyzing numbers to gauge something called brand awareness. Put simply, brand awareness is a gauge of how many people know your place, product, destination, nonprofit, school, hospital, whatever even exists (Keller, 1993). If someone does not know your organization or place exists, they cannot begin to learn more. Communicating the brand values and brand personality noted above is a good start to creating brand awareness. For managers in our study, social media were key tools to creating brand awareness, which then ideally translates into actual visits to the place—the economic impact. Measuring that link, however, is tremendously difficult.

This suggestion ties back into the topic of consistent brand identity. Visitors must know the social media site is legitimate. Indeed, Facebook officials demanded that governments change their names to include an official "government" moniker (Tepe, 2012). In a report featured in GovLoop, the communication manager for the City of Olathe, Kansas is quoted as saying this mandatory change will have a negative effect because, "First and foremost, 'City of Olathe, KS' is our brand. It is on all of our official correspondence. The Facebook URL is used on most if not all of our citizen communications" (Tepe, 2012, para. 5).

As one manager in the study described, "Our Facebook page, we have I think almost 70,000 Facebook fans now, so when you look at the interaction those people are having with us, it's a confirmation that our brand messaging is at least reaching them." Managers reported using free online tools (such as Google Analytics®) to evaluate upticks or downticks in fans and followers. Relatedly, another manager described their process of social media evaluation as such:

We know our followers or "likes" on Facebook have doubled and tripled and quadrupled over the last couple of years, so we know that we're reaching more people and we will very rarely have someone unlike us on Facebook or unfollow us on Twitter, so that tells us that they are at least somewhat satisfied with the information they're receiving.

As Mossberger et al. (2013) find, the evaluation component of social media success in government agencies is difficult to achieve because of the still-emerging and rapidly changing nature of the technologies. Within a private sector context, Hoffman and Fodor (2010) argue that metrics for evaluating social media success have to change to reflect the purpose of the tools—that measures cannot be connected to a direct return on investment in the traditional sense. Instead, "managers should begin by considering consumer motivations to use social media and then measure the social media *investments* customers make as they engage with the marketers' brands" (Hoffman & Fodor, 2010, p. 42, emphasis in original). This reflects closely with Bryer's (2011) concern regarding the costs of democratization, or the costs to both the public agency and citizen for utilizing the tools. Measuring success, then, can become difficult to achieve.

Practitioners ideally want to work toward devising measurements that are right for their organization and goals. Compiled from Hoffman and Fodor (2010), Mergel (2013a, 2013b), and Fisher (2009), along with findings from my own research, some good starting points for measurement metrics include: brand awareness, number of followers, unique visits to the sites, click-throughs back to agency communications, information shares, sentiment (tone), and participation in discussion/engagement. Additionally, DigitalGov, a service of the U.S. General Services Administration, suggests 10 measures for success, such as depth and breadth of social media communication, as well as a step-by-step implementation guide on its website (DigitalGov, 2014). Either way, practitioners should ideally take the extra step to use social media to evaluate how consumers are perceiving the place brand, a loop that is not often closed (Zavattaro et al., 2015). For example, social media managers could put simple survey questions on Facebook or Twitter about the place itself, brand values, brand awareness (how did you hear about our city, school, hospital, nonprofit, etc.?), and more. Staff can then analyze that information to give a different perspective on elements of brand saliency and brand loyalty, finding areas of strength and points for improvement.

Conclusion

For many public organizations, developing a strategic place brand identity is a difficult endeavor in and of itself. As Kotler and Levy (1969) note, everything about an organization can talk. That means everything in a city (or whatever entity is undertaking a branding initiative) conveys an image that is part of the overall brand identity. That means everything from uniforms, to landscape, to personnel appearance represent the brand. For organizations of any size, there certainly is bound to be pushback from internal and external stakeholders. As one of the managers in my study on DMO place brand management described her DMO's struggle with getting local stakeholder groups to adopt the brand identity, "They just don't use it, plain and simple. They just don't, whether they didn't like it, it wasn't their choice. Whatever it is, they just don't use it." Compounding these difficulties for brand identity adoption are all the necessary communications layers, including social media.

Based on a compilation of findings from my various research projects, I offered several best practices (items practitioners cited often or those that emerged through data analysis) to integrating branding practices into social media communications: maintain a consistent identity and voice, adopt a positive tone to increase engagement, strategically deploy social media platforms, and evaluate social media metrics. I tried to be clear throughout that managers are encouraged to work within their organizational capabilities and resource availabilities to develop the best social media program for them. If nothing else, I would encourage managers to really focus on the first suggestion of consistent brand identity across platforms. This way, users are clear that they are finding accurate, organizationally endorsed information rather than something random and unofficial. This can help consumers develop confidence in the brand and trust with the organization to bolster a positive organization–public relationship.

Of course, challenges remain when it comes to social media itself, including but certainly not limited to, time devoted to social media by public administrators and citizens, lack of dialogue, privacy, records retention, technology failure, technology availability in the community, and lack of consistent voice (Bryer, 2011; Franks, 2010; Mergel, 2013a, 2013b; Oxley, 2011; Picazo-Vela, Gutierrez-Martinez, & Luna-Reyes, 2012). Certainly these are not all insurmountable but definitely elements practitioners should consider when delving into social media sites.

As Jennifer Gregory notes, the benefits outweigh the costs when strategically communicating a brand identity via social media:

> We have more followers on Twitter than any Convention and Visitor's Bureau in the state, and we've been asked, I've particularly been asked, to speak at conferences and meetings across the southeast about branding a community and how to implement that brand specifically through social media. So we're very active on Twitter, we try to be very active on Facebook, we have a blog, our website is ever changing, but all of these things are connected and have a strategic purpose.

References

Aaker, D. A. (1991). *Managing brand equity: Capitalizing on the value of brand names.* New York: The Free Press.

Anholt, S. (2007). *Competitive identity: The new brand management for nations, cities, and regions.* New York: Palgrave Macmillan.

Bae, Y., & Lee, H. (2012). Sentiment analysis of Twitter audiences: Measuring the positive or negative influence of popular Twitterers. *Journal of the American Society for Information Science and Technology*, 63(12), 2521–2535.

Brainard, L. A., & Derrick-Mills, T. (2011). Electronic commons, community policing and communication: On-line police–citizen discussion groups in Washington, D.C. *Administrative Theory & Praxis*, 33(3), 383–410.

Brainard, L. A., & McNutt, J. G. (2010). Virtual government–citizen relations: Informational, transactional or collaborative? *Administration & Society*, 42(7), 836–858.

Brown, S., & Campelo, A. (2014). Do cities have broad shoulders? Does Motown need a haircut? On urban branding and the personification of place. *Journal of Macromarketing*, 34(3), 421–434.

Bryer, T. A. (2011). The costs of democratization: Social media adaptation challenges within government agencies. *Administrative Theory & Praxis*, 33(3), 341–361.

Bryer, T. A., & Zavattaro, S. M. (2011). Social media and public administration. *Administrative Theory & Praxis*, 33(3), 325–340.

Chung, H., & Ahn, E. (2013). Creating online brand personality: The role of personal difference. *Journal of Promotion Management*, 19(2), 167–187.

de Chernatony, L. (2010). *From brand vision to brand evaluation*. Burlington, MA: Butterworth-Heinemann.

DigitalGov. (2014). *Federal social media analytics toolkit*. Retrieved from www.digitalgov.gov/resources/federal-social-media-analytics-toolkit-hackpad.

Duggan, M., & Smith, A. (2013). *Social media update 2013*. Retrieved from www.pewinternet.org/2013/12/30/social-media-update-2013.

Eshuis, J., Braun, E., & Klijn, E. (2013). Place marketing as governance strategy: An assessment of obstacles in place marketing and their effects on attracting target groups. *Public Administration Review*, 73(3), 507–516.

Fisher, T. (2009). ROI in social media: A look at the arguments. *Journal of Database Marketing & Customer Strategy Management*, 16(3), 189–195.

Franks, P. C. (2010). How federal agencies can effectively manage records created using new social media tools. Retrieved from www.businessofgovernment.org/report/how-federal-agencies-can-effectively-manage-records-created-using-new-social-media-tools.

Hand, L. C., & Ching, B. D. (2011). You have one friend request: An exploration of power and citizen engagement in local governments' use of social media. *Administrative Theory & Praxis*, 33(3), 362–382.

Hatch, M. J., & Schultz, M. (2001). Bringing the corporation into corporate branding. *European Journal of Marketing*, 37(7/8), 1041–1064.

Hoffman, D. L., & Fodor, M. (2010). Can you measure the ROI of your social media marketing? *MIT Sloan Management Review*, 52(1), 40–49.

Holcomb, J., Gottfried, J., & Mitchell, A. (2013). News use across social media platforms. Retrieved from www.journalism.org/2013/11/14/news-use-across-social-media-platforms.

Keller, K. L. (1993). Conceptualizing, measuring, and managing customer-based brand equity. *Journal of Marketing*, 57(1), 1–22.

Kotler, P., & Levy, S. J. (1969). Broadening the concept of marketing. *The Journal of Marketing*, 33(1), 10–15.

Marketing Dictionary. (2014). Brand definition. Retrieved from www.marketingdictionary.org.

Mergel, I. (2013a). A framework for interpreting social media interactions in the public sector. *Government Information Quarterly*, 30(4), 327–334.

Mergel, I. (2013b). Social media adoption and resulting tactics in the U.S. federal government. *Government Information Quarterly*, 30(2), 123–130.

Mergel, I., & Greeves, B. (2012). *Social media in the public sector field guide.* San Francisco, CA: John Wiley & Sons, Inc.

Mossberger, K., Wu, Y., & Crawford, J. (2013). Connecting citizens and local governments? Social media and interactivity in major U.S. cities. *Government Information Quarterly, 30*(4), 351–358.

Munar, A. M. (2012). Social media strategies and destination management. *Scandinavian Journal of Hospitality and Tourism, 12*(2), 101–120.

Oxley, A. (2011). A best practices guide for mitigating risk in the use of social media. Retrieved from www.businessofgovernment.org/report/best-practices-guide-mitigating-risk-use-social-media.

Pew Research. (2014). Social networking fact sheet. Retrieved from www.pewinternet.org/fact-sheets/social-networking-fact-sheet.

Picazo-Vela, S., Gutierrez-Martinez, I., & Luna-Reyes, L. F. (2012). Understanding risks, benefits, and strategic alternatives of social media applications in the public sector. *Government Information Quarterly, 29*(4), 504–511.

Rishel, N. M. (2011). Digitizing deliberation: Normative concerns for the use of social media in deliberative democracy. *Administrative Theory & Praxis, 33*(3), 411–432.

Stieglitz, S., & Dang-Xuan, L. (2013). Emotions and information diffusion in social media: Sentiment of microblogs and sharing behavior. *Journal of Management Information Systems, 29*(4), 217–247.

Tepe, L. (2012). Local governments do not "like" Facebook's new name page policy. Retrieved from www.govloop.com/community/blog/local-governments-do-not-like-facebooks-new-page-name-policy.

Vicente, M. R., & Novo, A. (2014). An empirical investigation of e-participation: The role of social networks and e-government over citizens' online engagement. *Government Information Quarterly, 31*(3), 379–387.

Xiang, Z., & Gretzel, U. (2010). Role of social media in online travel information search. *Tourism Management, 31*, 179–188.

Yan, J. (2011). Social media in branding: Fulfilling a need. *Journal of Brand Management, 18*(9), 688–696.

Zavattaro, S. M. (2010). Municipalities as public relations and marketing firms. *Administrative Theory & Praxis, 32*(2), 191–211.

Zavattaro, S. M. (2013). *Cities for sale: Municipalities as public relations and marketing firms.* Albany, NY: SUNY Press.

Zavattaro, S. M., Daspit, J. J., & Adams, F. G. (2015). Assessing managerial methods for evaluating place brand equity: A qualitative investigation. *Tourism Management, 47*, 11–21.

Zavattaro, S. M., French, P. E. & Mohanty, S. D. (2015) A sentiment analysis of U.S. local government tweets: The connection between tone and citizen involvement. *Government Information Quarterly, 32*(3), 333–341.

Zavattaro, S. M., & Sementelli, A. J. (2014). A critical examination of social media adoption in government: Introducing omnipresence. *Government Information Quarterly, 31*(2), 257–264.

5 Social City Hall

Warren Kagarise

With the Seattle Seahawks bound for the Super Bowl, the City of Issaquah renamed itself to support the team in the big game. In a rally on the steps of City Hall, our mayor and a group of flag- and sign-waving fans proclaimed Issaquah's new name as 12SAQUAH—at least for February 2, 2014, the day of Super Bowl XLVIII. The name change attracted the attention of the Seahawks organization, as well as local, regional, and national media outlets. Most importantly, it helped the City of Issaquah connect with more than 1 million people in the span of a single weekend.

So, what do the Seahawks have to do with Issaquah? In short, not much.

Aside from the thousands of diehard fans within City limits, our connection to the Seahawks is no different than hundreds of other communities throughout Washington State and the Pacific Northwest. But the Seahawks fan base, collectively known as 12s, is regarded as one of the most passionate—if not the most passionate—in all of professional sports. By renaming the City as 12SAQUAH, we showed Issaquah as a place with a sense of community, creativity, and fun.

It offered us a chance to make a great first impression. Many of the more than one million people who engaged during the 12SAQUAH campaign interacted with the City for the first time. Though 12SAQUAH marked a special occasion, it offers a good example of the way the City of Issaquah approaches its social media presence. The focus on community and connection, delivered in a relatable, conversational way, defines the approach we bring to our day-to-day interactions across our eight (and counting) social media platforms. That ethos is reflected in our bio that appears on each platform: "The social side of City Hall."

A Connected Community

Our presence on social media is borne of necessity. In a dynamic, fast-growing city like Issaquah, citizen input is vital to help our elected leaders and municipal staff make the best decisions for the future. Spare time is scarce, especially in a community of busy young families with careers, school assignments, and extracurricular activities to balance. Attention spans continue to shrink, making the need for a concise, impactful message more important than ever.

In many ways, social media is the ideal medium to engage with this audience. It requires a minimal time commitment and we can literally reach citizens in the palms of their hands, via their smartphones and tablets. With engagement as our top goal, we launched on eight platforms (Facebook, Twitter, YouTube, Instagram, Pinterest, Foursquare, Vine, and Google+) in April 2013. Now, in our community of 32,000 people 15 minutes east of Seattle, we routinely connect with up to one million people in any given month. But our social media success did not occur overnight—it's the result of careful policymaking, planning, creativity, and a willingness to be bold.

Another critical piece of our success is the trust placed in the Communications team by the City administration and elected officials. We have been granted immense latitude to innovate, engage with citizens in ways outside of the City's past comfort zone, and, occasionally, push the envelope.

Our foremost commitment is to use social media to provide excellent customer service—a key tenet of our culture at the City of Issaquah. In fact, customer service is part of our City's overarching vision and our employee-developed mission, vision, and core values. Using social media, residents ask questions about policy initiatives before the City Council, share feedback about City services, and, most frequently, submit requests for assistance.

In addition to the usual questions about potholes and power outages, citizens are frequently curious about routine police or public works activity. During a November 2014 standoff between police and two teenagers barricaded inside a house, a steady stream of tweets about the incident allowed us to keep nerves from fraying further, steer drivers away from a potential traffic quagmire, and help protect neighbors and police during a tense situation. Overhead, a news helicopter buzzed, capturing a livestream for the station's website. Issaquah's police chief, concerned about the risk to officers' safety, asked me to put a stop to the potential security risk. Unable to reach anybody on the phone, I relayed our safety concerns to the station through a Twitter direct message. Within moments, a producer apologized and ended the live feed.

If the Communications team does not know or have easy access to answers, we reach out to the appropriate department. Within City Hall, the need to gather responses to citizen questions has facilitated better internal communications. For instance, during the November 2014 police standoff, support personnel answering phones at City Hall could direct callers with questions about the incident to follow live on Twitter. That simple gesture went a long way to reduce stress (for staff) and confusion (for citizens) during a hectic time. Usually, these customer service questions come to us after City Hall has closed for the day. To accommodate these requests, we committed to answering questions as quickly as possible, even if the initial answer is a simple acknowledgment.

Building a Foundation

We are constantly looking for new ways to connect social media to our citizens' everyday activities. For instance, during the holiday shopping season, when

Issaquah police typically notice an uptick in car prowls and thefts as shoppers leave items in plain sight inside their vehicles, we created a social media-focused safety campaign called #SantasBackup. As officers patrol shopping center parking lots in November and December, vehicles at risk of prowls or thefts receive a card reading, "You're on the naughty list." The card also includes safety information, ways to contact police, and, of course, the hashtag #SantasBackup.

Because the City of Issaquah launched its social media presence after the medium had become a part of everyday life, we had the advantage of learning from others' mistakes and successes. For instance, before the first tweet was sent or the first Instagram photo was shared, we undertook a comprehensive review of social media policies among government agencies at the federal, state, and local levels.

Drawing on guidelines and policies from the U.S. General Services Administration, Washington State Office of the Attorney General, City of Seattle, and the nonprofit Municipal Research and Services Center—as well as individual cities and counties—we created a flexible social media use policy and a handbook for City of Issaquah staff. In addition to setting parameters for official blogs and social media accounts, our handbook laid out ground rules for staff. If individual departments and programs expressed interest in establishing a social media presence, a roadmap is in place to ensure consistent branding and a uniform voice across platforms.

Our policy also created an umbrella for City-affiliated blogs and social media accounts. Overall, the Communications team oversees official accounts, but team members from throughout the organization are engaged to supply content to the Communications team for the City's social media feeds. Despite interest from other departments, no other group has made a formal request to establish a social media presence independent from the City's overarching accounts. If a department-specific account is approved, posting is outlined as the responsibility of department-level administrators.

A successful social media account or blog requires a dedicated administrator or team of administrators. But it also requires a sense of personality and a dedication to respond quickly to questions and maintain a dialogue with followers. Though our handbook offers advice about how to manage a successful social media account—"If possible, thank users that share your posts or pertinent information with a public reply," it reads—it is difficult to convey the need for a casual running dialogue that makes social media such a successful medium.

We greatly admired other agencies' official social media accounts that offered followers personality, humor, and, most importantly, a sense of community. With that in mind, we knew we would have to take some risks to get noticed, attract followers, and serve our customers.

Joining the Conversation

Not long after launching our social media presence, Jamaican musician Ziggy Marley stopped at Issaquah's Target to purchase socks. Though our single tweet about the episode failed to gain traction, it marked the first time we were willing to capitalize on a random occurrence to start a dialogue with our community.

For Valentine's Day 2014, we tempted followers with candy. Using the City's social media platforms, we put out a call for questions—with one caveat: answers would come only in the form of conversation hearts. Questions from intrigued Issaquah residents and businesses streamed in via Twitter and Vine. Using only the two dozen or so phrases present in a single bag of conversation hearts, the Communications team used the candy and props to craft cheeky responses. The queries ranged from where to find a romantic dinner spot in Issaquah to how to overcome a serious hankering for chocolate. While not as serious as the questions usually fielded by the City via social media, Candy Convos offered a chance to showcase the City's personality in a lighthearted, accessible way.

It was another candy—Skittles—and our embrace of the Seattle Seahawks that brought us our greatest social media success. After the initial 12SAQUAH announcement, the celebration generated more than one million impressions during Super Bowl weekend alone. While the campaign fostered a sense of community and rallied our community around the Seahawks, it also accomplished something far more practical.

In the run-up to the Super Bowl, with all attention focused squarely on football, it allowed the City to become part of the conversation that was swirling all around us. Rather than competing for attention, our decision to rename the City helped us weave Issaquah into the broader Super Bowl narrative.

In addition to cheering on the Seahawks in their second Super Bowl appearance, the City of Issaquah set out to:

- increase the number of community members engaging with us
- deepen the City's relationship with our existing followers
- strengthen community pride and sense of place
- raise the community's regional and national profile.

The overwhelming majority of user response was enthusiastic. Many followers marveled that a government agency—a suburb, no less—would have the audacity to rename itself for a sports team. Twitter user @chaseface16 summed up the sentiment with, "My hometown changed its name from #Issaquah to #12SAQUAH to prepare for Super Bowl. Ridiculous or proud? Proud! #gohawks." At the peak of 12SAQUAH fervor, hundreds of tweets, posts, and photos were shared each hour.

The real test came with the dawn of game day. Without any direction from the City, fans used the 12SAQUAH moniker in their celebrations, with hundreds of them sharing social media posts and photos highlighting 12SAQUAH on Super Bowl Sunday.

Wrigley, maker of Skittles—favorite snack of Seahawks running back Marshawn Lynch—sent us 30 pounds of candy and five bags of coveted Seattle Mix to celebrate our name change. Seizing the opportunity to reach high school students—one of our targeted audiences—we decorated bags of original-flavor

Skittles with the 12SAQUAH hashtag to encourage students to post about the experience on social media. With only a few hours' notice, we went to Issaquah High School and handed out 200 bags of Skittles in less than two minutes. Students immediately started sharing photos and posts about the experience.

A year later, when our mayor renamed Issaquah to 12SAQUAH for the Seahawks' Super Bowl XLIX appearance, we returned to the high school for a pregame rally. Many of the students remembered how the previous year's Skittles giveaway introduced them to the City's social media presence—and started a running dialogue with their local government.

Data Drives Dialogue

Metrics form the backbone of our social media activity. We use Facebook's built-in analytics tools to determine the best time to post, in order to reach the largest audience possible. (As of right now, it's Saturday evening, though the prime time fluctuates depending on the time of year and whether the Issaquah School District is in session.)

Even a small advertising budget can deliver outsized results. Using only $30, we expanded our Facebook reach to come into contact with more than 3,000 additional users during the Super Bowl celebration. On Facebook, a campaign to generate page likes can attract new followers for as little as two cents per like—a much more cost-effective strategy than hosting a public meeting or mailing a print newsletter to every household in the City. Such campaigns are often timed to coincide with periods when the City of Issaquah is in the news, such as the annual Salmon Days Festival, which attracts more than 150,000 people to our community each October.

With rare exceptions, posts chosen for promotion have already displayed some success in terms of likes, retweets, or shares. Gauging a post's shareability is a good indicator of whether it would be successful as a promoted post or tweet. Using the platforms' built-in advertising and promotion tools is a simple, effective way to reach a broader audience—or, as we learned through a recent tourism campaign, a targeted audience.

Using a $5,000 grant from the City's hotel-motel tax fund, we parlayed our social media success into a tourism campaign starring Sasquatch. We created a series of videos featuring the mythical creature in a variety of Issaquah settings and experiences, and then shared the videos via social media. The videos were produced on a shoestring budget, freeing up more than 80% of the grant for advertising.

Advertising is particularly effective to promote the reach of a video on Facebook or YouTube. By targeting audiences in the western United States and Canada, we reached more than 750,000 people in less than 90 days. Furthermore, we were able to examine how a video performed in a particular region, and then decide whether to increase the budget for that area or select a different place to target.

Using social media also offered us a way to multiply our message for free. By reaching out to businesses featured in the videos, key influencers in the Greater

Seattle region and even the cast of Animal Planet's *Finding Bigfoot* show, we were able to attract more attention to the campaign than we would have been able to do so alone.

Harnessing the power of force multipliers or using a national event with significant community interest—such as the Super Bowl—has enabled Issaquah to participate in the ongoing social media dialogue in a meaningful way. These steps have also enabled the City to remain relevant when the vast majority of social media users are focused on other topics, such as the roar of a Super Bowl or the annual churn of the holiday shopping season.

Every community is different, and a successful social media manager will learn to experiment to best connect with his or her citizens. Though social media success can seem fleeting, it requires managers to play the long game in order to build and maintain a successful social media presence. Creating a comprehensive policy, relying on the expertise of staff and allowing creativity to flourish are the keys to success.

6 Telling the Story of Boston through Social Media

Lindsay Crudele

The brutalist slab of Boston City Hall looks like a bleak relic of vintage government: inside, humming fluorescent lights cast a sallow glow on a line of citizens queued up to pay excise tax. However, a careful observer would see more: a soon-to-be-married couple clad in their finery riding the elevator to the clerk's office, or the slumber party energy of a volunteer shift manning the overnight call center through a snowstorm.

As Boston's first director of social media, it was my job to imagine how we could introduce new pathways for sharing the stories of City Hall that few citizens would otherwise have a chance to see, and inviting the public inside. Through social media, we had a means to democratize city communications. On our best days, social media served as a crowdsourcing channel for local music to be played in City Hall's telephone system, and a productive platform for constituent service requests. On our worst, it provided us with a fast and reliable method of disseminating accurate information during emergencies, and a powerful collaborative tool for recovery efforts. Today, the social media program of the city belongs to its people, and the expectation of two-way communication is carved into City Hall like waterways.

In spring of 2015, more than 400 local and state government social media managers met for the first national summit of its kind in Reno, Nevada. That event marked a groundswell in the way local government now embraced social media, as small and medium-sized cities dedicated resources to driving a culture of digital engagement across their teams. Not only were major cities adapting to a new, collaborative approach for city communications, but small and medium-sized communities were now embracing digital engagement. Hundreds of public servants were becoming skilled in the unique art of persuading city leaders to adopt social media tools, and helping their peers turn a lens on their own work for the public eye. Public officials recognize today that it says more to *not* maintain a social media presence than it does to maintain one.

Early Days

As a journalist and communicator before ever setting foot inside City Hall, I saw the early power of social media in lean, service-minded projects. I was organizing small community events to raise money for a local roller rink in danger of closing—some DJ friends would play music, artist friends designed posters, and I would provide media relations and promotion support to fill the roller rink with new guests. The rink served as a de facto community center, welcoming kids let out of school in the afternoon with nowhere else to go, guided by a grandmotherly rink owner who would check in with them, talk to them, and listen to their concerns. With no budget to speak of and all services donated in kind, I relied on partnerships such as donated advertisements in the pages of the Boston Phoenix. But social media allowed me to package up the news, hand it to the community, and allow them to share information with peers—an added benefit meaning the news was delivered by a trusted and familiar source. We could get the word out far and wide by offering a packet of information, if they deemed it useful and relevant, and we found a way to make it easy to do so.

Culture Change

Mayor Thomas M. Menino was the 53rd mayor of Boston. Known for his high-touch approach to community engagement, his philosophy to meet people where they were permeated city operations, such as through his team of neighborhood liaisons who cultivated personal relationships walking the districts, at community meetings, and in conversation. However, Mayor Menino realized an emerging digital community was not being reached. A former reporter, I was used to including him as a source in my print and radio work; in 2009, I joined him as his reelection campaign digital director, finding new ways to tell his story, creating a digital presence that opened up a new conversation between him and the community, and engaging his supporters through social media.

Any social media director would be grateful for the trust and enthusiasm of leadership, and it is useful to listen carefully to identify potential internal allies when breaking new ground. Mayor Menino was an evangelist from the start, bringing back a mandate to City Hall for other teams to dip their toe in the water in kind. As I worked to guide and manage many of those conversations, the need became clear for centralized governance, a clear policy, trainings and focus, and a social strategist role was formalized in 2011.

In this chapter, I will detail the birth and development of Boston's social media program; the processes and methods I used to construct it through a period of exploration and discovery, and lessons that may be useful to other practitioners wishing to do the same. Our story began in 2008.

Social Media in the City of Boston

Early on, we learned how the publicly accessible nature of social media turned transactions into transparent conversations, accessible to one another, and therefore not only connected them to us, but to one another. A favorite story told by the City's Innovation & Technology team involves a trashcan-bound possum, reported to public works, instead released by a neighbor who saw the report on the City website, all before crews were able to respond.

While strengthening central channels, we created a complementary suite of amplifying channels specialized to meet the specialized topics of each of the 51 departments—niche conversations that could be flipped into emergency mode in crisis times to create a massive, singular footprint. This was useful not only during crises, but during any major announcement. In order to support these channels, it was necessary to root out a digital team where there had never been one before, a virtual communication and response team embedded across departments carrying out a coordinated strategy. This required the ability to negotiate across teams and leadership styles, which meant customizing services: identifying champions and those in need of triage, applying tools and strategies to match all levels of competency, and raising the baseline. The virtual team included a range of job functions, from communications officers to the city's archaeologist himself, who shared live updates from a dig.

Notably, linking those accounts via a centralized engagement management platform provides common governance and oversight, increased security, and in crisis, a crucial central access point providing a superadmin with the ability to access all established channels. During the Boston marathon attack in 2013, this created a large "thunderclap" approach that helped deliver rapid response updates quickly and consistently, regardless of staffing structure and availability during the time of crisis.

By January 2015, the city's social community had grown to 1.5 million followers across all of its official platforms, doubled from the previous year. Brand awareness for a city holds value if a conversation has been underutilized, however, performance indicators transcend reach. Supported by social media campaigns, we not only promoted the benefits of interacting conversationally, but also encouraged users to report issues via the self-service mobile reporting app. That year, reporting doubled in kind.

The 2015 practitioner summit represents a culture change in the government sector not generally known for taking risks. These leaps have succeeded, by different methods in different communities, in the face of outdated procurement systems that fail to keep up to purchasing structures for modern tools, through near-constant demand on under-resourced teams, and rightfully skeptical public constituencies who wonder who really is listening behind the staff account. The doors have been opened in hundreds of communities across the country in places where a digital front door may be reflective of a truly accessible public representation; or, inadvisably, for those interested simply in the appearance of one.

Acronyms and dense policy reports hold meaning for policymakers, but prove myopic as a communication style in social media. I quickly discovered the need for the development of an internal digital communication agency of sorts in order to package noteworthy messaging in visually appealing, easy to understand formats that integrated with the natural culture of social media. A common practice included the development of what I called "shareables," a self-contained digital graphic that would contain pertinent information if shared organically via a single click through organic spread. We needed to pay attention to external terms of service, and be agile in adapting to evolving platform features. Our messages found themselves competing with major brands and media outlets; while it's doubtful the public expected the same sheen from local government, the most personal, engaging, and visual communications would travel further, in service to both daily quality of life and vital emergency messages.

Doubts and fears failed to actualize; by setting clear internal and external expectations, and communicating respectfully and personably, social media was welcomed by the community as it represented an extension of constituent service access. Social media simply amplifies an organization's existing culture and mission.

Central to all else was a daily strategy: everyday engagement positioned us for priority moments, whether a high-profile emergency, or simply a positive and exciting new announcement. Asking for attention and subscription only when needed by the city misses an opportunity to build trust and add value. While emergencies resulted in organic (or natural) spikes in followers, the potential was much higher with a daily commitment that showed attention to quality of life and constituent service.

What is the Voice of City Hall?

To effectively conduct conversations via social media, it was necessary to consider the voice and visual identity of City Hall, a potentially threatening principle to some who feared accessibility could threaten credibility and official status. Information-dense flyers crammed with text were rendered illegible if not distilled into simplicity for digital channels. We used social media as a laboratory to transform 70-page reports into a package of graphics, tweets, and videos, and tease that story out over time to make it easier to digest complex information and reach more users. Clear speech and straightforward design serves an agenda of transparency and access. Most surprisingly, we had the opportunity to be ourselves, and establish a new vision of public employees.

New ways of thinking were necessary to make this a daily way of life. Rarely does a state or local government consider seriously an advertising or marketing budget; formal press releases offer limited space for creativity. Social media production presented the opportunity to reimagine what the voice of a City Hall could be, if expressed as a personal, friendly, reassuring conversationalist. Simple messaging in language and visual presentation helped deliver information more efficiently to digital communities, and ensured it was easier than ever to share. We worked to translate press releases, pages of tips and densely worded signs into shareables, and injecting unexpected humor as appropriate.

My idea was to turn City Hall inside out, and one way to employ social media was as a channel by which to tell stories that would remain unseen unless we told them. For months, I could not understand why the front steps of the building were sometimes scattered with rice. I realized after more than a few elevator rides with brides that I had been an inadvertent wedding guest; we set up a mobile photo booth and created a blog hosting a digital gallery of the couples who married at City Hall and their "how we met" stories. It was our tribute to this heartwarming but hidden experience, in a historically significant location for the nation's marriage equality movement. Similarly, Instagram was a place in which to offer a behind-the-scenes glimpse that could not be visualized in a press release: for instance, line-ups of green cots for overnight call takers during a blizzard, in a parking ticket hearing room. I established a pipeline that made it de rigueur for the mayor to send us photos from the car as he rode around the city on a snow inspection, as well as secure methods for him to post and scan social content directly. We hosted Q&A sessions across multiple social media channels that functioned like office hours, and hosted the first summit of Boston's own social media team, with guests from Facebook and Tumblr. During the capture of the Boston marathon bomb suspect, a single cellphone photo, grainy in the late evening streetlight, said more in three words than any printed statement could. As the police commissioner leaned into the Mayor's car: "We got him." It was shared more than 20,000 times, a new record for the city.

The Toolkit

The visual nature of social media makes design resources vital, whether through a process of identifying existing resources, providing training to advance those skills, or adding expertise to the team, as well as securing licenses for design tools. Free, cloud-based tools continue to improve, with slick, versatile templates and myriad font sets, and provide low-cost agility especially valued during crisis, but limitations include the risk of lost work, and design sets that may not match established brand standards. During the marathon bombing, a tip line for the FBI was circulated, and we quickly created a digital card for social media use containing the information to avoid inevitable typos.

Social media should be viewed as one communication channel among a suite of touch points. In the City of Boston, the @NotifyBoston Twitter feed was a companion channel to the Mayor's 24-Hour Hotline, serving as a customer service platform for reporting issues and answering questions, as well as general citywide topics and announcements.

Establishing relationships that connect social efforts to your other digital platforms creates synchronicity of message, and the social program often inspired the creation of new channels in order to optimize this strategy. We reached regularly into new platforms as needed to express content: a public call recording hosted via a site typically used for music, or instructional GIFs hosted on a microblog.

Social listening supports service and crisis communications, while informing a more attuned content strategy. Typical tools emphasized three areas, particularly for situational awareness during major events:

- brand listening: emerging trends and related conversations outside existing search scope
- engagement management to monitor known conversations and branded hashtags
- geosocial monitoring for location-focused alerts.

The self-selected social community does not represent scientific polling itself, but it is often a telling litmus for community sentiment. By following cues in our social media analytics, I watched our snow communication reach vault from three million impressions per storm to 30 million, through a combination of scheduling structures and use of visual media, including infographics and PSA shareables. For organizations with financial means to do so, small investments in sponsored campaigns targeted toward specific audiences, elevating top-performing media further, often results in dramatically improved engagement based on 2015 models of Facebook algorithmic structure.

Terms of Engagement

The City's first social media policy defined the operating team, the tools employed, and guidelines for respectful and legal practice. Establishing terms of engagement as early as possible helps an organization navigate external platforms, subject to their own terms of service and culture. This guides internal communicators, and also sets community expectations. It is far easier to define terms in advance than steer a ship back around a crisis later. Engaging legal counsel is an essential step at this point. Here lies another opportunity to engage a designer to present these new standards in a way that is accessible to internal teams and easy to digest for the public as well. I conducted training sessions internally that transformed our policy document into infographics, for example, to illuminate key differences between official government and campaign accounts.

Internal Advocacy

Identifying and engaging influencers, social media personalities, or accounts may be useful to help create a larger footprint for priority announcements, due to their large community of followers or a smaller but passionate and quick-acting community. However, every voice should count to municipal government, not just those with the skills or resources of an influencer. Technology can support means of being a better listener, to uncover needs and concerns about neighborhood issues. Be influenced by every voice.

Influencers also exist within one's organization, and are often already amplifiers due to their pride and familiarity with organizational content. By providing them with tools and guidelines for employee advocacy, internal influencers can be organized into an amplifier layer, supported by those who know the stories better than anyone, and whose enthusiasm is first-hand. In the City of Boston, our suite of niche conversations also functioned in this way.

Strong internal communications are the backbone of vibrant external communications. Creating a clear protocol for sharing content with social media publishers, or empowering their first-hand use, will support more regular storytelling opportunities, and for those who are able, simple guidelines for how that content can be packaged and shared for easier dissemination. Humble public servants may be reticent to trumpet their work, but I reminded colleagues that telling the story of the service they provide, and their stories of impact, represent more than bragging: it is transparency.

Human Sustainability

The excellence of a robust social media engagement operation must be sustainably supported, recognizing social conversation is unconstrained by traditional office hours; public expectation for response will not be met with a 24–48 hour turnaround, and emergencies, which may stretch for long periods of time, are vital moments for city government to offer rapid-response communication. Redundancies in response team operations may be found by adding headcount, or by creating internal systems, training existing staff, and creating on-call schedules to ensure consistency.

Struggles to maintain work–life balance transcend sector and profession, but social media managers are especially vulnerable to the boundary-crossing pace of a vibrating, unpredictable city ecosystem. Conversations often spike as commuters travel to and from work, and weather events occur at will. Building team redundancies can support staff through operations that may stretch around the clock; we watched our snowstorms in Boston hit one after the next until reaching into the double digits. Managers should take care not to model unsustainable levels of service, or else risk breaking valuable community trust. Social media support centers can mirror call center operations, with users trained in shifts to respond to citizen needs.

Self-care is an often-neglected focus for a digital media manager, particularly those engaged in constituent service and emergency operations. Teams should step away from the screen glow and recall nature and activity. It is advice that is easier to give than to follow: I have sprinted from restaurants to live tweet a mayoral speech when a community must hear from him; however, it is a vital aspiration that supports sustained commitment to the work.

Standing Still Is Falling Behind

Too much sustainability, however, may be a warning sign for the practitioner. Maintaining a program that sustains itself, buoyed by community participation and supported by organizational participation, is a victory for social media adoption. The practitioner has succeeded in advancing transparency, access, and democracy. However, greater further impact may be achieved by identifying communities whose fledgling digital programs are in need of stewardship. An emerging community of social media evangelists will serve citizens well by establishing alliances of our own in order to exchange experience and best practices.

Social media should be considered as a partner to data initiatives, media relations, and design resources, supported by a well-considered voice and visual identity, which makes these communications easy to locate and relatable to its users. The task remains for cities to create a two-way digital conversation that not only generates a public dialogue, but also leverages resulting social data to inform policy and to craft a content strategy attuned to citizen preferences.

The responsible and forward-thinking practitioner is a social media strategist or manager who diligently commits to internal communications: summarizing social conversations to inform leadership through trends, sentiment analysis, and surfacing key conversations in the social sphere. The program is equal parts customer service, digital marketing, content strategy, data analysis, and what I have come to refer to as *internal journalism* in order to creatively tell the story of public service in action.

For a time, visitors to Boston City Hall who arrived on a Wednesday might encounter a sign that the city clerk's office was closed that day. Through the adoption of social media in cities, for many interactions, posted hours barely matter. The round-the-clock nature of digital conversations aligns city halls with the community's own lifecycle. The doors have been opened, and the citizens have entered. The call is irreversible. Is your city listening?

7 Digital Dashboards as Social Media

Using Data to Increase Transparency and Accountability

Nicole M. Rishel Elias and Peter S. Federman

Digital dashboards produced by government agencies have become means to communicate complex data and reach wide audiences, making them a new and unexplored social media tool. When considering how social media is impacting governance, the first question that arises is, what constitutes a social media? We apply the United States Federal Web Managers Council's definition of social media to the use of dashboards: the various activities that integrate technology, social interaction, and content creation (www.howto.gov/social-media/social-media-types). These elements of integrating technology, social interaction, and content creation provide for a more expansive understanding of "social media" than what is commonly a term reserved for Facebook, Instagram, Twitter, LinkedIn, blogging, and YouTube activity and content (Rishel, 2011). By the United States Federal Web Managers Council's definition, information sharing and content creation in the way data is represented can take place with the use of a wider variety of technologies, as long as there are multiple users interacting to create content. Beyond digital dashboards, additional forms of social media that share these basic characteristics include: wikis, discussion forums, and e-government (Rishel, 2011).

The purpose of this chapter is to introduce readers to digital dashboards and demonstrate the potential benefits and challenges of dashboards as innovative social media tools. We begin by defining "digital dashboards" and situating dashboards in larger social media literatures and federal policy history. To explore the practical dimension of dashboard use, we present interview data and analysis of federal employees who are involved in dashboard creation and utilization. Finally, we demonstrate how dashboards can positively contribute to our understanding of social media in the context of public administration practice.

Defining Digital Dashboards

There are numerous ways to define a "digital dashboard," and for the purposes of this chapter, we chose to distill our own definition from our federal employee interview data. We asked interviewees, "How would you define 'digital dashboard'?" Most responses included some or all of the following components: utilizing technology visualization, simplifying vast or complicated data, having a shared or social element, and the means of achieving a larger goal. One respondent defined a dashboard as: "The utility that provides user-friendly mechanism for users to gain access to data easily and present it in a way that makes it easy to consume. [It] provides a focused analysis of the data." In another interview the element of shared information was key: "Data visualization about key employee metrics to help with performance management, succession planning, programming. Visual metrics that managers can relate to about the work in their office and their employees." Finally, the larger end of dashboards was articulated: "Something that helps you identify areas of concern and progress, everything from action planning to data elements, my preference is the data elements.... Data accountability measures." From interview responses, we arrived at the following definition: a digital dashboard is a tool that uses technology visualization in order to simplify and share data for the purpose of achieving an organizational goal.

The Need for Dashboards

Collecting, synthesizing, and disseminating data on federal employees has been a central priority for agencies, particularly the Office of Personnel Management (OPM) and the Equal Employment Opportunity Commission (EEOC) since the passage of the Civil Rights Act of 1964. With the advent of personal computing and the Internet making the collection and distribution of data faster and simpler, most federal agencies increasingly use data in their everyday decision-making processes. Over the past several decades, there have been numerous attempts to improve the quality of the data collected and how it is accessed and displayed within and beyond federal agencies. This is critical for internal hiring and employment practices, as well as disseminating information to the public in order to increase transparency of federal operations. Scholars call for more research on the policy and practice surrounding federal data collection (Choi, 2009; Hendrick, 1994; Milliken & Martins, 1996; Pitts, 2009). As technology progresses at an exponential rate, including developments such as information dashboards, official government social media outlets, and devices or sharing portals that allow employees to work remotely, it is important to review both past and present usages of technology that collect, evaluate, and distribute data.

Challenges to Access and Usage of Data

In the past, data has been used sparingly within the federal government and has come from limited sources. According to Choi (2009), the primary sources of federal employment data has been the Central Personnel Data File (CPDF) and the periodically administered Federal Human Capital Survey, now called the Federal Employee Viewpoint Survey (FEVS). Newcomer and Caudle (1991) and Wallman (1998) also identify these surveys as the primary source of data on federal employees, but caution that while they capture overall employee perceptions of workplace dynamics, they are not comprehensive or tailored to agency-specific issues. Furthermore, despite the FEVS and the CPDF collection of data on demographics and perceptions of the workplace, the use of this data likewise has been limited to few government reports and scholarly articles. The major challenge surrounding these large datasets is that these sources are not easily accessed or used by managers within agencies.

Time lags from data collection to the presentation of results is another concern for these survey instruments. Wallman (1998) emphasizes this lag in updating the surveys themselves—the standards that are used to categorize race and ethnicity data were updated in 1998 for the first time since 1977, demonstrating a lack of attention to the categorization of responses within these surveys to that point. New tools such as dashboards have the potential to improve both the quality and dissemination of this and other data sets, but time and research are needed to assess the impact new dashboards will have on management practices, citizens, and the scholarly community.

Even when data are made accessible and displayed in such a way that it is useful to agency decision-makers, challenges remain for the public sector. According to Broadnax (2010), research using the data from the FEVS and CPDF federal surveys has improved significantly since the 1970s, when it was at best politely discouraged and at worst completely ignored. Hendrick (1994) points out that private organizations are significantly more advanced in utilizing data for decision-making purposes, because of both an increased focus within the private sector and the fact that businesses often have simpler mission statements and structures as compared to public organizations.

Data are often used to institute management practices within public organizations. Soni (2000) explains that within the Environmental Protection Agency, there are myriad issues with current usage of demographic data. She finds that in many cases a single training is provided for data techniques and lower-level employees view the data itself as unimportant. Gilbert and Ivancevich (2000) also point to a lack of accountability where data-based decision making leads to training that is implemented but then never fully integrated into the daily workflow. Managerial support and accountability as well as multiple measures of success all contribute to a successful data-based programs.

Unfortunately, there is not much research to indicate that public organizations have adopted policy and practice that integrate data into decision-making and performance measures. Mergel and Bretschneider (2013) point out that while social media systems are being implemented in government as innovative solutions to reach the general public and communicate data, they are still in the beginning phases of their usage as effective data delivery systems. She points out three stages to social media as a data delivery tool: Intrepreneurship and Innovation, Constructive Chaos, and Institutionalization. These stages trace social media usage within governmental organizations from rogue employee Twitter accounts to standardized and consolidated messaging, which in practice can both deliver data to the public.

Comprehensive information systems in the public sector lag behind their private sector counterparts. According to Hendrick (1994), there are implications for greater innovative management when information technology systems are used effectively. Hendrick specifies that a quality information system will be "accurate, timely, accessible, comprehensive and continuous" (1994, p. 543). Pitts (2009) and Soni (2000) both found such integration to be lacking when exploring information technology in public organizations. Newcomer and Caudle (1991) review the most essential elements of public sector information systems. They provide a list of indicators for assessing information systems, including usefulness, understandable output, timeliness, access, and adaptability.[1]

For public managers to use data effectively, it must be presented in a simple and direct way. Dashboards as social media tools can serve as an excellent starting point for further inquiry into data-based decision making by federal managers, as well as serve as an excellent tool for delivering data to the general public. Rather than expecting managers or citizens to access the FEVS as their main source of data, dashboards can significantly improve access to and reporting of all types of data. Large-N research, such as the work presented by Soni (2000) and Pitts (2009), can be enhanced and improved by successful implementation of dashboards that will allow researchers to access data quickly and easily.

Social Media and New Technologies

Dashboards are being used as social media tools and are continuing to evolve and change how we view communication and information technology. Social media use among government agencies is growing quickly and is without question a tool that requires further analysis (Bryer & Zavattaro, 2011; Mergel, 2012, 2014; Mergel & Bretschneider, 2013; Rishel, 2011; Zavattaro & Sementelli, 2014). Mergel and Bretschneider (2013) agree that while social media is an emerging tool, the first step in the adoption of these technologies within a government agency is chaotic and generally performed by "intrapreneurials," individuals who take it upon themselves to experiment with new technologies as they emerge.

There is little organization as to how and when social media is adopted by government agencies, nor how they might use these technologies to increase transparency and accountability with the general public (Mergel, 2012). Mergel gives the example of Marie Davie in the Federal Acquisition Service who informally collected information through social media, using her colleagues to create a best practice for acquisitions. This type of informal experimentation could lead to what Rishel (2011) refers to as unintended consequences, but experimentation and further research on the uses of social media will be required to determine what further accountability issues may arise. As governmental organizations find new approaches to using social media as a data distribution tool, there will no doubt be myriad issues to contend with, some of which are still unknown.

Furthermore, Mergel (2014) describes the various ways in which information is created and disseminated through social media. These include the "one-way push" to educate, "two-way pull" to engage, and "networking" to interact with other individuals on a community level. While dashboards are an example of a "one-way push," the implications for sharing and accessing the data provided may well lead to the use of other functionalities, some of which may come through social media. Zavattaro and Sementelli (2014) raise a related concern of the intended "dialogue" that social media promises to foster not being met in all contexts and how to better construct engagement through social media tools. Through dashboards, it may be possible to begin to overcome some of these social media obstacles by using data to further increase organizational commitment to issues of transparency, accountability, and management practice within and beyond the federal government.

Federal Policy and the Creation of Dashboards

The increased utilization of dashboards in the federal government is partly due to policies that have required greater measured government accountability and public transparency. The Government Performance and Results Act (GPRA) is one of the foundational policies calling for the concept of "measured" accountability, and it is the precursor to the increased usage of dashboards in the government (Office of Management and Budget, 2011). Enacted on January 5, 1993, GPRA sought to shift the focus of government decision-making and accountability away from activities that are undertaken (e.g., amount of grants made) to the results of these activities (e.g., program quality). Consequently, the focus was on performance indicators to measure agency outputs, service levels, and outcomes of program activities.

The George W. Bush administration introduced the President's Management Agenda (PMA) Scorecard in 2002 to grade agencies on their management practices. Similar to what is found in current dashboards, the PMA scorecard used a traffic light scoring system of "red," "yellow," and "green," in which the Office of Management and Budget (OMB) rated federal agencies on their efforts to improve in five government-wide areas. Critical success factors under this government-wide PMA initiative include: obtaining an unqualified audit opinion, eliminating material weaknesses and Anti-deficiency Act violations, meeting financial reporting deadlines, and using financial data to support daily and long-term management decisions (Office of Management and Budget, 2001).

Subsequently, the Bush administration established the Program Assessment Rating Tool (PART), which translated GPRA's focus on goals and measurement at the agency level to the program level. The OMB led the program reviews on four categories of questions (program purpose and design; strategic planning; program management; and program results/accountability). The OMB gave scores on each question and provided an overall rating based on the scores. The PART reviews, scores, and ratings were made publicly available through Expectmore.gov. Though these were not dashboard reports, they laid the groundwork for the performance indicators to be integrated with new forms of technology and social media (ExpectMore.gov, 2008).

Beginning around 2010, there has been a dramatic increase in the use of dashboards in the federal government. This is due to the Obama administration's work on several key initiatives, more specifically, the Memorandum on

Transparency and Open Government, which was issued by President Obama on January 21, 2009. This Memorandum espoused the principles of open government and would lead to the Open Government Directive. The Open Government Directive outlined three principles of open government, transparency, participation, and collaboration, as detailed below:

> Whereby, transparency promotes accountability by providing the public with information about what the Government is doing. Participation allows members of the public to contribute ideas and expertise so that their government can make policies with the benefit of information that is widely dispersed in society. Collaboration improves the effectiveness of Government by encouraging partnerships and cooperation within the Federal Government, across levels of government, and between the Government and private institutions.
>
> (Open Government Initiative, 2009)

The Directive established deadlines for actions to be taken by federal agencies: publishing government information online, improving the quality of government information, creating and institutionalizing a culture of open government, and creating an enabling policy framework for open government. The Directive further instructed federal agencies to have an Open Government Plan and to identify at least one specific, new transparency, participation, or collaboration initiative. Lastly, the Directive required creation of an "Open Government Dashboard."

The Open Government Dashboard (OGD) is used to track agencies' progress on the deliverables required by the Directive. The OGD makes each agency's Open Government Plan publicly available, while also presenting aggregate statistics and data visualizations to provide an assessment of the state of open government in the Executive Branch. The OGD contains an evaluation of the agencies based on 30 specific criteria drawn from the Open Government Directive, grouped into five broad areas: high-value data, data integrity, open web page, public consultation, and open government plan. By early April 2010, all federal departments published an Open Government Plan, specifying roadmaps for making operations and data more transparent, and expanding opportunities for citizen participation, collaboration, and oversight.

In addition to requiring all agencies to develop Open Government Plans and the creation of the OGD, the Obama administration launched Recovery.gov in February 2009, incorporating a dashboard to track federal stimulus funding under the 2009 American Recovery and Reinvestment Act. Subsequently, the U.S. Chief Information Officer, Vivek Kundra, implemented the "IT Dashboard" in June 2009 for accountability and transparency in federal IT investments. The "IT Dashboard," a one-stop information clearinghouse, allows the public to track federal spending on information technology initiatives (Ganapati, 2011).

Performance.gov, a website launched by the OMB in 2011, provides a dashboard reporting and performance tool that "gives the public, agencies, members of Congress, and the media a view of progress underway in cutting waste, streamlining government, and improving performance." The primary purpose of Performance.gov is to concisely communicate "what the Federal Government is working to accomplish, how it seeks to accomplish its objectives, and why these efforts are important" (Performance.gov, 2011). All cabinet departments and nine other major agencies have agency pages on Performance.gov. Each agency's page describes the agency's mission and lists the agency's strategic goals, objectives, and Priority Goals. Each agency's home page also provides links to the agency's strategic plan, annual performance plan, and annual performance report; reports agency progress on government-wide management initiatives; and shows agency contributions to Cross-Agency Performance (CAP) goals.

Agency Priority Goals are designed in the following manner: "Following successful evidence-based practices used in both the private and public sectors, the Administration engaged senior Federal leaders in establishing two-year Agency Priority Goals in areas where agencies were focused on accelerated performance improvement" (Performance.gov, 2011). Government-wide Cross-Agency Performance (CAP) goals were established by the administration in areas benefiting from collaboration across multiple agencies:

> At its core, these goals serve as a simple but powerful way to motivate people and communicate priorities in improving the Federal Government's performance and accountability. Agencies establish a variety of performance goals and objectives to drive progress toward key outcomes, while outlining long-term goals and objectives in their strategic plans. Leaders in states, local governments, Federal programs, and in other countries have demonstrated the power of using specific, challenging goals—combined with frequent measurement, analysis, and follow-up—to improve performance while being more efficient and effective for the taxpayer.
>
> (Performance.gov, 2011)

Overall, Performance.gov advances President Obama's commitment to communicate candidly and concisely what the federal government is working to accomplish, how it seeks to accomplish its objectives, and why these efforts are important (Performance.gov, 2011).

The Government Performance and Results Modernization Act of 2010 (GPRAMA) followed the launch of Performance.gov and expanded upon GPRA. Signed into law on January 4, 2011, GPRAMA sought to create a clearer performance framework by defining a governance structure and by better connecting plans, programs, and performance information. After a four-year phase-in period for the GPRA of 1993, along with 13 years of the law's full implementation, GPRAMA made substantial changes. Among other things, GPRAMA continues the three agency-level products from the GPRA of 1993, but with the following changes:

1   Establishes new products and processes that focus on goal-setting and performance measurement in policy areas that cut across agencies;

2   Brings attention to using goals and measures during policy implementation;
3   Increases reporting on the Internet; and
4   Requires individuals to be responsible for some goals and management tasks.

(Office of Management and Budget, 2011)

In making these changes, GPRAMA's design drew from multiple sources. These included the views of the law's authors, the Obama administration's approach to government performance, the Bush administration's approach to government performance, the work during the 111th Congress of a Senate Budget Committee task force, and the views of the Government Accountability Office (Brass, 2012).

Given this rich and relatively recent policy history that led to the creation of dashboards, it is important to understand the federal government's commitment to the practice of implementing dashboards. The next step is to explore how dashboards are being created and used today. The next two sections explain our research design and present our analysis of current federal employees engaged in the construction and use of current dashboards.

Research Design

We performed a qualitative analysis using open-ended interviews of 11 federal employees who were selected for their expertise in dashboard data visualization and decision-making using dashboards. Interviews were conducted over a two-month period from November 2014 through January 2015. Interviews took place over the phone and in person with four participants present at each interview: two researchers, one OPM representative, and the interviewee. Each interview lasted approximately one hour. All interviewees were OPM employees with the exception of one, who works closely with OPM to create dashboards.

During interviews, the OPM representative asked most questions and the researchers each took separate notes and asked follow-up questions. To process the results of the interviews, the two sets of notes for each interview were combined. This resulted in a master document for each interviewee that encompassed all of the major topics and some quotations from the interview. In total, 11 master documents (MDs) were created. These documents were imported into NVivo, where they were coded using the interview questions and themes that emerged during the interview.

In total, there were 19 questions asked (see Appendix 7.1). Each response to a particular question was coded as that question to facilitate analysis once themes were added. Then, each response was coded by theme. We used an open coding technique consistent with Berg's (2007) understanding; we sought to "open inquiry" widely in this stage (p. 317). The interview questions were the foundation of the analysis. We followed the Marshall and Rossman (2006) approach to theme creation: "For editing and immersion strategies, [the researcher] generates the categories through prolonged engagement with the data—the text. These categories then become buckets or baskets into which segments of the text are placed" (p. 159).

As we conducted the analysis, further refinement of these categories was necessary. Many responses contained multiple themes, while some did not contain any of the relevant themes. Marshall and Rossman (2006) emphasize that generating categories and themes is important:

> For researchers relying on editing or immersion strategies, this phase of data analysis is the most difficult, complex, ambiguous, creative, and fun. Although there are few description of this process in the literature, it remains the most amenable to display through example.
>
> (Marshall & Rossman, 2006, p. 158)

From the initial readings of the texts, we constructed general themes, or "categories," in which to code the text. In the next phase of the analysis, we began to refine these categories by distilling more precise descriptions of the ideas at work (see Appendix 7.2). The coding scheme was tested for inter-coder reliability.

Analysis and Results

We begin by examining the three major themes and then delve into the key subthemes that appeared most frequently in our analysis (see Appendix 7.2). The major themes received the following number of codes: Benefits of Dashboards (244 references), Challenges of Dashboards (273 references), Organizational Concerns of Dashboards (343 references), and Future Concerns of Dashboards (87 references). With Benefits and Challenges being relatively similar, Organizational and Future Concerns for Dashboard use prompt interesting questions surrounding the practice of creating and utilizing dashboards. Each of the four major themes are evaluated below, then the subthemes most relevant to social media are examined.

Benefits of Dashboards

The Benefits of Dashboards coding category is defined as "the positive utility dashboards provide for individuals within and beyond public agencies" and includes: internal and external accessibility, internal and external

Table 7.1 Occurrences of Major Themes

Categories	Occurrences of major themes
Benefits	244
Challenges	273
Organizational	343
Future	87

accountability and transparency, ease of use, and decision-making (see Appendix 7.2). To illustrate the types of responses that were coded as Benefits, two quotations from interviews that are representative of the most common responses are cited below. First, one interviewee explains the utility of a dashboard as means to track performance and make necessary changes within the organization:

> To determine whether or not we are meeting performance standards. The dashboard is the trigger or the indicator—you are doing well or you are not—beyond this you need to figure out why we are not meeting goals. Then, make measurable progress.

Many interviewees cited the "objective" approach to sharing organizational progress as positive approach, compared to managers selectively identifying organizational priorities or making judgments about performance in the absence of evidence.

One manager emphasized the benefits that dashboards provide in "seeing" the data and tracking progress over time:

> Dashboards bring data to the forefront—bottom line is whether or not there is a benchmark, if the data isn't combined with the goals/benchmarks, it has little meaning. It [data] is placed on a shelf after annual reports. Dashboards allow for continuous reporting, and continuous monitoring and greater transparency. If I only get briefed on something once a year, I don't think it's that important. If I have greater awareness, I understand and am engaged with the data ... this makes me a better leader, because I can identify areas I need to hone in on to make better decisions for the agency.

Dashboard users, particularly at the managerial level, emphasized the importance of dashboards for both large- and small-scale decision-making. Interviewees cited the ability to make better-informed decisions and share the rationale with their employees as major benefits of dashboards.

Challenges of Dashboards

The Challenges of Dashboards coding category is defined as "the negative utility dashboards create for individuals within and beyond public agencies" and includes: data is complex, data is poorly represented, level of detail, amount of information, decision-making, dashboards lead to over-quantification, and diversity and inclusion (see Appendix 7.2). Several dashboard users emphasized that the most significant challenges that dashboards pose is related to decision-making. Some managers emphasized to need to go beyond the dashboard by linking goals and performance measures to the data presented in the dashboard. One interviewee states, "It is nice to bring data to the forefront, but you won't have any accountability unless it's directly related to a performance measure or goal. Otherwise, it's just presenting the data." Overcoming this challenge is particularly difficult, according to several interviewees, because for data to be tied to performance goals, decision-makers and employees must share an understanding of the measures, goals, and desired outcomes. This shared understanding and organization congruence goes beyond the scope of the dashboard itself and requires a concerted effort by individuals, guiding policy, and actual practice to remain consistent.

Other concerns arose with the complexity and representation of data within dashboards. A dashboard developer explained that

> Complex data is narrowed down—this is both an advantage and disadvantage. You miss a lot of the nuance of the data. If you rely on dashboards to understand the data without an understanding of this, this can be harmful.... Leaders still have to make decisions and cannot only rely on dashboards.

Several dashboard developers reiterated this caution, and emphasized that the most productive uses of dashboards require developers and decision-makers to work together from the onset of the development process in order to foster a shared understanding of the dashboard's purpose and utility. In the absence of these collaborative efforts, confusion and over-reliance on the dashboard can occur when employees make decisions using dashboards that are misaligned with the function of the dashboard.

Similarly, both dashboard developers and users voiced the caution of relying on dashboards too much, especially in two key areas: first, in terms of responsibility for understanding what the data is representing, and second, having too much information presented for a user to easily process the information. One manager who uses dashboards regularly explained that others tend toward "Overuse and relying exclusively on dashboards." This was problematic according to this interviewee, because there were many other sources of information that should not be overlooked, especially employee perspectives. Another interviewee stated that

> information overload for decision-makers [could occur] if the information is not conveyed in an easily understandable way. This could make the decision harder, rather than easier. This can add confusion and uncertainty for decision-makers. Because dashboards can be interpreted in so many ways, this can add to many choices and difficulty for decision-makers.

Both dashboard creators and users voiced cautions along these lines with dashboards causing the decision-making process to be more complicated and cumbersome. This is interesting, because a number of interviewees likewise spoke to the efficiency and expediency of dashboards for decision-making. Ultimately, shared developer–user understandings, realistic expectations of a dashboard's utility, and appropriate levels of reliance on dashboard information are central to alleviating what interviewees saw as the greatest dashboard challenges.

Organizational Concerns

Defined as "the ongoing issues that impact multiple users and developers, or all employees, within public agencies," the Organizational Concerns category includes: willingness to use dashboards, leadership, linking dashboards to performance, communication, support for arguments/justification for decision-making, lack of shared understanding among developers and users, visual representations, and collaboration. The most commonly cited concern within the category was visual representations, which was also by far the most common node within the entire scope of the interviews (i.e., with more than twice the number of occurrences than the next most common node). As dashboards are a visual medium, this is not necessarily unexpected, but it is certainly notable that nearly every interviewee saw visual representations as important.

One interviewee described their use of dashboards within their organization as follows:

> Different dashboards [are] used for different parts of my work life—Unlocking Federal Talent [is] used as a quick visualization of what is occurring within my group, [including] job satisfaction [and] demographics. [When I was] briefing agency heads and associate directors, showing them the dashboard and how to utilize the dashboard, this was the first time the data was able to jump off the screen and smack me in the face. The dashboard was able to capture the nuance of what is happening in terms of engagement within agencies. Dashboards allow data to come to life.

The visual aspect of "seeing" the data has a strong impact on interviewees, and in turn, communicating their decisions was made easier by sharing this visual representation with others in their agency. These themes of visual representation, collaboration, and leadership were echoed by others, including one interviewee who said:

> [Dashboards] improve transparency—sometimes you don't know what you don't know. The dashboard gives you a very quick easily digestible snapshot so that you can see at a glance what is going on. If the dashboard is really good, all the dots are connected and this presents a very rich story.

This term "snapshot" was used by several interviewees, indicating that the interviewees were primarily focused on using dashboards as a visual medium to provide quick and simple overviews of data to their colleagues within their agency as well as others in the federal government and the general public.

Finally, both dashboard creators and users expressed concern about how dashboards are used, as well as the implications of their increased usage. One interviewee stated that the federal government is in the midst of a

> new "dashboard movement". We must be cautious that we are not creating dashboards for dashboards sake. OPM is creating different visual tools for a dashboard to give agencies a snippet of their recruitment initiatives, [and

the] dashboard movement is catching fire. OPM in the process of creating visual tools [and using] dashboards as recruitment initiatives.

Over-reliance on visual representation could be seen as negative if the rationale and nuance behind the simplified visual is lost. Having too many visuals, especially when visuals contradict one another, was emphasized as a significant challenge for decision-makers.

Future Concerns

The Future Concerns of Dashboards coding category is defined as "the issues that users and developers foresee being concerns as dashboards advance, multiply, and are relied upon more heavily in the future within public agencies" and includes: number of dashboards, maintaining and storing dashboards, dashboard sophistication level, real-time data, and interactive and customizable (see Appendix 7.2). Dashboard users expressed some concern surrounding the possibility of collecting too much or irrelevant data. Other users and developers felt that over-reliance on dashboards for decision-making was a distinct possibility. According to one dashboard creator, "Once you start collecting the data, it's hard to stop. [By] creating tools that make the collection of data easier, we are now beginning to make this standard operating procedures." Though this seems positive, dashboard creators saw many challenges with storing, updating, and continuously processing data that is so easily collected.

The expectation for greater sophistication of dashboards was another future concern voiced by dashboard creators. One interviewee stated that it would "greatly impact the future of decision-making if the dashboard showed relevant timely data in a snapshot form with all the dots connected. This makes decision-making easier, [but you] run the risk of over-relying on dashboards." Continually maintaining this level of sophistication for numerous Dashboards would be quite costly and challenging, according to several dashboard creators. These concerns stemmed primarily from the current level of detail and abundance of dashboards that require regular maintenance today. Interviewees saw the future demand for greater breadth and depth of dashboards growing rapidly in the future.

Other users were concerned about coordination and collaboration among agencies using dashboards, as well as how and when those dashboards would be used. One user stated,

> [I'm] not sure how other agencies use Dashboards, [I'm] assuming financial and atmospheric [agencies] use them. OPM doesn't use them enough, there is room for growth. In the future, [I] see Dashboards guiding decision-making and resources similar to police forces using CompStat. Dashboards should be much more dynamic and based in real time, not in lag time capturing past data as they do now.

Several other interviewees expressed this same concern for increased capacity. Dashboard users appeared to be apprehensive about the possibility of sharing data with other agencies, and what that might mean for their agency in particular. Dashboard creators did not voice this concern with sharing dashboards across agencies. One interviewee explained,

> When I first started out as an analyst, it was to run fast programs and write up reports and that was really it. Now, with dashboards and these connected systems, as a manager I have to be cognizant of the issues of the data [and that] not all data is created equal. Collaborating with other groups [and] breaking down silos is great, but I have to have a relationship with other groups.

While the concepts of collaboration, cooperation, and data-sharing are certainly seen as positive by many of these developers and users, it is clear that many users harbor concerns about the impact of actually implementing some of these dashboard-generated relationships in practice.

Major Subthemes

The occurrence of the four most-coded subthemes were: Visual Representation (from the major theme, Organizational Concerns), Linking Dashboards to Performance (from the major theme, Organizational Concerns), Decision Making (from the major theme, Benefits), and Internal Accountability and Transparency (from the major theme, Benefits). Visual representations, or, according to interviewees, how dashboards tell a story and display data easily and simply, was a node within the Organizational Concerns theme and by far the most referenced subtheme of our interviews (see below). Mentioned at least once by each interviewee, the idea of dashboards visually representing data is the most relevant aspect of the dashboard discussion in the federal workplace. One interviewee explained, "By visualizing data, it helps determine if new policy, training or programs are needed. [Dashboards] help agencies move in the right direction and drives decisions." Visualization was often linked to positively aiding in decision-making, particularly because interviewees saw dashboards simplifying and expediting the decision-making process. Another interviewee mentioned that "[dashboards are] much faster and easier to visualize than raw data. [We] can see how much time to take and at the end of the development cycle [we] can see everything. Data is easier to interpret." Other data users noted that the visual representation of data created an equalizing dynamic within the workplace; namely, that data visuals are easy to share and discuss at all levels of the organization, not just the managerial level. One dashboard user said,

> This is the huge benefit of dashboards—the complexities are challenging, but the biggest benefit of dashboards is that we can use a dashboard to make data simple to understand by anyone. Creating a visual of complex data from many different pieces to convey a message for anyone to get their message across is very powerful.

Table 7.2 Major Subthemes

Categories	Major subthemes
Visual Representations (Organizational)	111
Linking Dashboards to Performance (Organizational)	62
Decision Making (Benefits)	54
Internal Accountability and Transparency (Benefits)	48

The second most common subtheme among interviewees was the idea that dashboards are inherently linked to performance: striking a balance between what is presented via dashboard and what is accomplished in practice. Many dashboard users emphasized the benefit that dashboards provide in increasing transparency and accountability related to performance, but they were also cautious about the need to allow for flexibility in meeting deadlines and goals and the intention to improve practice when performance is measured by dashboard. As one interviewee put it, "We have to update dashboards monthly and to hold [ourselves] accountable—[both] for our agency head to ascertain what we are working on and as an accountability metric by putting it out in the public." This idea of accountability and performance evaluation was expressed by multiple interviewees, including one who explained that their office used dashboards to

determine whether or not we are meeting performance standards. The dashboard is the trigger or the indicator—you are doing well or you are not—[and] beyond this you need to figure out why we are not meeting goals. Then, make measurable progress.

Multiple users at the managerial level noted similar steps taken to improve performance based on dashboards, especially going beyond what the dashboard presents to uncover the organizational issues taking place in practice.

Interviewees also made it clear that one of the primary ways they used dashboards within their agencies was to help with decision-making. The benefit of dashboards for decision-making was the third most-coded subtheme. Many users and creators mentioned that dashboards can help decision-makers access relevant data, as well as positively influence the decision-making process through shared understandings and increased efficiency. One interviewee highlighted the benefits of using dashboard in decision-making: "I think with the increased use of dashboards, people can look historically and can clarify the decision-making process. [Dashboards] help make better decisions." Having the simplicity of the data display compared to complicated charts and spreadsheets saves time and effort on the part of the decision-maker.

The fourth most-coded subtheme was the benefit of internal accountability and transparency. There was significant discussion among interviewees about the importance of internal accountability and transparency, or dashboards being shared among federal employees to support decision-making, policy, and practice. One interviewee stated,

Dashboards increase accountability when the stakeholders have some action items or responsibility for influencing the data. This creates peer pressure for success, especially when presenting a strong/weak performance via dashboard. Just the knowledge that dashboards exist has made internal leaders more aware of needs.

With motivation to perform like this, dashboards can be used as tools to improve accountability and transparency in order to meet these performance goals. However, some users and developers urged caution, including one who said that "definitely increase transparency, but some agencies are careful and take controls to massage data. [Dashboards are] not that transparent. If you can centralize and have independent reporting [they could be], but it will be tough." This observation raises several red flags for practice and the possibility that dashboards may be too strong a motivator to *demonstrate* performance in certain organizational contexts. The distinction between actual performance improvements and the ability to document performance improvement has been prevalent since the onset of policy calling for greater performance measures and accountability. However, it was clear that an overwhelming majority of users supported the use of dashboards in this way and that they could be a central tool for promoting greater accountability and transparency within the federal government.

Implications for Dashboards as Social Media

As dashboards continue to be improved and refined, we will see increased usage and interaction both within the federal government and with the public who access the data made available through dashboards. When considering the social media capabilities of dashboards, the three themes of accountability, transparency, and visualization are particularly relevant for dashboards in practice. Just as we have seen how other forms of social media such as Wikis or Twitter can increase accountability, transparency, and visualization, be it among politicians, corporations, individuals, or social movements, dashboards can be used in a similar manner by the federal government.

There was strong evidence for the values of accountability, transparency, and visualization in the social media context of dashboards. We created a matrix to demonstrate the most commonly coded references to specific questions and themes related to dashboards as social media tools (see Appendix 7.3). For example, when asked if dashboards have increased internal and external accountability and/or transparency (Q10, Q11), most interviewees respond that they had (1C, 1D), indicating, among other things, that "dashboards have increased accountability internally and externally by taking all the data and having it at the fingertips of the leader/manager, [so] it's hard to deny what's there. Especially when other agencies see similar trends." Another manager put it this way: "Yes, most people are sensitive to social pressure (for example, the Hawthorne effect[2]). A dashboard makes the information public and by doing this, it makes the decision-maker more accountable and the process more transparent." Just as social media has become the hallmark of a transparent and open society, with corporations and individuals sharing their values and data, dashboards serve the same purpose within the federal (and, potentially, in the future other levels of) government.

Improving the social or communicative aspects of dashboards should be a top priority in practice, especially when considering who is able to access dashboard data and how readily available this information is to internal and external users. One interviewee believed that "dashboards aren't that transparent. You can skew the facts to lead to different decisions and outcomes, especially based on the data that is put into the dashboard. Leaders need to [build] community from the top-down, [through] social media." Strong leadership paired with greater accountability is critical to making the data and the process of visualizing data more transparent. Beyond the transparency of dashboard creation and visualization, the social or sharing component of dashboard dissemination should be carefully considered by federal agencies. Dashboards that are made publicly available through government websites are not enough and lag behind the common practices of social media outlets today. Rather, agency leaders should work closely with those publishing social media posts to ensure that dashboards are regularly posted and updated on federal social media accounts.

For dashboards to generate greater accountability and transparency, visualization for public consumption likewise should be taken seriously. Increasingly, social media has become a visual medium with graphic-heavy applications like Instagram and Snapchat, for example, becoming major outlets that trump text-heavy outlets. When considering the visual elements of dashboards as social media tools, many users and developers found that the way in which data was presented visually in a dashboard was a critical element to how it would be interpreted and (potentially) further disseminated. One interviewee in response to Q1 explained,

> [There are] different interpretations [of dashboards]—static dashboards are a snapshot in time. [There are also] more exciting, interactive dashboards with data points that you can remove or add and tell stories from different angles. Interactivity is key for effectiveness.

Providing actors external to the federal government the same ability to "see" and engage with dashboards is essential to their prolonged success as social media tools.

As dashboard technology improves and more agencies, federal employees, and the general public are integrated into the usage of these tools, according to one federal manager, we will have "More accessibility, more interaction, more users will have interest. The more traffic coming to the dashboard, the more data can be analyzed. Making the dashboard public-facing and connecting it easily to social networks and media [is critical]." In large part, the success of dashboards in the end will depend on how well federal agencies are able to strike a balance between increased accountability, transparency, and visualization. A dashboard user explained that "[dashboards allow] communication via domino effect, and social media makes the dashboard modern and sexy to the user." The prospects for dashboards as social media tools are exciting, with these insights from current federal employees along with strong policy support, the hope is for continued improvements to the way dashboards are presented and shared, ultimately increasing accountability and transparency in the future.

Acknowledgments

We would like to thank the Office for the Advancement of Research at John Jay College, CUNY and PSC CUNY for funding this work. We would also like to acknowledge the U.S. Office of Personnel Management for research access and support of this research project.

Appendix 7.1: Interview Questions

1   How do you define a dashboard?
2   What dashboards did you help create?
3   What dashboards do you utilize in decision-making?
4   How are dashboards being used in your agency and government-wide?
5   What is your role in creating dashboards?
6   What is your role in utilizing dashboards?
7   What is the intended use for decision-making?
8   How have dashboards helped decision-makers?
9   How have dashboards made decision-making more challenging?
10 Have dashboards increased accountability? If so, internally and/or externally? How?
11 Have dashboards increased transparency? If so, internally and/or externally? How?
12 What could be done to dashboards to increase accountability?
13 What could be done to dashboards to increase transparency?
14 How do dashboards impact the future of data management?
15 How do dashboards impact the future of data representation?
16 How do dashboards impact the future of decision-making?
17 What do diversity and inclusion dashboards provide?
18 How are diversity and inclusion dashboards challenging for decision-making?
19 How do dashboards impact diversity and inclusion policy and practice?

Appendix 7.2: Coding Scheme by Theme

1   Benefits of Dashboards: the positive utility dashboards provide for individuals within and beyond public agencies

    a   Internal Accessibility—individuals within organization having access to data that has been complex/difficult to obtain in the past
    b   External Accessibility—citizens outside of organization having access to data that has been complex/difficult to obtain in the past

c   Internal Accountability and Transparency—dashboards being shared among federal employees to support decision-making, policy, and practice

d   External Accountability and Transparency—dashboards being shared publicly to support federal decision-making, policy, and practice

e   Ease of Use—federal employees being able to complete tasks more efficiently and/or effectively with a dashboard

f   Decision-making—dashboards help decision makers access helpful data; dashboards positively influence decision-making.

2   Challenges of Dashboards: the negative utility dashboards create for individuals within and beyond public agencies

a   Data Is Complex—challenging and/or unclear for individuals to understand what is being represented by the dashboard

b   Data Is Poorly Represented—challenging and/or unclear for individuals to see how data is being represented by the dashboard

c   Level of Detail—challenging to design a dashboard that provides the appropriate level of detail for all individuals utilizing the dashboard

d   Amount of Information—challenging to design a dashboard that provides the appropriate amount of data for all individuals utilizing the dashboard

e   Decision-making—dashboards hinder decision makers by the type and level of data presented; dashboards negatively influence decision making

f   Dashboards Lead to Over-quantification—some aspects of internal and external outcomes are difficult to quantify

g   Diversity and Inclusion—demographic data does not capture what could be most helpful to decision-makers, but it is the only data available.

3   Organizational Concerns: the ongoing issues that impact multiple users and developers, or all employees, within public agencies

a   Willingness to Utilize Dashboards—buy-in from individuals who could but potentially do not utilize dashboards

b   Leadership—buy-in from leaders who potentially do not recognize the utility of dashboards; leaders need help understanding dashboards and make strategic decisions about dashboard use

c   Linking Dashboards to Performance—striking a balance between what is presented via dashboard and what is accomplished in practice (i.e., allowing for flexibility in deadlines and goals), intention to improve practice

d   Communication—dashboards as tools for communication data internally and externally

e   Support for Arguments/Justification for Decision-making—dashboards presenting quantifiable measures to eliminate arbitrary or personal preference impacted decision-making; dashboard data strengthens rationale for policy and practice f   Lack of Shared Understanding among Developers and Users—the intended purpose and utility of dashboards is inconsistent among developers and users

g   Visual Representations—dashboards tell a story, dashboards display data easily and simply

h   Collaboration—the need to work together in constructing and understanding dashboards.

4   Future Concerns: the issues that users and developers foresee being concerns as dashboards advance, multiply, and are relied upon more heavily in the future within public agencies

a   Number of Dashboards—concern as to how many dashboards will be created, maintained, and utilized due to the amount of work this requires

b   Maintaining and Storing Dashboards—concern as to how to manage, regularly update, and store dashboard data due to the amount of work this requires

c   Dashboard Sophistication Level—concern as to how to maintain a balance between individual decision-making and dashboards "deciding for" the individual versus no guidance on next steps

d   Real-time Data—desire for timely data in the future

e   Interactive and Customizable—desire for a user-centered, flexible dashboard experience in the future

Appendix 7.3: Social Media Node/Question Matrix

	1: C	1: D	3: D	3: E	4: C	4: D	4: G	4: H
Q1	1	1	2	2	4	3	9	1
Q7	2	2	0	0	5	1	8	2
Q8	2	2	0	0	3	3	7	0
Q9	3	3	1	1	5	0	6	0
Q10	11	11	0	0	2	1	3	0
Q11	10	8	0	0	2	3	2	0
Q12	3	3	0	0	3	3	3	1
Q13	0	0	0	0	0	4	6	4
Q16	0	0	3	2	0	1	4	0
Q18	0	0	0	0	4	1	2	1

Notes

1 Further information on these concepts is found in Newcomer and Caudle (1991, p. 380), which will be useful in evaluating the use of social media, Dashboards, and other innovate technologies.

2 An explanation and more information on the Hawthorne effect, an influential human relations concept, can be found at the Harvard Library website: www.library.hbs.edu/hc/hawthorne/intro.html.

References

Berg, B. L. (2007). *Qualitative research methods for the social sciences* (6th ed.). Boston, MA: Allyn and Bacon.

Brass, C. T. (2012, February). Changes to the Government Performance and Results Act (GPRA): Overview of the new framework of products and processes (Publication No. 7-5700 R42379). Retrieved from www.fas.org/sgp/crs/misc/R42379.pdf.

Broadnax, W. D. (2010). Diversity in public organizations: A work in progress. *Public Administration Review, 70*, s177–s179.

Bryer, T. A., & Zavattaro, S. M. (2011). Social media and public administration: Theoretical dimensions and introduction to the symposium. *Administrative Theory & Praxis, 33*(3), 325–340.

Choi, S. (2009). Diversity in the U.S. federal government: Diversity management and employee turnover in federal agencies. *Journal of Public Administration Research & Theory, 19*(3), 603–630.

Expectmore.gov. (2008). The Program Assessment Rating Tool (PART). Retrieved from http://georgewbush-whitehouse.archives.gov/omb/expectmore/part.html.

Ganapati, S. (2011). Use of dashboards in government. IBM Center for the Business of Government. Retrieved from www.federalnewsradio.com/pdfs/080111_dashboard_report_ibm.pdf.

Gilbert, J. A., & Ivancevich, J. M. (2000). Valuing diversity: A tale of two organizations. *Academy of Management Executive, 14*(1), 93–105.

Hendrick, R. (1994). An information infrastructure for innovative management of government. *Public Administration Review, 54*(6), 543–550.

Marshall, C., & Rossman, G. B. (2006). *Designing qualitative research* (4th ed.) Thousand Oaks, CA: SAGE Publications.

Mergel, I. (2012). The public manager 2.0: Preparing the social media generation for a networked workplace. *Journal of Public Affairs Education, 18*(3), 467–492.

Mergel, I. (2014). A manager's guide to assessing the impact of government social media interactions. *IBM Center for the Business of Government: Research, trends, reports*. Retrieved July 2, 2014, from www.businessofgovernment.org/report/manager's-guide-assessing-impact-government-social-media-interactions.

Mergel, I., & Bretschneider, S. I. (2013). A three-stage adoption process for social media use in government. *Public Administration Review, 73*(3), 390–400.

Milliken, F. J., & Martins, L. L. (1996). Searching for common threads: Understanding the multiple effects of diversity in organizational groups. *Academy of Management Review, 21*(2), 402–433.

Newcomer, K. E., & Caudle, S. L. (1991). Evaluating public sector information systems: More than meets the eye. *Public Administration Review, 51*(5), 377–384.

Office of Management and Budget. (2001). *Office of Federal Financial Management: President's management agenda*. Retrieved from www.whitehouse.gov/omb/financial_fia_pma.

Office of Management and Budget. (2011). *Government Performance and Results Act (GPRA) related materials*. Retrieved from www.whitehouse.gov/omb/mgmt-gpra/index-gpra.

Open Government Initiative. (2009). *Open government directive*. Retrieved from www.whitehouse.gov/open/documents/open-government-directive.

Performance.gov. (2011). *About this site*. Retrieved from www.performance.gov/about.

Pitts, D. (2009). Diversity management, job satisfaction, and performance: Evidence from U.S. federal agencies. *Public Administration Review, 69*(2), 328–338.

Rishel, N. M. (2011). Digitizing deliberation: Normative concerns for the use of social media in deliberative democracy. *Administrative Theory & Praxis, 33*(3), 411–432.

Soni, V. (2000). A twenty-first-century reception for diversity in the public sector: A case study. *Public Administration Review, 60*(5), 395–408.

Wallman, K. K. (1998). Data on race and ethnicity: Revising the federal standard. *The American Statistician, 52*(1), 31–33.

Zavattaro, S. M., & Sementelli, A. J. (2014). A critical examination of social media adoption in government: Introducing omnipresence. *Government Information Quarterly, 31*(2), 257–264.

8   Dashboards as Social Media Tools
Practitioner Perspectives

Ray Parr

The growing acceptance of digital technology along with the need to under-stand complex data sets has resulted in a significant increase in the number of Dashboards being used across the federal government. However, it can be diffi-cult for practitioners to bridge the gap between what is proposed in theory and how these methods can be applied in practice. In this perspective piece, as a Personnel Psychologist with the U.S. Office of Personnel Management (OPM) in the Office of Diversity and Inclusion (ODI), I present my assessment of how Dashboards are being used and their potential as social media tools within this agency and across the federal government.

My office leads and manages government-wide diversity and inclusion (D&I) efforts within OPM. Known around the office as the "data guru," I am respons-ible for developing government-wide D&I data metrics. I speak regularly with federal employees about the importance of measureable outcomes for diversity and inclusion programs and firmly believe that D&I metrics must be accessible not only to analysts but also to senior leadership through effective analysis and data visualization.

In an effort to help practitioners bridge the gap between theory and practice, this piece provides a mix of insights and suggested best practices taken from my experience working with Dashboards. While all government employees have their own individual and unique experiences that influence their work style and preferred tools, it is useful to be aware of others' experience to avoid some of their missteps and build on their successes. I hope this experience working with Dashboards can provide such insight into a practitioner's perspective on Dash-boards as social media tools.

What Do All Successful Dashboards Have in Common? They Are SMART

One common theme driving Dashboard usage within the federal government is the concept of measured accountability, which places emphasis on specific measurable outcomes that can be used to evaluate organizational performance. The concept of measured accountability is consistent with SMART criteria, an acronym that outlines the primary objective of any goal as *specific, measur-able, achievable, relevant,* and *time-bound*.[1] When those involved in creating

Dashboards design them with these criteria in mind, the result is consistently a stronger product. It is important that developers and practitioners have a clear understanding of what the Dashboard is measuring and how it functions in order to gain useful information about organizational performance from the dashboard.

The Federal IT Dashboard provides an excellent example of a successful Dashboard that fits the concept of measured accountability and closely follows the SMART criteria. Launched on June 1, 2009, the Federal IT Dashboard's *specific* purpose is to provide information on the effectiveness of government IT programs to help guide decisions around the management of federal IT resources.[2] To accomplish this purpose, the Federal IT Dashboard provides a *measurable* assessment of IT programs by capturing general information of over 7,000 federal IT investments and detailed data for over 700 investments that agencies have classified as major.[3] Additionally, the Federal IT Dashboard provides data on awarded contracts including the contract amount, vendor, and start and end dates; performance metrics, such as the Chief Information Officer's (CIO) rating of a program, baseline results, target results, and actual results; and cost and schedule information. The Federal IT Dashboard also sets an *achievable* goal of helping to improve or guide the management of the estimated $80 billion in federal IT spending. Accordingly, the Federal IT Dashboard is able to shed light on potential areas of concern and possible inefficiencies, which has resulted in an estimated savings of $3 billion dollars.[4,5]

The Federal IT Dashboard is *relevant* by seeking to improve the management of IT resources and increase transparency. For other Dashboards, the SMART criterion of relevancy can lead to difficulties, which are discussed in the following paragraph. Since the Federal IT Dashboard is aligned with the annual Federal Budget and the Dashboard is set up to track IT investment progress over time, the goals of the Dashboard are inherently *time-bound*. Furthermore, every agency's CIO is responsible for evaluating and updating the data on a regular basis.

From a practitioner's perspective, the Federal IT Dashboard is easy to understand and a useful tool for decision-making, because this Dashboard encompasses the concept of measured accountability and closely follows the SMART criteria by providing insights into inefficient policies, underperforming programs, and areas of potential concern. However, like many Dashboards, the major weakness of the Federal IT Dashboard resides in the accuracy and timeliness of the data contained within, which in turn can affect the relevancy of the dashboard. A Government Accountability Office (GAO) report publicly released on January 13, 2014 found that some CIOs' ratings of risk associated with IT projects as depicted on Dashboard were inconsistent. In fact, the report stated that "of the 80 investments reviewed, 53 of the CIO ratings were consistent with the investment risk, 20 were partially consistent, and seven were inconsistent." According to the report, since the OMB did not update the public version of the Dashboard as the President's Budget Request was being created, the public version of the Dashboard was not updated for 15 of the past 24 months prior to the report's release.[6] While not utterly detrimental to the goals or purpose of the Federal IT Dashboard, similar issues surrounding the accuracy and timeliness of the data is a troubling trend across the federal government. For Dashboards to be useful to the community of users, information accuracy is critical.

Why Use a Dashboard?

There are numerous approaches to guiding an agency to focus on measured accountability, and Dashboards provide one of many avenues to achieve this goal. Consequently, one must understand the motivations behind using a Dashboard over other approaches, and specifically what Dashboards can provide an agency. Dashboards can show the areas where an agency is meeting or exceeding its mission and goals as well as areas where improvement in performance is needed. Government leaders can use this insight to determine program viability, identify weaknesses and make changes, and reallocate resources if necessary. In particular, a Dashboard can provide a clear summary of key performance metrics in a central location. For example, the Federal IT Dashboard has a section dedicated to summarizing government-wide performance in critical areas (see Figure 8.1).

Dashboards can also be useful for synthesizing multiple sources of data through the use of informative graphics or "data visualizations." The Federal IT Dashboard uses a motion trend chart, which can combine multiple agencies' spending data to compare how it changes over the years; see Figure 8.2.

A treemap data visualization (see Figure 8.3) from the Federal IT Dashboard depicts the comparative size of IT investments by agency, showcasing the overall IT spending budget and the agencies that encompass the majority of said budget. Data visualizations like this allow users to understand complex data in less time than it would take to read a traditional report or budget. Key pieces of information stand out and are easily discernable by those who do not have data backgrounds.

Dashboards as a Social Media Tool

The Dashboard movement began as a popular internal tool of the federal government, but developers and users must be smart about the data they are attempting to relay and to whom. Dashboards as social media tools and Dashboards that capture public trends could be helpful for both federal agencies and the public. For example, in one particular effort, OPM is in the process of creating different visual tools for Dashboards to give agencies a snippet of their recruitment initiatives. If designed with a social media focus in mind, the new recruitment Dashboard could target the public, and even potential applicants by providing information regarding the application process, statistics on hiring trends, and other information that would be pertinent to both potential employees and employers. Dashboards should be thought of as two-way social media tools that both disseminate information to a community of users and that capture information for agency users.

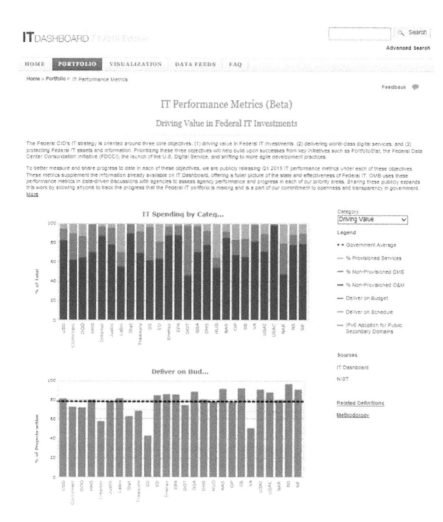

Figure 8.1 Federal IT Dashboard IT Performance Metrics.

A major challenge that should be addressed in current Dashboard design and use is that most Dashboards are static. Data are not constantly updated, but instead is filled on annual or semi-annual basis, which is detrimental to the use of Dashboards as social media. In order to function as a form of social media, Dashboards should be dynamic, interactive, and socially integrated. A dynamic Dashboard can provide metrics in real time, similar to web traffic analytics tools such as Google Analytics. Using web analytics as an example, a dynamic Dashboard would allow a website owner to have access to real-time data on website users, approximate location of traffic, at what point users lost interest in their website, and areas of the site where users are interacting the most. This technology would be very useful in designing publicly facing programs and information outlets.

Figure 8.2 Federal IT Dashboard IT Spending Trend Data Visualization (Motion Trend Chart).

Figure 8.3 Federal IT Dashboard Investment and Budget Allocation by Agency (Treemap).

In fact, Dashboards already exist that aggregate social media data, including from real-time update formats such as Twitter or Instagram. These services not only provide users with an avenue to constantly communicate through the Internet and update other users, but also provide a rich source of dynamic data that can be analyzed through Dashboards. For example, an application called TweetDeck is a social media Dashboard for Twitter account users that allows a user to follow real-time trends on Twitter. This can be used not only for keeping up with friends and family, but also to keep tabs on world events and emergencies. TweetDeck and other applications can be set up to provide alerts based on keywords, geographic location, or even publicly traded stock symbols. If the federal government were to adopt this form of dashboard as a two-way social media tool, up-to-date information could be disseminated to a community of followers and the agency could map information gathering and other social media activity trends.

Flexibility is another key element that should be incorporated into Dashboards in order to maximize social media function. User control or freedom to manipulate the information being provided by the dashboard is key to creating more dynamic interfaces. Many web-based dashboards use interactivity, partly due to the fact that they inherently allow for a greater degree of user control. However, current federal Dashboards often lack the social integration that is required for it to become the center of a community and truly a social medium—this requires greater flexibility. Up to this point, Dashboards within the federal government have been useful as one-way conversation devices, providing information on events that have already occurred, ongoing progress on previously made commitments, and future actions to be taken. However, this current configuration of communication limits the ability of users to fully take part in the conversation.

Thinking back to when Dashboard technology was first introduced in the federal government, there was a lot of interest in Dashboards. Developers must keep Dashboards relevant, fresh, and publicly available in order to maintain that momentum. To expand their application, Dashboards should be shared publicly not only through agency websites but also on popular social media government sites such as Facebook and Twitter where the public searches for timely information. By increasing the usage of Dashboards as social media tools, these outlets would generate greater accountability to the public and better serve the decision-makers within federal agencies. For Dashboards to become truly social, they must continually increase their ability to be dynamic and interactive, and attempt to create a community around itself.

Notes

1 Poister, T. H. (2008). *Measuring Performance in Public and Nonprofit Organizations*. John Wiley & Sons.
2 https://itdashboard.gov/faq#faq1.
3 https://itdashboard.gov/faq#faq1.
4 www.whitehouse.gov/economy/reform/cutting-waste.
5 http://fedscoop.com/kundra-on-white-house-white-board-it-dashboard-saved-3-billion.
6 www.gao.gov/products/GAO-14-64.

Part III

Social Media

External Relations

9 Fostering Engagement Through Social Media?

The Case of the Washington, DC, Metropolitan Police Department

Lori A. Brainard[1]

In fall 2014, a grand jury in Ferguson, Missouri, chose not to indict a white police officer who shot a young black man. The case received a great deal of attention because of reports that the young man, Michael Brown, was unarmed and in a posture of surrender (though witness testimony is conflicted). Following the grand jury decision, protests—often including the destruction of property—ensued. Protestors were met with a police department mobilized with military-style weaponry and combat gear, escalating tensions. This is but one example, admittedly an extreme example, of poor relations between a police department and the residents it serves.

In recent years, a focus on a declining government–citizen relationship—and movements toward improving that relationship—has emphasized the possibilities of using technology and, in particular, social media to engage citizens. This is especially relevant in the area of policing. With the widespread adoption of community policing, police departments are searching for new methods of engaging with residents, and social media may provide one means. Nevertheless, there are no existing best practices, and the adoption and use of social media vary greatly from one department to another. In fact, according to one survey, police chiefs identify learning to use social media for resident engagement as a clear priority (Police Executive Research Forum, 2012).

This chapter provides a case study of the Washington, DC, Metropolitan Police Department's (DC MPD) use of social media to engage residents. DC MPD has been on the leading edge of social media use to engage with residents, beginning with its adoption of Yahoo! Groups in 2004 and its subsequent adoption of Facebook, Twitter, and YouTube. This chapter asks: (1) How has DC MPD come to adopt social media technologies? (2) How does DC MPD use its social media, and what role does it play in engaging residents? (3) What might we learn from the DC MPD experience with social media, especially as it relates to prospects for relationship-building with residents?

I find that DC MPD has embraced each technology as it has become widely available, but also that police have come to dominate these technologies. In practice, these venues are primarily forums for information distribution. While that is a valuable service, it does not reflect the more relationship- and collaboration-building emphasis of community policing. In order to achieve these benefits, if police departments wish to get online, they should consider how they structure the technologies and their participation and presence on them.

Government, Citizens, and Social Media

Though definitions of social media vary, one basic and very useful definition comes from Bryer and Zavattaro, who note that social media are "technologies that facilitate social interaction, make possible collaboration, and enable deliberation across stakeholders. These technologies include blogs, wikis, media (audio, photo, video, text) sharing tools, networking platforms (including Facebook), and virtual worlds" (2011, p. 327). Importantly, Bryer and Zavattaro note that social media do not *inherently* lead to social interaction, deliberation, and collaboration. People—those in government agencies and citizens—need to *use* them interactively, collaboratively, and deliberatively. Further, social media are not necessary for interaction, collaboration, and deliberation in a networked environment as the case studies—ranging from the use of clay tablets in the Roman era, to the use of hand-copying during the Protestant Reformation, to the use of broadsides in the American revolution—in *Writing on the Wall: Social Media—The First 2000 Years* (Standage, 2013) make clear. The key is for government and citizens to use social media in ways that foster participation, deliberation, and collaboration.

The particular social media technologies that DC MPD uses include Yahoo! Groups, Facebook, Twitter, and YouTube. Yahoo! is a combination web portal, search engine, and news curating site. It allows for interaction through its Yahoo! Groups, which are essentially old listserv technologies. Facebook and Twitter allow for the creation of content and enable interaction through social networking (the individual development of lists of friends and followers). Twitter posts are limited to 140 characters, while Facebook posts are not. YouTube is a network of "channels" that people can follow and on which video can be posted. MPD also began using Instagram, a networked photo-sharing site, at the beginning of 2014.

There are various reasons why government agencies wish to use social media. These include the desire to lower costs (Johnston & Hansen, 2011), enhance existing activities (Meijer & Thaens, 2013), and to connect with and engage residents. The latter includes a wide range of activities, from providing information to citizens, to conducting transactions, collaborating with citizens (defining problems and developing solutions), and deliberating with them (considering various options and deciding together). Though different scholars use different terms to mean often similar ideas, we can make use of two definitions of citizen/public engagement/participation. In a report on "civic engagement," Roberts notes that

> Public engagement is people's direct involvement in community affairs rather than reliance on indirect representation mediated by others such as subject-matter experts, elected officials, or bureaucracies. Based on what

people perceive to be important to them, they engage in problem-solving and decision-making in order to make a difference in their world.

(Quoted in Svara & Denhardt, 2010, p. 5)

Nabatchi (2012, p. 6) defines citizen participation as "processes by which public concerns, needs, and values are incorporated into decision-making." Citizen participation happens in many places (e.g., civil society and electoral, legislative, and administrative arenas) and can take many forms (e.g., methods may range from information exchanges to democratic decision-making). This chapter relies on Nabatchi's broader definition in order to remain open to all forms of participation, including exchange and transactions. It understands Roberts' definition of engagement in problem-solving and decision-making as one end of a continuum of engagement with less intense forms of engagement such as the exchange that Nabatchi discusses at the other end. Rather than citizen, this chapter uses the term "resident," in recognition that police departments are to serve all residents in a community, not just legal citizens.

Engagement with residents is especially important to police departments (PDs), which emphasize community policing—in which the police and the community work together to define problems and develop solutions (Skogan, 1994, p. 1). PDs potentially have much to gain from using social media to engage with residents. Using social media as an adjunct to community policing can enhance existing efforts by bringing more residents into a relationship with police, allowing for asynchronous communication and thereby lowering the costs associated with participation, allowing for anonymity, etc. Nevertheless, use of social media by PDs is in its infancy, and they want to learn more about how to use these technologies (Police Executive Research Forum, 2012). Through an in-depth case study, this chapter attempts to draw some lessons.

Methods

This chapter provides a case study of DC MPD's use of social media to engage residents. An in-depth case study should prove useful for a variety of reasons. First, many studies of police use of social media are focused on one city's use of one platform (Brainard & Derrick-Mills, 2011; Brainard & McNutt, 2010). Others focus on several or many cities but on a single platform (Crump, 2011; Heverin & Zach, 2012). Still others focus on many cities and many platforms (Brainard & Edlins, 2014). This study focuses on one city and its several platforms. By focusing on one city and its several platforms, we are better able to draw some specific lessons. Especially in a period in which police–resident relations appear to be quite tense, drawing such lessons is important.

DC MPD was chosen in part out of convenience, as I reside in DC and, more importantly, have previously collected data on DC MPD's use of Yahoo! Groups from earlier studies (Brainard & Derrick-Mills, 2011; Brainard & McNutt, 2010). To that extent, this chapter builds on and extends those earlier studies. Three research questions guide this study: (1) How has DC MPD come to adopt social media technologies? (2) How does DC MPD use its social media, and what role does it play in engaging residents? (3) What might we learn from the DC MPD experience with social media, especially as it relates to prospects for relationship-building with residents?

Data for this study come from various sources. I have pre-existing data on DC MPD's use of Yahoo! Groups, and I maintain membership data, data about posts and threads, and descriptive, textual data. These data are from 2006, the first full year in which all seven of DC MPD's police districts had active Yahoo! Groups. These data were reported and analyzed in "Virtual Government–Citizen Relations: Informational, Transactional, or Collaborative?" (Brainard & McNutt, 2010). The data are re-presented here in order to serve as a benchmark for similar 2014 Yahoo! Groups data. These data also include membership numbers, data on posts and threads, and textual data. Thus, I am able to compare DC MPD's use of Yahoo! Groups in 2006[2] with its use in 2014. Additionally, I collected posts and threads from Facebook and Twitter for June 2014. June was chosen for the latter because it is also the last month for which the author has Yahoo! data. So while much of the Yahoo! Group data can be compared over time, Facebook and Twitter cannot. However, we can make some rough comparisons across platforms in 2014.

I performed both quantitative and qualitative thread analysis. For quantitative analysis, I analyzed the number of posts and threads, the number of threads of two posts, the number of threads of three or more posts, and their varying percentages. Additionally, this chapter uses the number and percentage of PD posts to social media to understand levels of police dominance. For qualitative analysis, I read each thread of two posts and each thread of three or more posts in order to identify whether exchange (such as a question and answer) occurred and whether there was any ongoing discussion reflective of deliberation and collaboration.

There are several limitations to this study, some of which relate to the nature of the technologies and their development over time. Regarding Yahoo! Group data, I was not able to collect 2014 data that is perfectly comparable to the 2006 data. Thus, for example, the 2006 data showed membership by month. Yahoo! Groups no longer displays monthly membership data; rather it displays yearly data. I thus needed to use the membership data for 2014 as of June 30 (the end date for data collection). Similarly, I was unable to collect a full year of Yahoo! Group posts for 2014, as the cut-off date for data collection was June 30. Twitter presented its own problems. While I could collect all posts by DC MPD, including posts that replied to others, I was unable to collect posts initiated from outside DC MPD and tweeted at DC MPD (unless DC MPD replied). Tweets from residents to DC MPD do not show up on DC MPD's Twitter feed unless DC MPD responds. The next section presents the data in sequence of research question. Finally, I do not investigate YouTube or Twitter because MPD does not attempt to use either in a participatory way.

DC MPD and Social Media

DC MPD has two tracks for its social media. One is primarily for public relations purposes and is targeted at children; DC MPD's Sam the Bloodhound launched his Facebook page on February 12, 2014, and began tweeting on April 9, 2014. The other social media track is dedicated to engaging all residents and stakeholders in the *work* of DC MPD (versus for public relations and marketing). This includes Yahoo! Groups, a Facebook page, and a Twitter account. I have chosen not to include YouTube. The research questions focus on the police–resident relationship online. DC MPD uses YouTube exclusively for posting videos on police recruitment, traffic safety information, safety education, and cold case profiles. Instagram is used in a similar way. They are excluded from this study.

DC MPD adopted Yahoo! Groups, Facebook, and Twitter as these technologies came online. With its use of Yahoo! Groups in particular, DC MPD put itself at the forefront of using social media to engage with residents. Over the course of approximately one year, DC MPD got all of its police districts up on Yahoo! It launched its first Yahoo! Group, that of the Third District, in March 2004 in order to engage in "dialogue between the Police and residents, activists, DC Government agency representatives, and elected leaders" (Smith, n.d.)—and for "coming together to solve problems" (Moisan, 2005). District commanders and public information officers moderate the Yahoo! Groups. DC MPD launched its Facebook page in 2008. While a few of the police districts also have their own Facebook pages, not all do, and so the DC MPD-wide Facebook page is the primary mechanism for Facebook-based engagement with citizens. DC MPD began tweeting in 2011 and has one MPD-wide feed. Both Facebook and Twitter are populated by the Command Center—the central dispatching unit of DC MPD—rather than mediated by public information officers.

DC MPD's Use of Social Media

This section presents the data demonstrating how DC MPD uses Yahoo! Groups, Facebook, and Twitter for engaging residents. Findings are discussed in the next section.

Yahoo! Groups. Table 9.1 demonstrates growth in membership from 2006, the first year for which complete membership data are available (Brainard & McNutt, 2010, p. 844), through the first half of 2014. The table shows that the Seventh District began its group with the fewest members. The Third District,

Table 9.1 Membership by District, 2006 vs. 2014

District	2006	As of June 30, 2014	% change
1st	236	2,947	115
2nd	130	1,340	931
3rd	452	1,725	282
4th	393	1,825	364
5th	394	1,957	397
6th	158	774	390
7th	45	891	188

the first to launch, began its group with the most members. As of June 30, 2014, the First District had the most members, while the Sixth District had the fewest. In terms of percentage change in membership between 2006 and 2014, the Second District achieved the highest, with 931% growth, while the First District achieved 115% growth in membership.

Table 9.2 shows population and crime data by police district. Poverty and unemployment data are tracked by Police Service Area (PSA—neighborhood sub-stations). In the portrayal of poverty and unemployment in Table 9.2, the number to the left shows the highest rate of all PSAs in the relevant district while the number to the right shows the lowest. Thus, for example, among all seven districts, District Seven has the highest crime rate. Similarly, the Seventh District has the highest poverty rate (among all PSAs in all districts), with its highest PSA poverty rate (44%) being the highest of all PSAs and its lowest (22%) being the highest of all PSAs. This same pattern is reflected in unemployment rate. Similarly, the Seventh District's total number of violent crimes is highest among all PSAs (tied with that of the First District). Table 9.2 shows the Third District with the lowest poverty rate. While its PSA with the highest unemployment rate is midway between the highest and lowest in other districts, its lowest unemployment rate is among the lowest. The Seventh District and the First District have the most violent crime, followed by the Sixth District and then the Fourth District.

We get further insight by looking at the number of posts to Yahoo! Groups in each district by year. Table 9.3 shows that District Seven, the poorest district, consistently has had the fewest or among the fewest posts. This shows that the digital divide *may* be alive and well in DC. On the other hand, District Seven also experienced the most growth in posts between 2006 and the first half of 2014—404%—only outdone by District Two's 832%. In the First and Third Districts, we also see *negative* change, the significance of which varies depending on whether one looks at growth through 2013 or through June 2014.

The level of activity within each Yahoo! Group is also important. One indicator of activity level is number of posts per person (= no. of year X posts/no. of year X members). In order to attain the most accurate number, we would need the number of posts in a complete year *and* the number of members for the same complete year. Unfortunately, while we have the original posts per person by district for 2006, we do not have directly comparable data for 2013, for two reasons. First, Yahoo! does not make annual membership data available. Second, at time of writing (December 2014), we do not have a full year of data for 2014. Nevertheless, data for the first half of 2014 at least can give us some insight into posts per person—and thus into current levels of activity. In short, more posts per member indicate (and *only* indicate) conversation in some form—either a simple back and forth or an ongoing dialogue; in any case, more than a single post, which indicates simple information distribution. Comparing the posts per member across each district, Table 9.4 shows an across-the-board decline in posts per member from 2006 through the first half of 2014. Within 2014, we see the Seventh District has the highest number of posts per person (1.6), as it did in 2006, followed by the Sixth District (1.3) and the Second District (1). The

Table 9.2 Poverty, Unemployment, and Crime by District

	First District	Second District	Third District	Fourth District	Fifth District	Sixth District	Seventh District
Population, 2010	73,991	123,950	80,987	106,833	61,701	70,206	69,800
% Poor persons, 2007–2011; high/low PSA	36/7	29/4	20/6	19/10	35/13	38/17	44/22
% Unemployed, 2007–2011; high/low PSA	19/2	5.7/1.9	13/3.5	16/7	22/8.5	24/14	31/17
Violent crime, 2011	160	31	123	74	118	137	160

Source: www.neighborhoodinfodc.org/comparisontables/comparisontables.html (December 3, 2014).

Table 9.3 Posts to Yahoo! Groups by District and Year

District	2006	2007	2008	2009	2010	2011	2012	2013	2014 (as of June 30)	% change through 2013	% change through June 30, 2014
1st	1,381	3,468	3,508	2,556	2,543	2,399	2,214	2,015	1,317	-42	-4
2nd	144	644	1,370	1,518	1,570	1,978	1,272	2,216	1,342	244	832
3rd	1,263	2,554	1,534	1,905	1,589	1,805	1,719	1,493	904	-42	-28
4th	1,142	1,951	3,174	2,717	3,193	2,527	2,978	2,437	1,393	25	22
5th	648	1,002	2,421	2,213	2,397	2,726	2,285	3,274	1,485	227	129
6th	241	1,202	1,392	1,347	1,421	1,475	1,353	1,562	986	30	309
7th	279	916	1,437	1,232	1,172	1,417	1,114	1,411	1,408	54	404

Table 9.4 Posts per Member

District	2006 Posts per member	Members as of June 30, 2014	Posts as of June 30, 2014	Posts per member as of June 30, 2014
1st	5.9	2,947	1,317	0.45
2nd	1.1	1,340	1,342	1
3rd	2.9	1,725	904	0.52
4th	2.9	1,825	1,393	0.76
5th	1.6	1,957	1,485	0.76
6th	1.5	774	986	1.3
7th	6.2	891	1,408	1.6

First District has the lowest number of posts per person (.45), though it had the second highest in 2006. This suggests that for 2014 thus far, the Seventh District and the Sixth District *may* have more conversation than the First District.

It is also important to know who does most of the posting to the Yahoo! Groups. The higher percentage of posts by MPD employees indicates that police dominate group activity. Table 9.5 shows the percentage of police posts of the 50 most recent posts as of June 30, 2014, and compares them with the same data from 2006. Overall, we see that *every* district became *much* more dominated by MPD in 2014 than in 2006. More specifically, in 2006, District Four was the least dominated by MPD posts, and District Seven was the most dominated by MPD posts. In 2014, District Four remained the least dominated by MPD, and District Three became the most dominated by MPD. Interestingly, District Seven moved to become among the least MPD dominated. The Chief of Police occasionally participates in the Seventh District group.

While understanding the amount of activity and who is performing the activity is important, it is also necessary to understand the nature of the activity. This requires qualitative thread analysis, which involves a careful read and categorization of each thread and each post within each thread. Given the amount of data involved, it is necessary to select a subset of districts for this analysis. The data above suggest that our understanding of the nature of activity within each group can most benefit from further detailed investigation of the activity within the Third, Fourth, and Seventh Districts. The Third District has the

Table 9.5 DC MPD Posts to Yahoo! Groups

District	# MPD posts 2006	% Police posts 2006	# MPD posts through June 30, 2014	% Police posts through June 30, 2014
1st	12	24	45	90
2nd	18	36	41	82
3rd	20	40	49	98
4th	9	18	36	72
5th	20	40	39	78
6th	20	40	43	86
7th	47	94	42	84

highest percentage of police posts; the Fourth District has the lowest percentage of police posts; and the Seventh District sits at the median. Specifically, we want to know the actual MPD role in these groups (as the numbers above are indicators only) and/or whether there is any exchange or dialogue taking place. This analysis investigates all of the posts in each of these three districts for January–June 2014.

Tables 9.6, 9.7, and 9.8 display the numbers of posts, the number of threads, the number of threads of two posts (indicating exchange), and the number of threads of three or more posts (indicating dialogue) for each of Districts Three, Four, and Seven. As Brainard and Brinkerhoff (2006) note, "The ratio of threads to messages demonstrates interaction among members" (p. 41S). Reading through each of these threads helps us understand whether they actually are exchange and/or dialogue and the qualitative extent to which DC MPD may or may not dominate the Yahoo! Groups.

The data in Tables 9.6–9.8, taken together with the data in Table 9.5 (on posts by DC MPD), tell us that the overwhelming number of posts in each district are one-directional, single posts from MPD personnel and that there are many fewer exchanges (threads of two posts) and even fewer potential discussions (threads of three or more posts). The data also show that the Fourth District had significantly more threads of three or more posts than the Third District. Are these actually conversational? A deeper investigation can tell us.

Looking first at the Third District, we investigate the threads of two posts. Again, a thread of two posts suggests some sort of exchange, perhaps a question and answer. What we see when we look closely is that of the 31 such threads

Table 9.6 Third District Thread Analysis

Month	# Posts	# Threads	# Threads of two posts	# Threads with three or more posts
June	136	2 (2%)	1 (1%)	1 (1%)
May	171	5 (3%)	3 (2%)	2 (1%)
April	146	6 (4%)	6 (4%)	0
March	152	4 (3%)	2 (1%)	2 (1%)
February	150	12 (8%)	6 (4%)	6 (4%)
January	157	15 (10%)	13 (8%)	2 (1%)

Table 9.7 Fourth District Thread Analysis

Month	# Posts	# Threads	# Threads of two posts	# Threads with three or more posts
June	225	34 (15%)	12 (5%)	22 (10%)
May	274	49 (18%)	18 (7%)	31 (11%)
April	235	34 (15%)	13 (6%)	21 (9%)
March	217	25 (12%)	8 (4%)	17 (8%)
February	212	34 (16%)	16 (8%)	17 (8%)
January	237	44 (19%)	11 (5%)	33 (14%)

Table 9.8 Seventh District Thread Analysis

Month	# Posts	# Threads	# Threads of two posts	# Threads with three or more posts
June	209	9 (4%)	7 (3%)	2 (1%)
May	219	13 (6%)	5 (2%)	8 (4%)
April	289	28 (10%)	11 (4%)	17 (6%)
March	244	13 (5%)	4 (2%)	9 (4%)
February	217	15 (7%)	4 (2%)	11 (5%)
January	249	22 (9%)	10 (4%)	12 (5%)

over the six-month period January–June 2014, all but six were informational in nature. The overwhelming majority of these were announcements from MPD—crime statistics, update on a crime, etc.—followed by a "thanks" from a resident. The remaining six threads of two posts were residents asking questions or reporting a crime with an officer response. These were straightforward exchanges of routine information. Of the 13 threads with three or more posts, three were true exchanges in which either a citizen asked a question and got an MPD response (with a subsequent "thanks" from the resident); or MPD posted information, a resident asked a question, and an officer answered. The other 10 threads consisted of MPD providing information followed by "thanks" from a resident, an MPD employee, or both.

Turning our attention to the Fourth District, we see that there were 78 threads of two posts. Of these, the majority (56) were simple exchanges. Again, for example, MPD would send an informational post (a crime report), and a citizen would reply "thanks," or a resident would ask a question and an officer would respond. Twenty-two of the threads with two posts raise some concern from a resident engagement perspective. In these 22 posts, MPD initiated the thread by sending out information (a crime report, a status update, announcement about a community meeting, etc.), a resident responded with a substantive question, and the police did not answer. The exchange thus ended with the resident's question. There were 141 three-post threads. Overwhelmingly, these were routine in nature.

For example, many were initiated when MPD posted information (for example, the daily crime report), followed by a citizen question about the report, followed by more detail from the officer. Or a resident would begin a thread with a question, subsequently answered by MPD, and the resident thanked MPD. Some of the larger threads were larger simply because more people reiterated what others were saying, or more people thanked MPD. Only one of the threads was ended by MPD not responding. Only two of the threads of three or more posts were significant in that they were non-routine and involved MPD and residents working together even in some minimal way. One thread began when a resident asked where 911 calls go if one lives on the border of DC/MD. MPD responded that the call could go to either jurisdiction. A second resident also aired the concern. When MPD responded that they are working on the problem, the original resident asked MPD to inform the public. Finally, a

13-post thread began when a resident posted a concern about poor driving at traffic circles. Other residents expressed their concerns—both related to this particular traffic circle and also related to other problem spots in the district. MPD responded by confirming that pedestrians have the right-of-way and that MPD would conduct traffic enforcement.

In the Seventh District, the overwhelming majority of two-post threads were routine in that they were either questions and answers or information with a follow up (again, often "thank you"). There were only three threads abandoned by MPD. Of the 59 threads of three or more posts, four can be characterized as non-routine conversation and involved residents and MPD working together in some way. One thread of 10 posts included several exchanges of information between residents and an officer that led to an offline meeting. A second thread, of 14 posts, involved residents and police working together to exchange information about All Terrain Vehicles. Residents reported the various locations in which ATVs were in neighborhoods illegally, and MPD canvassed those areas. A thread of 18 posts involved a scam in which a tow truck was backing up to cars, pretending to tow them but, in fact, stealing them. Various residents included the location(s) of the truck, types of vehicles pursued, and details of the truck's appearance. MPD officers investigated the various reports and included real-time updates (though the truck was not caught). Finally, a thread of 25 posts was about gunshots. The thread shows residents reporting gunshots and possible locations and MPD officers clarifying various locations with each other. MPD followed up on these reports, again providing real-time updates. One point of interest worth noting is that the MPD Chief participated in several of the threads in the Seventh District.

In general, membership in DC MPD Yahoo! Groups appears to be growing. There has been general growth in the number of posts, though some instances of negative growth. There has been an overall decline in posts per member and an overall growth, across every district, in police dominance. As a result, most threads—even threads of two, three, or more posts—tend to be one-way information distribution, with perhaps some follow-up "thanks" in the case of threads of two or more posts. Only the Seventh District has experienced anything that comes close to police–resident collaboration.

Facebook. The kinds of data available for understanding DC MPD's use of Facebook for engaging residents are far more limited than those of Yahoo! Groups. I do not have data previous to June 2014 but do have all Facebook posts for that month.[3] Unlike DC MPD's Yahoo! Groups, the MPD's Facebook page is citywide, so most data are inherently incomparable to those of Yahoo! Groups.

As with Yahoo! Groups, the 50 most recent posts (as of June 30, 2014) were analyzed to understand whether MPD dominated the page in postings and, if so, to what extent. These data are somewhat comparable to those of Yahoo! Groups, as the 50 most recent posts to groups as of June 30, 2014, were also analyzed. As with Yahoo! Groups, MPD dominated its Facebook page. According to Table 9.9, of the 50 most recent posts (as of June 30, 2014) 39 (78%) were made by MPD. This is approximately the same level of dominance by MPD of

Table 9.9 DC MPD Posts to Facebook Page

Posts by MPD employee	% Police posts (of 50 most recent)
39	78

Yahoo! Groups, which ranged from 72% of posts by MPD to 98% of posts by MPD.

Analyzing threads and posts for the month of June is enlightening. Table 9.10 shows us that there is a higher percentage of threads of two and three posts than we saw in the Third District and Seventh District Yahoo! Groups for June, but a lower percentage than in the Fourth District Yahoo! Groups.

Additionally, most of MPD's Facebook page consists of posts that are identical to—and often fed by—its Twitter posts. Thus, much of the Facebook page simply reflects the Twitter content. There are additional posts that are unique to MPD's Facebook, however. These are mostly human-interest posts about police officers and the department, often accompanied by photos. Of the Facebook threads of two or more posts, all are routine and consist mostly of announcements with resident replies thanking MPD, similar to that which occurred in the Yahoo! Groups. There is one thread in which MPD posted information and a resident asked for clarification and MPD did not respond, and another in which MPD posted information and a resident responded with a racist remark. Threads with as many as six or seven posts were little more than an MPD announcement followed by thanks. Given the ease of including photos on Facebook, many of the threads include photos of MPD officers with replies from individual residents simply commenting on the photo.

Twitter. As with Facebook, only data for June 2014 are available for Twitter. DC MPD's Twitter page is also citywide. Returning to the question of MPD dominance, we see that 100% of posts are by DC MPD. Again, we are only able to see posts originated by DC MPD and MPD responses to posts originated by residents. We are unable to see posts tweeted at DC MPD to which MPD did not respond and, in fact, DC MPD notes on its page that it will not respond to tweets immediately or in real time. Given this limitation, Table 9.11 shows that all 50 of the most recent posts, as of June 30, 2014, were made by DC MPD. Because we cannot see any posts tweeted at MPD to which MPD did not

Table 9.10 MPD Facebook Thread Analysis

Month	# Posts	# Threads	# Threads of two posts	# Threads with three or more posts
June	109	9 (8%)	4 (4%)	5 (5%)

Table 9.11 DC MPD Tweets

Posts by MPD employee	% Police posts (of 50 most recent)
50	100

respond, we are unable to say whether there are any orphaned or abandoned potential conversations, as we saw in the Yahoo! Groups. What we can say about DC MPD's Twitter page is that it lacks the human-interest stories contained on MPD's Facebook page and the indicators of discussion used above.

Also, it is not a venue for discussion or collaboration, as shown in Table 9.12. None of the DC police tweets received responses. There were no MPD responses to resident tweets. That means that many resident tweets—*if* any—received no reply.

Findings and Discussion

I return now to the research questions on DC MPD's adoption of social media technologies; how DC MPD uses those technologies to engage residents; and lessons to be learned about resident engagement via social media from DC MPD.

DC MPD has adopted Yahoo! Groups, Facebook, and Twitter in turn as they have become available. In these ways, DC MPD has put itself at the forefront of social media use for police–resident relations. DC MPD chooses to use all of these technologies, rather than to rely on just one, on the assumption that the technologies capture different audiences, with Yahoo! Groups being attractive to older people, while younger folks flock to Twitter and Facebook (Personal communication, May 13, 2014).

It has made some specific choices about the way it structures its use of those technologies. Yahoo! Groups are structured along the lines of police districts. There are seven Yahoo! Groups—one for each police district. DC MPD has chosen to maintain Facebook and Twitter pages that are citywide. Twitter makes obvious sense as a citywide technology because people tend to rely on Twitter for real-time information related to traffic or emergencies. To the extent that Facebook and Twitter are co-populated by the Command Center, Facebook also makes sense as a citywide platform.

The question of how DC MPD uses its social media to engage residents is tricky, but we can approach this question from both a longitudinal and cross-technology perspective. Adopting the various social media technologies as they appear over time ensures that DC MPD is staying current with the venues in which residents "gather." Yahoo! Groups, for which we have data for two years eight years apart, demonstrate that DC MPD's use of Yahoo! Groups to engage residents is mixed, at best. Membership numbers appear to have increased, but it is impossible to know with certainty. It is unclear how many members are members in name only and are not actively participating *nor* even reading or

Table 9.12 DC MPD Twitter Thread Analysis

Month	# Posts	# Threads	# Threads of two posts	# Threads with three or more posts
June	879			

receiving the posts. Membership merely tracks the number of people who are signed up as members. Similarly, the number of posts has increased, in some cases quite significantly. For example, the Second District has witnessed a 244% increase in posts as of the end of 2013 and an 832% percent increase as of June 30, 2014. On the other hand, two districts have experienced decline. The First District has experienced a 42% decrease in the number of posts as of the end of 2013 and a 4% decrease as of June 30, 2014. The Third District has experienced a 42% decline in posts as of the end of 2013 and a 28% decline as of June 30, 2014. Police presence and dominance of the Yahoo! Groups have increased significantly, with huge increases in the percentage of posts contributed by MPD. The one exception is District Seven, which has experienced a decline in DC MPD presence/dominance.

The data indicated three districts for further investigation. The numerical indicators were not promising. Most of the posts on the Yahoo! Groups were single posts. The Fourth District's Yahoo! Group contained anywhere between 4% and 8% of threads of two posts (indicating some form of exchange) and between 8% and 14% of threads were of three or more posts (suggesting some form of conversation). These were the highest percentages. The Seventh and Third Districts had lower percentages of threads with two or three posts. Interpreting these threads was even more disappointing. There was even less interaction than the numbers indicate. The threads of two posts overwhelmingly were standard informational posts, with a "thanks" for a follow-up. Most threads of three or more posts were similar—though with more "thanks" posts. Some threads of three or more posts were exchanges. The only district that came close to collaborative conversation on the Yahoo! Groups was the Seventh District, which has the highest poverty rate, the highest unemployment rate, and the highest crime rate. This, perhaps, is the silver lining in the cloud of findings. Interestingly, the Chief of Police occasionally posted to the Yahoo! Group in the Seventh District. Both over time and across districts, the Seventh District has been the most engaged via Yahoo! Groups.

Across technologies, the data suggest that Yahoo! Groups appears to be the most effective venue for participation and engagement approaching discussion and collaboration. Twitter is most effective for push announcements. Interestingly, though the data are not strictly comparable, they do indicate that Facebook is roughly about as popular for "discussion" as Yahoo! Groups (indicated by the number and percentage of threads of two and three or more posts). However, investigation of those threads reveals less actual discussion than in Yahoo! Groups. Finally, Yahoo! Groups are, occasionally, used for real-time communication with residents from the crime scene or search area.

Conclusion

There are several lessons to be learned from DC MPD's use of social media to engage with residents. First, in keeping with the discussion defining social media by Bryer and Zavattaro (2011), these technologies—despite the name—are not inherently social. They must be used actively and deliberately in order to leverage their potential as venues or forums for discussion and collaboration. The oldest technology discussed here—Yahoo! Groups—is the technology that most closely approaches a venue for discussion and collaboration. New technologies are not inherently social, and old technologies are not inherently asocial.

DC MPD has adopted the various technologies as they have been developed. In terms of resident engagement, we can learn from DC MPD that new technologies do not need to—and perhaps should not—supplant older technologies. A social media strategy for engaging residents should use various kinds of technology because, or so that, the different technologies can be used in different ways.

Technology, however, is not just "used." Police departments must pay attention to how they structure the use of these technologies. The most collaborative of the three technologies is organized at the police district level, while the less collaborative are organized citywide. Facebook, which other research has shown to be *used* for purposes of discussion and (potentially) collaboration, is used for announcements by DC MPD. If MPD does truly want to engage with residents, it might consider district-level Facebook pages. Another way in which the use of technologies is structured is by police department participation and management. Yahoo! Groups, organized by districts, are moderated by both the district commander and the district and administrators. Facebook and Twitter are fed by the DC MPD Command Center, which coordinates field activities for the police and monitors the computer-aided dispatch system (Personal communication, May 13, 2014). The Command Center obviously emphasizes push information distribution rather than conversation facilitation. Police departments seeking to use social media for interaction with residents must decide the purpose to which they want to put Facebook. If they wish to use Facebook for engagement, they might consider facilitation by public information officers or district commanders.

This gets at the question of police involvement in the very sites they created. MPD dominates all three technologies. This is not to say that the information DC MPD is putting out is not valuable. It is merely to say that this does not constitute working together socially in order to deliberate and collaborate. These venues might be more inviting of resident participation if they were not dominated by MPD. A similar challenge arises around the issue of abandoned threads. These are threads in which residents participate and ask questions, but the questions are not responded to by MPD. If we use Nabatchi's (2012) inclusive and broad definition of citizen engagement and imagine a continuum, of which one end consists of information to and from citizens and the other consists of government–citizen collaboration in the form of joint problem definition and deliberation about solutions, it is clear that DC MPD's use of social media has resulted in activity on the thin end of the continuum.

We return to the question of government–citizen (or resident) relations. Obviously, technology is not a panacea for any decline or diminishment of the relationship between PDs and residents. This drives home the notion that social media are not inherently social (Bryer & Zavattaro, 2011). Even when they are intentionally used by government agencies to work with citizens, those good intentions are not realizable without deliberate attention to how the technologies, police participation, and citizen participation are structured. More to the point for this topic, PDs need more than a mere presence on social media in order to enhance the "community" in community policing.

Behind all of the literature on social media and government–citizen relations is a set of normative assumptions. One assumption is that technology adoption by government agencies is inevitable. A second assumption is that engagement with citizens ought to be collaborative; that is, government and citizens working together to define problems, identify proposals, and deliberate on solutions. A third assumption is that technology, especially social media technologies, can and should be used to engage citizens and residents in a collaborative way.

DC MPD is motivated by all of these assumptions. As described above, it adopted Yahoo! Groups in the first place in order to have a place for dialogue and for police and residents to work together. It has not achieved those goals and that is disappointing. To be clear, it is not disappointing that DC MPD has not lived up to the assumed ideals present in the academic literature. It is disappointing that DC MPD has not achieved its *own stated* goal.

That DC MPD (and perhaps other police departments and government agencies in general) has not lived up to the normative assumptions in the literature does not necessarily suggest that it needs to make changes in order to do so. To the contrary, perhaps it is the set of assumptions in the literature that need to change in order better to reflect reality.

Nevertheless, if an agency claims that it is or will be using social media to host dialogue and collaborate with citizens and residents then it should at least attempt to do so and/or make progress over time. In the case described here, DC MPD has not made progress. Rather, the technologies seem to be used less collaboratively than they were when first adopted, and they have become yet another tool through which to send information to citizens.

It is the contradiction between assumptions, goals, and reality that needs to be resolved. While scholars continue to test their assumptions against reality, PDs and government agencies need to decide the purposes for which they want to use social media. If they wish to use social media for collaboration then, as discussed above, they need to rethink how they structure the technologies and their patterns of use. If they use social media for non-social purposes—whether because they do not want to do so or because they want to but do not seem to be able to do so—then they risk raising expectations of residents only to disappoint.

Notes

1 The author thanks Gretchen Wieland for her valuable research assistance. Gretchen is an MPA student in the Trachtenberg School of Public Policy & Public Administration at the George Washington University. The author also thanks John McNutt, Professor in the School of Public Policy and Administration at the University of Delaware, with whom the original study that provided the 2006 data used here was conducted.
2 All 2006 data are from Brainard and McNutt (2010).
3 The author and research assistant were prevented from scrolling down to earlier months of the feed. Attempts were made using different browsers and on different computers.

References

Brainard, L. A., & Brinkerhoff, J. M. (2006). Sovereignty under siege, or a circuitous path for strengthening the state? Digital diasporas and human rights. *International Journal of Public Administration, 29*, 595–618.

Brainard, L. A., & Derrick-Mills, T. (2011). Electronic commons, community policing, and communication: On-line police–citizen discussion groups in Washington, DC. *Administrative Theory & Praxis, 33*(3), 383–410.

Brainard, L. A., & Edlins, M. (2014). Top 10 US municipal police departments and their social media usage. *The American Review of Public Administration,* 0275074014524478.

Brainard, L. A., & McNutt, J. (2010). Virtual government–citizen relations: Informational, transactional, or collaborative? *Administration & Society, 42*, 836–858.

Bryer, T. A., & Zavattaro, S. M. (2011). Social media and public administration: Theoretical dimensions and introduction to symposium. *Administrative Theory & Praxis, 33*(3), 325–340.

Crump, J. (2011). What are the police doing on Twitter? Social media, the public, and the public. *Policy & Internet, 3*(4), 1–27.

Heverin, T., & Zach, L. (2011). Law enforcement agency adoption and use of Twitter as a crisis communication tool. In C. Hagar (Ed.), *Crisis information management: Communication and technologies* (pp. 25–42). Oxford: Woodhead Publishing.

Heverin, T., & Zach, L. (2012). Use of microblogging for collective sense-making during violent crisis: A study of three campus shootings. *Journal of the American Society for Information Science and Technology, 63*(1), 34–47.

Johnston, E. W., & Hansen, D. L. (2011). Design lessons for smart governance infrastructures. In A. P. Balutis, T. F. Buss, & D. Ink (Eds.), *Transforming American governance 3.0: Rebooting the public square?* Armonk, NY: M. E. Sharpe.

Meijer, A., & Thaens, M. (2013). Social media strategies: Understanding the differences between North American police departments. *Government Information Quarterly, 30*(2013), 343–350.

Moisan, A. (2005, May 16). Bringing down crime: Ward 4 residents' intensive efforts produce results. *The Common Denominator.* Retrieved from www.thecommon denominator.com/051605_news1.html.

Nabatchi, T. (2012). A manager's guide to evaluating citizen participation. *Fostering transparency and democracy series.* Washington, DC: IBM Center for the Business of Government.

Police Executive Research Forum. (2012). *How are innovations in technology transforming policing?* Retrieved from www.policeforum.org/assets/docs/Critical_Issues_Series/how% 20are%20innovations%20in%20technology%20transforming%20policing%202012. pdf.

Skogan, W. (1994, November). *Community participation and community policing.* Paper presented at the Workshop on Evaluating Police Service Delivery, Evanston, IL.

Smith, Y. (n.d.). *MPDC listserv subscribership continues to grow.* Retrieved from http:// mpdc.dc.gov/mpdc/cwp/view,a,1239,q,562082.asp.

Standage, T. (2013). *Writing on the wall: Social media—the first 2,000 years.* New York: Bloomsbury USA.

Svara, J., & Denhardt, J. (2010). *The connected community: Local governments as partners in citizen engagement and community building* (White Paper 2-124). Retrieved from http://icma.org/Documents/Document/Document/301763.

10 Social Media and the Boynton Beach, Florida Police Department

Stephanie H. Slater

When Boynton Beach (FL) Police Department Officers Barry Ward and Terrence Paramore walked out of a house following a 911 hang-up call, they looked at each other and knew they had to do something about what they had just seen.

They went to Home Depot, bought a Christmas tree and all the fixings, and went back to the house to give it to a seven-year-old girl who was devastated that her family couldn't afford to celebrate the holidays.

The surprise delivery was captured on Officer Ward's body camera and then uploaded to the Boynton Beach Police Department's Facebook page. The headline read, "Caught on Camera: What these two cops did after responding to a 911 hang-up call will have everyone talking … because it's awesome!"

Within a few hours, the video was seen and shared several hundred times. The next day, the numbers were in the thousands. The third day, it was featured on *Good Morning America*. By the fourth day, Hoda Kotb and Kathie Lee Gifford were talking about it on the *Today Show* and the video had been viewed more than one million times. As of January 1, 2015, the video had been viewed 10.4 million times, shared 135,739 times, liked 278,711 times, and commented on 22,840 times. It went viral.

It's not uncommon for the Boynton Beach Police Department to post videos and photographs of officers doing good deeds online. The Office of Media Relations has been uploading positive content since we began using social media in September 2007.

So then why did this video get as much attention and global exposure as it did—and in such a short period of time? We believe the public needed to see and hear police officers doing something positive. Our video was posted online on December 1, 2014, just a few weeks after the grand jury's decision not to indict Ferguson Police Officer Darren Wilson for the death of Michael Brown. Two days later, a grand jury declined to indict New York Police Officer Daniel Pantaleo in the death of Eric Garner. Both deaths sparked tremendous outrage against police, protests throughout the country, and a social media firestorm that continues today.

For whatever reason, the video of Officer Ward and Officer Paramore bringing Christmas joy to a seven-year-old girl struck a chord with the public. It resonated around the world and positively changed public perception. That is the power of social media for law enforcement.

The Boynton Beach Police Department began to explore social media by creating a YouTube channel in September 2007. It was around the time that our local media outlets were going through a series of layoffs, and there were not many reporters around to come to the station and pick up patrol car dashcam or surveillance video of suspects. We began uploading the videos to YouTube and emailing the links to reporters. They loved it because they could use the videos on their websites, which by this point had become 24/7 breaking news platforms.

We also noticed that it was becoming increasingly difficult to get reporters to cover anything but breaking news stories. There was no guarantee they'd cover a story about the officer who stopped his patrol car to block traffic so that a turtle could make it across the road safely or the officer who went home to get clothing, shoes, and food for a homeless veteran he encountered during his shift.

However, those were stories we could share ourselves if we became our own news outlet. In April 2008, we became the first law enforcement agency in Florida to create a Facebook fan page. We expanded our social media program to Twitter in January 2009, followed by Pinterest in 2011, and then Instagram in early 2013. Our goal when using any social media is simple: humanize our officers, engage our community, and ensure their safety by keeping them informed.

For most people, encounters with law enforcement are not typically under the best of circumstances. If you've just been the victim of a crime, you are likely to feel extreme stress and a slew of emotions including fear and anger. If you've ever seen a police car in your rearview mirror, it is likely your heart beats a little faster. And if you've been the recipient of a speeding ticket, it is even more likely that you drove away from that encounter with less than positive feelings about police officers in general.

Then you scroll through Facebook on your smartphone and see a photograph of an officer holding his newborn son in his arms; watch video of a police officer dancing to Pharell's "Happy"; read a Tweet about a blood drive for an officer's daughter who was born prematurely at 20 weeks and is fighting for her life; see a post on Instagram that shows officers decorating cupcakes with children to raise money for a local food pantry.

You realize that there are human beings behind that badge—there are fathers, sons, and brothers; mothers, daughters, and sisters. They get up every day, put on a bulletproof vest, kiss their loved ones goodbye, and go to work to protect the rest of us from the evils in this world. They hope to come home safely and have dinner with their family. Maybe your perception of police changes a little, and then we've accomplished one of our goals for using social media.

In November 2012, we began a Twitter campaign to encourage our community to learn more about what it's like to be a police officer in the City of Boynton Beach. Our thought was that if people understood the actual job of a police officer, it would lead to better community relationships. We came up with the hashtag #ridewithbbpd and promoted it as a virtual ride along via Twitter.

For several hours a couple times a month, I rode in a patrol car with a police officer and live tweeted every call we responded to. I was careful not to identify anyone by name or give our exact location so as not to violate anyone's civil rights, interfere with the call for service, or jeopardize officers' safety.

On one ride-along, we responded to a domestic dispute between an elderly couple.

We tweeted:

> It's a husband and wife arguing. She hit him with her cane and left the house. #ridewithbbpd.

> We can't prove actual physical violence so no charges here. #ridewithbbpd

The virtual ride-along was also a chance for Twitter followers to learn about our officers. I took a selfie with each officer inside the patrol car and tweeted a few fun facts about that officer. For example, one officer named her dogs Felony and Justice. Another officer revealed that he likes to play "Call of Duty" on Xbox during his time off.

The end of each tweet had the #ridewithbbpd hashtag so that our virtual ride along became a brand. The #ridewithbbpd campaign quickly caught on in our community. People who had never used Twitter before created accounts so that they could ride along with us from the comfort of their homes.

We read their tweets back to us and learned that they were fascinated by the work police officers do on a daily basis and wanted to learn more. So, in January 2014, we expanded the #ridewithbbpd and trained three police officers to use Twitter and occasionally live tweet during their 11.5-hour shifts. The officers learned how to write in 140 characters or less; how to retweet and reply to tweets; and were given guidelines based on Florida's public record laws as to what they could and could not legally tweet about.

Officer Ron Ryan was the first to take on the #ridewithbbpd challenge. From 5:30 p.m. until 5:00 a.m., he tweeted about calls he responded to, things he observed throughout his shift, and tips to keep residents safe. He posted several photos and gave people insight into his personality through his writing style.

Here are few examples:

> Ofc. Ryan#920 going 10–8 in car 4603. Sit back and enjoy the ride. #Ridewithbbpd

> Disturbance was all over baby mama drama via Facebook. Parties separated. No one injured. #ridewithbbpd

> 51 to Bonefish Grill – CPR in progress – be back in a bit #ridewithbbpd

> Two people who were arguing over a cellphone on our arrival are now best friends again. Can you hear me now? #ridewithbbpd

Our guys/gals took an illegal gun off the street & saved a life with CPR. Not bad! Thanks for riding along. Over and out! #ridewithbbpd

The ride-along was so successful that it made national news and Officer Ryan was a guest on the Rick Sanchez radio show. A month later, Officer Nasim Davis live tweeted his shift from 3:30p.m. to 3:00a.m. A few hours into his shift, he locked himself out of his patrol car—and tweeted about it.

What a genius, I locked myself out of the car! Help! #ridewithbbpd

https://twitter.com/BBPD/status/445695297088679938/photo/1

"It's always refreshing to see that cops are people to," @jortron wrote in reply to the tweet, which became a top post on Reddit.com within a few hours.

Humanize officers—check! Engage the community—check! Now, how could we keep our community safe by using social media?

At the beginning of the school year in 2013, we saw a significant increase in complaints from parents about drivers speeding through school zones. Officers regularly enforced the speed in school zones, so why not live tweet and Facebook and Instagram post the enforcement initiatives?

One afternoon, I went out to a school zone with two of our motorcycle officers and within two minutes, their radar gun caught a driver traveling 37 in a 20mph zone. They pulled the driver over and I took a picture of the officer standing next to the car. I posted it on Facebook, Instagram, and Twitter with the hashtags #slowdown and #ridewithbbpd. It was immediately retweeted and the Facebook comments started pouring in with parents thanking us for being out there and urging us to do it in other school zones throughout the city. So we did and continue to do so in elementary school zones through the city throughout the school year. We post the speeds people are going, videos of them being pulled over, and photographs of the costly citations they received. We are careful not to post anyone's personal information and photographs of faces and license plates.

Some bloggers have criticized the department for "twitter shaming" drivers who were caught speeding in school zones. We're fine with that critique because it means people are talking about what we're doing, and the more conversations are being had about speeding in school zones, the more likely it will register for people when they are actually driving through a school zone. For us, this equates to saving children's lives.

Last spring, detectives mentioned that they were seeing an increase in robberies occurring during Craigslist transactions. Victims reported that they met a potential buyer and were robbed of their merchandise, often at gunpoint. Detectives suggested we offer up our lobby, which is open 24/7/365, as a safe place for people to buy or sell products on Craigslist. We posted an infographic about it on our social media and our local media publicized it in print, on air, and online. Other police agencies in our area followed suit in using social media to promote use of their lobbies. Response from the public has been overwhelmingly positive, and detectives have reported a decrease in Craigslist-related robberies since we began the education campaign.

It's generally always warm in South Florida; however, the summer months are brutal, and can be deadly for children and animals left in a vehicle. In June 2014, we saw a significant increase in calls for service about dogs being left unattended in cars. When officers responded to those calls, they found that people had no idea it was against the law to leave their pet alone in the car, even for just a few minutes. We saw this as a perfect opportunity to educate our community, so we reached out to the department's animal cruelty investigator and asked if she would be interested in doing a live chat via Facebook to answer the public's questions about the law as it pertains to pets in vehicles.

We posted an infographic on our social media and sent a press release to our local media to promote the live chat.

On July 1, 2014, from 10:00 a.m. to 11:00 a.m., Investigator Liz Roehrich fielded questions and comments from more than two dozen people about the county ordinance that makes it illegal to leave a dog in a car for any period of time. She explained how quickly a dog can overheat and die, and offered suggestions as to what someone can do when they see a dog alone in a car.

Every day is another opportunity for us to use social media to promote the good work of our agency, get assistance in solving crimes, hear from the community about their concerns, and talk about crime trends and prevention. Social media has become a tremendous part of our identity—so much so that we put our Twitter handle @BBPD on the rear panels of all our marked patrol cars, and display the web addresses for our pages on our business cards and email signatures.

The Boynton Beach Police Department's Facebook page has more than 16,400 likes on Facebook, more than 9,500 people follow us on Twitter, and our YouTube videos have been viewed 3.1 million times. Every like, view, share, comment, and follow on social media is an opportunity to change perception, engage, and educate. Now that's powerful.

11 Social Media for Emergency Management

Clayton Wukich and Alan Steinberg

On April 15, 2013, the Boston Marathon was in full swing when at 2:49 p.m., near the finish line on Boylston Street, two improvised explosive devices detonated just 12 seconds apart. The blasts killed three people, injured over 200, and inflicted considerable shock and concern across the country. As first responders rushed to the scene to treat victims, news of the terrorist attack spread via traditional media outlets as well as social media. Many citizens sought out information on what was happening and, in addition, advice on how to protect themselves and their families. Government agencies obliged via social media with advisories, road closure updates, and other relevant information (Sutton, Johnson, Spiro, & Butts, 2013). Law enforcement agencies specifically sought citizen involvement to identify the perpetrators. The result was an engaged population which more closely followed and participated in the subsequent manhunt.

The Boston Marathon bombing represents just one crisis in which social media directly link response agencies with the constituents they serve. These types of examples suggest that social media holds significant value as a crisis communication tool both for government agencies and citizens. Furthermore, research findings and guidance from early adopters such as the Federal Emergency Management Agency (FEMA) suggest that social media platforms provide value as a means to promote preparedness and risk reduction well before a disaster occurs (Crowe, 2012; FEMA, 2013; Mergel, 2014; Wukich & Mergel, forthcoming).

In this chapter, we demonstrate how social media sites contribute to emergency management before, during, and after disasters, enumerating three specific approaches outlined by the existing literature: (1) information dissemination; (2) intelligence gathering; and (3) use of social media to engage in conversations that may lead to the co-production of public goods and services. This framework conforms with past research (see Wukich, forthcoming), and represents specific phases of social media use that move from one-way communication tactics to more interactive and deliberative strategies that engage an array of actors (see Wukich & Mergel, forthcoming). We then provide specific examples from both academic research and news reporting that span mitigation, preparedness, response, and recovery operations and conclude by discussing the limitations of social media use in emergency management.

Unpacking the Roll of Social Media in Emergency Management

Social media, as we think of it today, has been available for over a decade. Facebook went live on college campuses in 2004 and was available to the general public by 2006. Twitter started in 2007 and quickly reached mass audiences. Users quickly began to apply these technologies to disasters. Twitter hashtags were first used to organize disaster information in late 2007 during San Diego-area wildfires by people who could not find salient information about risk and response efforts via traditional news sources (Messina, 2007; NetSquared, 2008). One of the first tweets to make use of #sandiegofire was by Nate Ritter when he tweeted, "#sandiegofire south shores, ski beach open to motor homes. fiesta island is open to first 500 livestock that come in." Later that day, other people in the area were using the hashtag to ask questions and post information regarding the fire (Messina, 2007).

As more people use social media to seek out hazard-related information (see American Red Cross, 2012), it is important for emergency management agencies to effectively integrate new technologies and strategies into their communication repertoire (Crowe, 2012; White, 2012). Emergency managers, however, must be prepared to interact with a public who increasingly expect not only increased attention from emergency managers (Kapucu & Van Wart, 2006), but a consistent online presence and prompt feedback on social media (Zavattaro & Sementelli, 2014).

Until relatively recently, government agencies relied on a combination of traditional media outlets and direct communication (e.g., warning sirens, reverse 911 telephone calls, and, to a lesser extent, face-to-face interaction) to get information to the public during disasters (Tierney, Lindell, & Perry, 2001). Organizational and special purpose websites such as Ready.gov were created after the September 11, 2001 attacks with the expressed purpose of providing disaster-related information; however, most people bypassed these sites in favor of traditional media sources such as television, radio, and newspapers (Pew Research Center, 2002). Citizens have long relied on those sources to accrue information during extreme events (Lindell & Perry, 2012). The increased use of social media, however, is changing that dynamic by making it easier for emergency managers to reach out directly to constituents, and allowing constituents, in turn, to connect both with responders and with each other, which creates valuable two-way connections (Ambinder et al., 2013; Bruns, Burgess, Crawford, & Shaw, 2012; Fugate, 2011; Mergel, 2014; Wukich & Mergel, forthcoming). Ideally, this type of activity increases communication between disparate actors and in doing so facilitates more informed and resilient communities (Dufty, 2012). Although social media use occurs more frequently in urban and suburban communities and among younger populations, adoption and usage rates are increasing (Duggan, Ellison, Lampe, Lenhart, & Madden, 2015), and a growing percentage now turns to these platforms for information during disasters (American Red Cross, 2012).

Social media sites such as Twitter and Facebook allow anyone with Internet access and an email address to seek out and/or share information with large audiences (Kaplan & Haenlein, 2010). Users often make these sites part of their everyday lives by sharing their thoughts, scanning information shared by others, and passing along news and other information within their network (Hansen, Shneiderman, & Smith, 2010; Lee & Ma, 2012). Users create open conversation topics by employing hashtags, thus creating self-organized conversations that bring together an array of participants (Leaman, 2009). Increasingly, hashtags such as #sandiegofire, #bostonstrong, and #gldfloods have been used during disasters (Bruns et al., 2012; Messina, 2007; Sutton, Spiro, Johnson, Fitzhugh, & Butts, 2013; Wukich & Steinberg, 2014). Whether through hashtags, posts, or direct messages, social media facilitate relatively open exchanges of information.

These sources of information possess potential value; disaster-related social media networks draw strength from their diversity because individuals hail from multiple scales of action (i.e., households, government agencies, nonprofit organizations, etc.) each with unique needs and perspectives that potentially affect other participants (Wukich & Steinberg, 2014). This diversity reduces information asymmetries between not just government agencies (Mergel, 2010), but other actors as well (Bruns et al., 2012; Wukich & Steinberg, 2014).

Social media offer agencies the opportunity to build trust with constituents, promote risk reduction activities, and increase operational effectiveness (Mergel, 2014; Rive, Hare, Thomas, & Nankivell, 2012). Three approaches to social media use facilitate those ends including (1) various forms of information dissemination; (2) social media monitoring to accrue situational awareness; and (3) interaction with users to generate knowledge and at times co-produce public goods and services (Wukich, forthcoming). The next sections illustrate these steps and enumerate examples across different phases of emergency management, prevention, mitigation, preparedness, response, and recovery.

Information Dissemination

Issuing alerts and warnings represents a long-standing practice in emergency management (King, 2004; Lindell & Perry, 2012; Mileti, 1999). The timely and effective distribution of this information can mean the difference between life and death and also influence outcomes related to community recovery (Comfort, 1999). Emergency managers who have long relied on third party go-betweens such as traditional media outlets to reach the public can now quickly disseminate warnings as well as protective action information directly to constituents (Hughes & Palen, 2012; Hughes, St. Denis, Palen, & Anderson, 2014; Sutton et al., 2014). Social media platforms facilitate other types of messages as well, including preparedness and recovery information (Mergel, 2014). Wukich and Mergel (forthcoming), for example, evaluated the tweets of state-level emergency management agencies and noted that over 40% of all messages were preparedness-related. Examples range from risk awareness messages to specific tips on how to prepare for hazards and keep your household and family safe. In the following sections, we describe a number of message types employed.

Social Media Monitoring and Analysis

Spontaneous reporting of disaster-related events provide valuable intelligence for emergency managers (Tobias, 2011; Vieweg, Hughes, Starbird, & Palen, 2010). This information may come from constituents, traditional media, or from other organizations. Additionally, analysis of public sentiment provides emergency managers with an indication of community reaction to specific directives and cases of urgent need. However, especially in large communities, the amount of social media data can be overwhelming. Data may be irrelevant, contradictory, and/or inaccurate (Castillo, Mendoza, & Poblete, 2011; Gupta & Kumaraguru, 2012). Worse, individuals with malicious intent may seek to mislead responders (Lindsay, 2011) and pranksters may inject false information into the conversation (Eveleth, 2012; Shih, 2012). During Superstorm Sandy, for example, Photoshopped images widely circulated depicting a submerged New York Stock Exchange (Shih, 2012) and a shark-infested New York City Subway system (Eveleth, 2012). Not realizing they were fake, CNN aired the Stock Exchange photos as breaking news, which contributed to the public's general confusion (Eveleth, 2012). It is, therefore, important that emergency managers be involved in creating, disseminating, and evaluating information to ensure accuracy and reliability.

There are potential problems with relying on social media, such as incomplete or inaccurate information. However, this is something that can be dealt with by authenticating and verifying information via multiple sources (Defrancis, 2011). Content, sentiment, and veracity analyses provide related information, monitoring strategies, and tactics used across different phases of emergency management. We describe analytic tactics in the next sections. In order to implement those tactics, however, resources are needed. Emergency managers analyze available data either (a) manually (St. Denis, Hughes, & Palen, 2012); (b) via machine-assisted approaches (Yin, Lampert, Cameron, Robinson, & Power, 2012); or (c) using a combination of both methods (Wukich, forthcoming). Relatedly, recent research has found that the majority of local agencies still do not use analyze social media data, so an understanding of available approaches is important for practitioners still examining their options (Mergel, 2014; Su, Wardell, & Thorkildsen, 2013).

Conversation and Coordinated Action

In her book on social media use in federal agencies, Mergel (2012) described the tendency of personnel to recycle press release content into social media messages, enabling only a one-way flow of communication between government and citizen. Several prominent emergency managers, however, have recognized the value of engendering conversations (Defrancis, 2011; Fugate, 2011). FEMA's official guidance on social media use advises practitioners to converse with constituents, develop shared expectations, and create and pursue shared objectives (FEMA, 2013). This advice mirrors the types of deliberative communication strategies used across other policy domains to facilitate meaningful public engagement in face-to-face settings (Gastil, 2008; Nabatchi, 2012). Research suggests that those types of interactions are beginning to take place. While Wukich and Mergel (forthcoming) illustrated only limited conversations between state agencies and the public over their period of observation, they highlighted several examples in which agencies asked the public to provide specific types of information, resources, and/or services to help solve shared problems. Sutton, Spiro, Butts et al. (2013) described how, after the Deepwater Horizon 2010 oil spill, federal and state agencies created information networks to share official information with each other and converse with the affected public. Conversations and subsequent crowdsourcing each occurs over a range of emergency management activities and are discussed in the following sections.

Social Media Use Before, During, and After a Disaster

During a disaster, communication is paramount, but social media also has uses in other phases of emergency management. In this section, we address how social media can be used before, during, and after a crisis, and we provide specific examples of how platforms are currently used. While best practice is widely available (FEMA, 2013), adoption and implementation rates vary (Mergel, 2014; Su et al., 2013; Wukich & Mergel, forthcoming). The three approaches of social media use—information dissemination, monitoring and analysis, and engaging others in conversation and coordinated action—are given particular attention. The vast majority of social media research on disasters focus on the response phase of emergency management, and that is where we will begin.

Social Media in Emergency Response Operations

During disasters, traditional modes of communication can be disrupted, and important information may not always make it to those who need it most (Comfort, 2007a). Social media is seen by many as a solution—albeit one part of a solution—to the problem (Fugate, 2011; Hughes et al., 2014; Sutton, Spiro, Butts et al., 2013). Much research has focused on social media use during disasters (St. Denis, Palen, & Anderson, 2014; Steinberg, Wukich, & Wu, forthcoming; Sutton, Johnson et al., 2013), and each of the previously discussed approaches—information dissemination, intelligence gathering, and engaging others—has been addressed to varying extents.

We first consider information dissemination. During disasters, citizens and other agencies must make protective action decisions in response to the hazards that they face (Lindell & Perry, 2012). Government agencies generate a range of message types via social media, including alerts and advisories and descriptions of hazard impact to help people make informed decisions (Bruns et al., 2012; FEMA, 2013; Olteanu, Vieweg, & Castillo, 2014; Sutton et al., 2014). While social media use may increase the speed at which agencies release information, this type of usage can be seen as an extension of traditional communication activities (Hughes & Palen, 2012). During the lead up to Superstorm Sandy, for example, multiple officials and agencies issued and amplified evacuation orders via Twitter, including messages from governors, local elected officials, and federal, state, local agencies. These multiple points of contact extended the reach of the initial set of evacuation orders. Other messages addressed post-storm issues such as clean-up, road closures, and the availability of resources such as shelters and food supplies (Hughes et al., 2014).

In addition to targeting the public at large, agencies at times develop and disseminate messages specifically for other agencies (Wukich, forthcoming). During Superstorm Sandy, for example, local agencies chose to update their colleagues on specific action items and damage assessments (Hughes et al., 2014). One specific example of this was when the Atlantic County Office of Emergency Management tweeted "Per order of Atlantic County Emergency Coordinator Vince Jones, (NJSA A:9–33) all first responders are to cease operations as of 10/29/2012 at 1600 hrs." Other messages informed responders about available resources and important deadlines. In addition, reports on the presence, or the lack thereof, of needed personnel and other resources are useful to other responding agencies. Wukich and Steinberg (2014), however, pointed out that only limited exchanges took place between agencies during four high-profile disasters in 2013. The resulting information gaps could lead to suboptimal disaster management outcomes because not all responders would have the same level of situational awareness upon which to make informed decisions.

Agencies that share information enhance the situational awareness, which ideally improves decision making and subsequent performance (see Comfort, 2005, 2007b; Kapucu, 2006). Emergency managers can also accrue situational awareness from the posts of citizens. A variety of approaches has been developed with regard to this type of data monitoring and analysis, including manual review and machine-assisted tactics. Manual analysis offers a resource-light approach. One person can review data to illicit situational awareness. Such low resource engagement still holds the potential for strong positive effects. For example, during Hurricane Earl in 2010, an emergency manager in Catawba County, North Carolina was able to accrue actionable intelligence by following the hashtag #Earl (Opshi, 2010). Even just searching for terms like *explosion* can provide useful information, as evidenced by FEMA Administrator Craig Fugate's experience during the 2010 gas pipeline explosion in San Bruno, California (Spellman, 2010).

A problem with the manual review of data, however, is that individuals can easily become overwhelmed by the sheer volume of messages (Hughes & Palen, 2012). One solution is to increase the number of people analyzing the data. St. Denis et al. (2012) documented a case in rural Oregon in which emergency managers organized several trusted digital volunteers to monitor social media during a large wildfire. Those volunteers identified points of need and communicated findings back to responders.

Another approach is to adopt machine-assisted strategies and tactics that involve tailored software systems (Yin et al., 2012). The American Red Cross has been a major advocate for using this type of approach (Defrancis, 2011) and has developed a strategy that mixes manual team monitoring with software analysis of big data. Wukich (forthcoming) described how the Red Cross teamed with Dell Computers to convert marketing software into a tool to identify public sentiment during disasters and pinpoint specific cases of need. The system, named the Digital Operations Center, was implemented with success during Superstorm Sandy and was later replicated in Texas.

During disasters, social media platforms provide mechanisms for two-way and multi-way communication. During the Superstorm Sandy event, staff and volunteers identified people in need and redirected personnel and resources accordingly (Wukich, forthcoming). The digital team engaged with them to ensure they received help. The New York City Fire Department fielded requests directly from citizens who were unable to get through via congested 911 lines (Shih, 2012). This type of two-way interaction holds potential in augmented traditional land-line approaches to crisis communication.

In some cases, emergency managers engaged a wider audience to participate in the provision of public goods and services by requesting help from the public to solve shared problems (Haddow & Haddow, 2014). Some agencies make open calls for information on hazard impact. For example, whenever significant seismic activity is detected, the U.S. Geological Survey asks social media users whether they felt the earthquake and the extent of any damage experienced (Atkinson & Wald, 2007). This type of information provides situational awareness to the agency and identifies potential need, which is intelligence that can be passed along to responding organizations. Mashup software such as Ushahidi allow users—government agencies and citizens alike—to incorporate pictures and other data to create maps illustrating damage and need (Bruns et al., 2012; Rive et al., 2012). However, according to Su et al. (2013), the vast majority of state and local agencies have not incorporated such technology into their repertoire. Resource seeking represents another type of crowdsourcing activity in which agencies request volunteers, funds, and/or other resources (Wukich, forthcoming). However, according to Wukich and Mergel (forthcoming), only a handful of state agencies employed this tactic during response operations.

Social Media in Disaster Recovery Operations

While much research has been conducted on the role of social media in response operations, less has been conducted on disaster recovery, particularly long term. As an extension of the response phase, social media have been used to notify the public about available resources and to broadcast steps taken toward recovery. For example, Bennett (2014) evaluated social media activity by one local emergency management agency following a tornado in Oklahoma and found that 33% of all messages addressed available services and resources such as food, small business loans, debris removal, and the provision of health care. With respect to engaging the public in conversations, Bennett (2014) noted that 17% of all recovery-related posts were part of an exchange between the agency and constituents.

Again as an extension of the response phase, crowdsourcing during the recovery phase represents a valuable tactic for emergency managers. Wukich and Mergel (forthcoming) noted calls for volunteers and donations initiated by state agencies following the 2013 Colorado floods and a 2013 tornado in Iowa.

Social media use theoretically makes recovery more efficient and improves coordinated efforts, both between those agencies charged with recovery operations and with the public at large. Promoting assistance programs and being able to engage with others regarding questions provide value to the process. Sutton, Spiro, Butts et al. (2013) documented the valuable content provided by agencies contributing to recovery operations following the 2010 Deepwater Horizon oil spill. The idea that agencies will continue to adopt social media as an official communication channel following disasters indicates that the resulting information networks might provide value to those interested in grasping the larger common operating picture as well as specific points relevant to their operations.

Social Media for Preparedness, Prevention, and Mitigation

The role of social media is not limited to only response and recovery operations, despite the preponderance of research on those phases. Social media can be a useful tool to encourage the public and other agencies to prepare for potential disasters. This can be done through the dissemination of educational information and by using communication channels to build community trust and generate a shared sense of risk (Mergel, 2014; Wukich, forthcoming). Agencies appear to be quite active in this area. In their analysis of state-level emergency management agency tweets across all phases of emergency management, Wukich and Mergel (forthcoming) noted that over 48% of all messages were directed toward preparedness, prevention, and/or mitigation activities.

Education-oriented messages represent one prominent type and include information regarding potential hazards, safety tips, links to websites with additional insights, and notices about events in the area where the public can become more informed. These types of messages instruct the public on how to improve personal and household preparedness and serve to guide people toward best practices (Wukich & Mergel, forthcoming). A related message type promotes coordinated preparedness activities such as the Great ShakeOut, in which schools, businesses, and other organizations conduct earthquake drills in anticipation of significant seismic activity.

With regard to the Great ShakeOut, several agencies asked for and retweeted pictures and descriptions of public participation to engender a conversation regarding best practices (Wukich & Mergel, forthcoming). Other types of conversations take place as well. Clark County, Washington State, for example, has initiated an annual game entitled "30 Days, 30 Ways" in which they encourage constituents to contribute comments and photos related to specific household-level preparedness activities. Each day a winner is chosen and given a prize. The agency's goal is to increase online participation and build awareness around preparedness activities (Wukich, forthcoming). Clark County also monitors social media accounts on a continual basis to accrue situational awareness even during so-called blue sky days when no disasters are on the horizon. This case represents a holistic implementation strategy.

With respect to crowdsourcing, the preparedness phase is an ideal time for agencies to recruit and train volunteers and build trust in the community (Perry & Lindell, 2007). Wukich and Mergel (forthcoming) pointed out that over 50% of all solicitations for volunteers were not sent during response or recovery operations, but during the preparedness phase of emergency management. This evidence suggests that some agencies engage with the public to build trust and organizational capacity well before a disaster actually takes place.

Discussion and Recommendations for Future Research

As demonstrated in this chapter, social media platforms possess the potential to improve performance along a number of fronts: (1) information dissemination; (2) intelligence gathering; and (3) engaging citizens in conversations, which may lead to the co-production of public goods and services. In this chapter, we have addressed how emergency managers employ social media before, during, and after disasters, and have highlighted the successes that they have achieved. Social media, however, is not a panacea to cure all the ills facing emergency management. While platforms are valuable, they represent just one piece of a larger set of crisis communication tools (see Haddow & Haddow, 2014; Hu & Kapucu, 2014; Walker, 2012), and have yet to be thoroughly implemented across different levels of government to maximize potential benefit (Su et al., 2013). Additionally, uneven adoption and use among citizens (see Duggan et al., 2015) means that emergency managers can only reach a segment of the population via social media. The number and diversity of social media users are growing, however, so further examination of how to more effectively implement the technology is warranted.

Despite the optimism expressed by researchers and practitioners (Sutton, Johnson et al., 2013; Wukich & Steinberg, 2014), emergency managers confront significant challenges that impede effective implementation. For example, skeptics in leadership positions may still question the value of such technology (Su et al., 2013). Fountain's (2001) research on enacting information technology demonstrated that implementation decisions were largely driven by the opinion that tools perpetuated existing organizational values and clearly improved work processes. Mergel and Bretschneider (2013) pointed out that social media use generally develops first by personnel experimenting with tools outside of official policy, and then after they demonstrate proof that a concept is effective, policies shift to enumerate acceptable applications. This process may take place in the context of emergency management.

Another consideration is the availability of resources. Many emergency managers operate with limited numbers of personnel and available resources; this presents certain obstacles for implementation (St. Denis et al., 2012; Wukich, forthcoming). With limited resources, agencies must often weigh the benefits of expanded social media use, especially when one considers that all of the other demands of emergency managers are still in place. One innovation to address resource scarcity has been the formation of volunteer groups to augment paid staff (Griswold, 2013; St. Denis et al., 2012; White, 2012). These challenges and potential solutions deserve the research community's continued attention.

In terms of additional future research, despite the growing number of valuable how-to manuals (Crowe, 2012; FEMA, 2013; White, 2012), and the strong descriptive research that indicates how social media has been used in specific cases (Hughes et al., 2014; Olteanu et al., 2014; St. Denis et al., 2012; Sutton, Johnson et al., 2013), there is still a need for theory grounded in systematic work that links these best practices with tangible results. This type of research will provide for a more robust understanding of how to use social media tools for the benefit of both emergency managers and their constituents. Research on the efficacy of flood alerts and warnings as well as protective action information represents a step in the right direction (Mileti, 2014), as does the research that links extreme weather alerts and warnings with increased social media activity (Ripberger, Jenkins-Smith, Silva, Carlson, & Henderson, 2014). Understanding key aspects of how data monitoring influences the decisions of emergency managers and how crowdsourcing impacts emergency management outcomes represent additional areas to examine. We challenge researchers to evaluate how specific strategies and tactics influence emergency management outcomes and determine how social media can be more effectively implemented to make communities more resilient.

References

Ambinder, E., Jennings, D. M., Blachman-Biatch, I., Edgemon, K., Hull, P., & Taylor, A. (2013). The resilient social network: @OccupySandy #SuperstormSandy. Falls Church, VA: Homeland Security Studies and Analysis Institute.

American Red Cross. (2012). Red Cross poll shows social media and apps motivate people to prepare [Press release]. Retrieved from www.redcross.org/news/press-release/ More-Americans-Using-Mobile-Apps-in-Emergencies.

Atkinson, G. M., & Wald, D. J. (2007). "Did you feel it?" Intensity data: A surprisingly good measure of earthquake ground motion. *Seismological Research Letters, 78*(3), 362–368.

Bennett, D. M. (2014). How do emergency managers use social media platforms? *Journal of Emergency Management, 12*(3), 251–256.

Bruns, A., Burgess, J., Crawford, K., & Shaw, F. (2012). #qldfloods and @QPSMedia: Crisis communication on Twitter in the 2011 south east Queensland floods. In *Media ecologies project* (pp. 1–58). Kelvin Grove, Queensland: ARC Centre of Excellence for Creative Industries & Innovation (CCI).

Castillo, C., Mendoza, M., & Poblete, B. (2011). *Information credibility on Twitter.* Paper presented at the International World Wide Web Conference, Hyderabad, India.

Comfort, L. K. (1999). *Shared risk: Complex systems in seismic response.* New York: Pergamon.

Comfort, L. K. (2005). Risk, security, and disaster management. *Annual Review of Political Science, 8*, 335–356.

Comfort, L. K. (2007a). Asymmetric information processes in extreme events: The December 26, 2004 Sumatran earthquake and tsunami. In D. E. Gibbons (Ed.), *Communicable crises: Prevention, response, and recovery in the global arena* (pp. 84–137). Charlotte, NC: Information Age Publishers.

Comfort, L. K. (2007b). Crisis management in hindsight: Cognition, communication, coordination, and control. *Public Administration Review, 67*(s1), 189–197.

Crowe, A. (2012). *Disasters 2.0: The application of social media systems for modern emergency management.* Boca Raton, FL: CRC Press.

Defrancis, S. (2011). Testimony of American Red Cross chief public affairs officer, Suzy Defrancis to the Senate Committee on Homeland Security and Governmental Affairs, Subcommittee on Disaster Recovery and Intergovernmental Affairs. *Hearing on "Understanding the Power of Social Media as a Communication Tool in the Aftermath of Disasters."* May 5, 2011, Washington, DC. Retrieved December 9, 2014, from www.hsgac.senate.gov/subcommittees/disaster-recovery-and-intergovernmental-affairs/hearings/understanding-the-power-of-social-media-as-a-communications-tool-in-the-aftermath-of-disasters.

Dufty, N. (2012). Using social media to build community disaster resilience. *The Australian Journal of Emergency Management, 27*(1), 40–45.

Duggan, M., Ellison, N. B., Lampe, C., Lenhart, A., & Madden, M. (2015). Social media update 2014: Pew Research Center. Retrieved from www.pewinternet.org/2015/01/09/social-media-update-2014.

Eveleth, R. (2012). Hurricane Sandy: Five ways to spot a fake photograph. BBC.com. Retrieved from www.bbc.com/future/story/20121031-how-to-spot-a-fake-sandy-photo.

FEMA. (2013). *IS-42: Social media in emergency management.* Washington, DC: Retrieved from http://training.fema.gov/is/courseoverview.aspx?code=is-42.

Fountain, J. E. (2001). *Building the virtual state: Information technology and institutional change.* Washington, DC: Brookings Institution Press.

Fugate, C. (2011). Written Statement of Craig Fugate Administrator Federal Emergency Management Agency Understanding the Power of Social Media as a Communication Tool in the Aftermath of Disasters before the Senate Committee on Homeland Security and Governmental Affairs, Subcommittee on Disaster Recovery and Intergovernmental Affairs. *Hearing on "Understanding the Power of Social Media as a Communication Tool in the Aftermath of Disasters."* May 5, 2011, Washington, DC. Retrieved December 9, 2014, from www.hsgac.senate.gov/subcommittees/disaster-recovery-and-intergovernmental-affairs/hearings/understanding-the-power-of-social-media-as-a-communications-tool-in-the-aftermath-of-disasters.

Gastil, J. (2008). *Political communication and deliberation.* Los Angeles: SAGE Publications.

Griswold, A. (2013). Digital detectives and virtual volunteers: Integrating emergent online communities into disaster response operations. *Journal of Business Continuity & Emergency Planning, 7*(1), 13–25.

Gupta, A., & Kumaraguru, P. (2012). *Credibility ranking of tweets during high impact events.* Paper presented at the Proceedings of the 1st Workshop on Privacy and Security in Online Social Media, Lyon, France.

Haddow, G. D., & Haddow, K. (2014). *Disaster communications in a changing media world* (2nd ed.). Waltham, MA: Butterworth-Heinemann.

Hansen, D., Shneiderman, B., & Smith, M. A. (2010). *Analyzing social media networks with NodeXL: Insights from a connected world.* Boston, MA: Elsevier.

Hu, Q., & Kapucu, N. (2014). Information communication technology utilization for effective emergency management networks. *Public Management Review,* 1–26.

Hughes, A. L., & Palen, L. (2012). The evolving role of the public information officer: An examination of social media in emergency management. *Journal of Homeland Security & Emergency Management, 9*(1), 1–20.

Hughes, A. L., St. Denis, L. A., Palen, L., & Anderson, K. M. (2014). *Online public communications by police and fire services during the 2012 Hurricane Sandy.* Paper presented at the 2014 International Conference on Human Factors in Computing Systems (CHI 2014), New York, NY.

Kaplan, A. M., & Haenlein, M. (2010). Users of the world, unite! The challenges and opportunities of social media. *Business Horizons, 53*(1), 59–68.

Kapucu, N. (2006). Interagency communication networks during emergencies: Boundary spanners in multiagency coordination. *The American Review of Public Administration, 36*(2), 207–225.

Kapucu, N., & Van Wart, M. (2006). The evolving role of the public sector in managing catastrophic disasters: Lessons learned. *Administration & Society, 38*(3), 279–308.

King, D. (2004). Understanding the message: Social and cultural constraints to interpreting weather generated natural hazards. *International Journal of Mass Emergencies and Disasters, 22,* 57–74.

Leaman, R. (2009). An introduction to Twitter hashtags. Retrieved from www.wild apricot.com/blogs/newsblog/2008/03/11/an-introduction-to-twitter-hashtags#.

Lee, C. S., & Ma, L. (2012). News sharing in social media: The effect of gratifications and prior experience. *Computers in Human Behavior, 28*(2), 331–339.

Lindell, M. K., & Perry, R. W. (2012). The protective action decision model: Theoretical modifications and additional evidence. *Risk Analysis, 32*(4), 616–632.

Lindsay, B. R. (2011). *Social media and disasters: Current uses, future options, and policy considerations.* Washington, DC: CRS Report for Congress.

Mergel, I. (2010). The use of social media to dissolve knowledge silos in government. In R. O'Leary, D. M. Van Slyke, & S. Kim (Eds.), *The future of public administration, public management and public service around the world: The Minnowbrook perspective* (pp. 177–187). Washington, DC: Georgetown University Press.

Mergel, I. (2012). *Social media in the public sector: A guide to participation, collaboration, and transparency in the networked world.* San Francisco: Jossey-Bass/Wiley.

Mergel, I. (2014). *Social media practices in local emergency management: Results from Central New York* (pp. 1–41). Syracuse, NY: Institute of National Security and Counterterrorism & Moynihan Institute of Global Affairs.

Mergel, I., & Bretschneider, S. I. (2013). A three-stage adoption process for social media use in government. *Public Administration Review, 73*(3), 390–400.

Messina, C. (2007). Twitter hashtags for emergency coordination and disaster relief. Retrieved from http://factoryjoe.com/blog/2007/10/22/twitter-hashtags-for-emergency-coordination-and-disaster-relief.

Mileti, D. S. (1999). *Disasters by design: A reassessment of natural hazards in the United States.* Washington, DC: Joseph Henry Press.

Mileti, D. S. (2014, June 23). *Keynote address.* Paper presented at the 39th Annual Natural Hazards Research and Applications Workshop, Broomfield, CO.

Nabatchi, T. (2012). Putting the "public" back in public values research: Designing participation to identify and respond to values. *Public Administration Review, 72*(5), 699–708.

NetSquared. (2008). Twitter and the San Diego fires: An interview with Nate Ritter. Retrieved from www.netsquared.org/blog/britt-bravo/twitter-and-san-diego-fires-interview-nate-ritter.

Olteanu, A., Vieweg, S., & Castillo, C. (2014). *What to expect when the unexpected happens: Social media communications across crises.* Paper presented at the CSCW '15, Vancouver, BC, Canada.

Opshi, A. (2010). County experiments with monitoring social media in emergencies. *Government Technology*. Retrieved from www.govtech.com/public-safety/County-Monitoring-Social-Media-Emergencies.html.

Perry, R. W., & Lindell, M. K. (2007). *Emergency planning*. Hoboken, NJ: Wiley.

Pew Research Center. (2002). Public's news habits little changed by September 11. Washington, DC: Pew Research Center. Retrieved from www.people-press.org/2002/06/09/publics-news-habits-little-changed-by-september-11.

Ripberger, J. T., Jenkins-Smith, H. C., Silva, C. L., Carlson, D. E., & Henderson, M. (2014). Social media and severe weather: Do tweets provide a valid indicator of public attention to severe weather risk communication? *Weather, Climate, and Society*, 6(4), 520–530.

Rive, G., Hare, J., Thomas, J., & Nankivell, K. (2012). *Social media in an emergency: A best practice guide*. Wellington, New Zealand: Wellington Region CDEM Group.

Shih, G. (2012, November 1). Twitter a hurricane lifeline: Millions turned to the social network for news, help as Sandy struck. *Reuters*.

Spellman, J. (2010, September 22). Heading off disaster, one tweet at a time. *CNN*. Retrieved from www.cnn.com/2010/TECH/social.media/09/22/natural.disasters.social.media.

St. Denis, L. A., Hughes, A. L., & Palen, L. (2012). *Trial by fire: The deployment of trusted digital volunteers in the 2011 Shadow Lake fire*. Paper presented at the 9th International ISCRAM Conference Vancouver, BC, Canada.

St. Denis, L. A., Palen, L., & Anderson, K. M. (2014). *Mastering social media: An analysis of Jefferson County's communications during the 2013 Colorado Floods*. Paper presented at the Information Systems for Crisis Response and Management Conference (ISCRAM 2014), State College, PA.

Steinberg, A., Wukich, C., & Wu, H. (forthcoming). Central social media actors in disaster information networks. *International Journal of Mass Emergencies and Disasters*.

Su, Y. S., Wardell III, C., & Thorkildsen, Z. (2013). *Social media in the emergency management field: 2012 Survey Results*. Arlington, VA: CNA.

Sutton, J., Johnson, B., Spiro, E., & Butts, C. (2013). Tweeting what matters: Information, advisories, and alerts following the Boston Marathon events. Online Research Highlight. Retrieved from http://heroicproject.org.

Sutton, J., Spiro, E., Butts, C., Fitzhugh, S., Johnson, B., & Greczek, M. (2013). Tweeting the spill: Online informal communications, social networks, and conversational microstructures during the Deepwater Horizon oilspill. *International Journal of Information Systems for Crisis Response and Management (IJISCRAM)*, 5(1), 58–76.

Sutton, J., Spiro, E., Johnson, B., Fitzhugh, S., & Butts, C. (2013). Tweeting Boston: The influence of microstructure in broadcasting messages through Twitter. Online Research Highlight. Retrieved from http://heroicproject.org.

Sutton, J., Spiro, E. S., Johnson, B., Fitzhugh, S., Gibson, B., & Butts, C. T. (2014). Warning tweets: Serial transmission of messages during the warning phase of a disaster event. *Information, Communication & Society*, 17(6), 765–787.

Tierney, K. J., Lindell, M. K., & Perry, R. W. (2001). *Facing the unexpected: Disaster preparedness and response in the United States*. Washington, DC: Joseph Henry Press.

Tobias, E. (2011). Using Twitter and other social media platforms to provide situational awareness during an incident. *Journal of Business Continuity & Emergency Planning*, 5(3), 208–223.

Vieweg, S., Hughes, A. L., Starbird, K., & Palen, L. (2010). *Microblogging during two natural hazards events: What Twitter may contribute to situational awareness* Paper presented at the CHI 2010: Crisis Informatics, Atlanta, GA.

Walker, D. C. (2012). *Mass notification and crisis communications planning, preparedness, and systems*. Boca Raton, FL: CRC Press.

White, C. (2012). *Social media, crisis communication, and emergency management: Leveraging Web 2.0 technologies*. Boca Raton, FL: CRC Press.

Wukich, C. (forthcoming). Social media use in emergency management. *Journal of Emergency Management*.

Wukich, C., & Mergel, I. (forthcoming). Closing the citizen–government communication gap: Content, audience, and network analysis of government tweets. *Journal of Homeland Security & Emergency Management*.

Wukich, C., & Steinberg, A. (2014). Nonprofit and public sector participation in self-organizing information networks: Twitter hashtag and trending topic use during disasters. *Risk, Hazards & Crisis in Public Policy, 4*(2), 83–109.

Yin, J., Lampert, A., Cameron, M., Robinson, B., & Power, R. (2012). Using social media to enhance emergency situation awareness. *Intelligent Systems, 27*(6), 52–59.

Zavattaro, S. M., & Sementelli, A. J. (2014). A critical examination of social media adoption in government: Introducing omnipresence. *Government Information Quarterly, 31*(2), 257–264.

12 Social Media in Emergency Management

Examples from the Field

Suzanne L. Frew and Alisha Griswold

In recent years, social media has empowered emergency and disaster managers, communities, and organizations to improve their ability to build disaster-resilient communities, protecting them from the harm caused by all forms of hazards—natural, technological, and human-caused. By building upon these toolsets, officials and community leaders (formal and informal) are sharing and better utilizing critical information from partners and the community to perform more effectively to meet the disaster mission. The use of social media in emergency management is forcing a fundamental paradigm shift in government, building linkages, creating relationships, and moving data in real time, facilitating greater effectiveness and efficiency.

Public and private sector players are working together in new, unexpected ways to integrate collaborative business solutions into what was traditionally the government's resilience mission; short-term housing and hostel intermediary Airbnb has partnered with the City of San Francisco to provide emergency housing following a crisis (see, for example, http://blog.seattlepi.com/tech-chron/2014/07/29/airbnb-partners-with-s-f-for-emergency-response-plan. Social media is also driving change in unexpected areas, such as the "sharing economy" movement, which allows owners of equipment and resources to loan them to other individuals when they are not being used (see, for example, www.sunset.com/home/sharing-economy).

Many key disaster events over recent years have driven home the unique value of using social media tools before, during, and after emergencies. One of the first events that drew awareness to the power of mobile technologies was the 2007 Virginia Tech campus shooting. When a senior student killed 32 people and injured 17 more, university students, family members, and communities related to the school used social media such as Twitter and Facebook to communicate details of the shootings to each other, while only generic information was being published by popular media (see http://sites.duke.edu/socialmediacoverage/personal-impact/2007-virginia-tech-massacre).

During the 2010 earthquake response in Haiti, a group of volunteers used Ushahidi, the free and open source mapping technology, to collect, process, and map the most urgent tweets with geotagged location data to find survivors buried in rubble. Ushahidi (the Swahili word meaning *testimony*), originally developed to report the 2008 post-election violence in Kenya, uses a variety of sources, including SMS (text messages), Twitter, and radio. The Haiti response demonstrated how social technologies, the use of offsite volunteers, and maps that visualized collected data offered a new and innovative approach to support the daunting response and recovery tasks faced by first responders and emergency managers (see http://voices.nationalgeographic.com/2012/07/02/crisis-mapping-haiti). Internationally, emergency management practitioners and researchers took notice.

When Superstorm Sandy hit the East Coast in October 2012, Morris County, New Jersey, already proactively engaged with social media, aggressively ramped up their efforts before, during, and after the storm. Local officials used an integrated platform strategy. According to Carol Prochazka Spencer, the digital social media manager at the time, the county focused on utilizing their Twitter, Facebook, blogs, and website to push out information, as well as monitor and interact with their community members. They reached out and engaged the business community before the storm hit and during the storm, and used information provided by sources outside their government agency, particularly concerned community members. Their analytics proved their strategy successful. The county's "MCUrgent" Facebook page following increased by 138% (of which 50% of the likes were from mobile devices) and Twitter followers increased by 66%. Key takeaway lessons included using photos when possible, responding to posts, having backup team members with multiple people trained to handle the social feeds, and keeping their "online voice" consistent. Their online response resulted in building a new level of trust with their community and increasing future opportunities for enhanced dialogue and relationships.

Benefits of Using Social Media in Emergency Management

There are many benefits for using social media in disaster and emergency management and for building disaster resilience. A few key benefits are described here.

Builds Relationships

Social media has many benefits when used for improving and maintaining a community's resilience to disaster. Perhaps one of the most challenging aspects of government (at all levels) is building and maintaining a sustainable, robust relationship that engenders trust and credibility when risk is involved. Social media enables the multidirectional dialogue between key stakeholders and the community, both those affecting and those who are interested in following and understanding the events. Fostering the relationships before the disaster pays off by having ready access to needed information, resources, and support during the event. Social engagement can provide a platform for and with individuals and community subcultures whose voices are traditionally not heard, a critical aspect of learning about risks, sharing concerns, and building both pre-disaster resilience strategies and post-disaster recovery strategies that reflect the needs and desires of a greater number of the community.

Improves Communications

Social media gives authorities the ability to reach community members with new methods for delivering alerts and warnings, messages of preparedness, public notices, and press releases, as well as time-sensitive response and recovery information. This ability to cast wide and narrow nets provide rapid real-time communications to the general public at large, geographically targeted populations at risk, or specific groups of individuals that have signed up for services. An integrated strategy combining social with traditional media and other outreach methods increases the overall penetration of a diverse and often complex community.

Expands Research

Social media platforms offer opportunities to solicit feedback and monitor and track engagement and levels of interest on safety and risk issues of concern to the community. Based on the research, clarification on message meaning, resilience strategies and solutions, and effective response activities can be dynamically adjusted to better customize the community's needs and desires. New information can be crowdsourced, gathered from the crown and compiled. Social media tools empower an interested public to participate in developing their own recovery solutions to help them get back on their feet faster, with more long-lasting buy-in.

Improves Situational Awareness

Mobile technologies enable community members to provide timely field information that can be critical to decision makers as an event unfolds. Posting informational updates, geotagged photographs, videos, and other data are invaluable to building the common operating picture (COP), or painting the big picture, for officials to adequately stay abreast of rapidly moving wildfires, flooding rivers, or the status of members of a neighborhood being evacuated. Social media platforms enable information to be transmitted in ways that improve understanding, such as data visualizations on maps. By pulling and pushing information through social media tools and platforms, community members can be more inclusively involved in the disaster resilience planning process, more adequately work with authorities when an event occurs, and improve their awareness and educational levels of what they need to do to improve their safety.

Prevention and Protection

Use of social media for preventing disasters is primarily through the collection and analysis of open-source data. Methods for collecting information is dependent upon the platform; consider Facebook, where users post updates and comments to networks that mirror their real-world relationships (primarily peer groups, colleagues, and academic cohorts). Digital detectives need only identify an affiliate or relative of any given individual and to track down the target profile or page. Other platforms, such as Yik Yak, focus on geographic co-location and leverage relative anonymity for the users, making identification of specific individuals challenging. However, perceived online anonymity can create a sense of false security and facilitate posting politically contentious and sometimes threatening content (see, for example, http://statenews.com/article/2015/01/mullen-pleads-guilty).

Preparedness and Mitigation

Comprehensive communication between the government and community members presents a significant challenge. Historically, elected officials have opted to address their constituents in one-directional means, primarily through speeches, press releases, and broadcasts over television and radio; social media provides a new method of engaging with the public, in a two-directional and sometimes group discussion. Twitter is a particularly popular platform for these virtual "town halls," with President Obama, heads of state, and several members of Congress conducting question-and-answer sessions (see, for example, www.nextgov.com/technology-news/tech-insider/2012/01/on-town-halls-and-social-media/55150).

The complement to government being able to reach stakeholders is public access to government. By allowing local agencies, and their subsidiary departments, to tailor their engagement strategies, stakeholders can more readily access services and resources (for instance, see: www.kingcounty.gov/about/news/social-media.aspx).

Prepositioned social strategies and tools pay off. When the 2014 SR530 "Oso Slide" spilled thousands of cubic yards of mud out over a square mile (in some areas more than 60 feet deep) in a rural section of central Snohomish County in the State of Washington, the county's existing network of social media followers allowed information to reach roughly 3,000 people instantly. The slide destroyed homes, knocked out phone service, and blocked traffic to surrounding cities. The county did not have to rely on media to provide details, but became the best source for reliable, timely incident information. County PIOs used their Facebook and Twitter pages to push out verified information while at the same time reaching out to media and the public to answer questions, correct misinformation, address rumors before they got out of hand, and communicate with community members in the affected slide area. The response was impressive. Many Facebook posts received upwards of 10,000 views, and tweets reached nearly 100,000 people through retweets. Good examples can be found at: www.wsdot.wa.gov/Projects/SR530/Landslide and www.llis.dhs.gov/sites/default/files/Innovatie%20Practice%20SR530%20Mudslide%20and%20Social%20Media.pdf.

Response and Recovery

Once a threat or hazard is identified, the next step is to notify the community members most likely to be impacted. The "Fast Follow" feature on Twitter allows users to subscribe to another user's tweets and receive them via SMS text message. Twitter does not charge individuals who use Fast Follow, although charges could be incurred through the subscriber's mobile service provider. Use of social media to get the word out as quickly as possible can save lives and help prevent property damage (see, for example, https://support.twitter.com/articles/20170004-fast-following-on-sms).

When disaster strikes, the American Red Cross (ARC) deploys their team of social media specialists called "DigiVols." These digital disaster volunteers dig through piles of tweets and Facebook posts pulling out calls for assistance and connecting community members in need with vital resources. DigiVols are vetted through the same channels as traditional ARC volunteers with a formal application process, core competency training, and background checks, before signing up for their first shift (see http://redcrosschat.org/disaster-digital-volunteer-training/#sthash.sBGO1Hc9.dpbs.

After the 2010 Deepwater Horizon oil spill in the Gulf of Mexico, photos of birds covered in oil texted by community residents to the Louisiana Bucket Brigade were used to create maps identifying areas needing cleaning (see www.nejm.org/doi/full/10.1056/NEJMp1103591).

Social media became vibrant platforms for global communications exchange during the 2011 Japan earthquake and tsunami. At one point approximately 1,200 tweets per minute were being generated, with trending hashtags such as #prayforjapan, #earthquake, and #japan (see http://idisaster.wordpress.com/2011/03/12/social-media-and-the-japan-earthquake-and-tsunami-what-we-can-learn).

Conclusion

Significant industry trends within the disaster management profession as well as technology are influencing social media's application to disaster management. The use of mobile devices, such as smartphones, now enables the average community member to capture, transmit, and receive pictures, videos, text messages, and informational posts during event. This emerging phenomenon known as "citizen journalism" provides invaluable field intelligence to those receiving or monitoring social media feeds. The growing popularity of wearable net-connected devices, such as augmented reality glasses and fitness trackers, have generated a fascinating mashup of social media and tangible technology. In August 2014, Jawbone, an exercise fitness tracker, documented Californians in the San Francisco Bay Area being woken by a 6.0 earthquake. Use of similar data sets could be used to build heatmaps of affected areas to compare against geological data to better portray impact and support resource allocation for response and recovery. See examples at: https://jawbone.com/blog/napa-earthquake-effect-on-sleep and www.washingtonpost.com/news/the-intersect/wp/2014/08/25/what-personal-fitness-trackers-like-jawbone-tell-us-about-earthquakes-public-health-and-just-about-anything-else.

With every incident, new stories are shared on the invaluable role of social media. It is no longer a matter of *if* social media should be used, it is now a matter of how effectively and creatively it can be used. The "online social party" will take place, and the cost for those responsible for public safety or the resilience of their community is too high to not join the conversation.

13 Hashtag Activism at Its Best?

A Comparative Analysis of Nonprofit Social Media Use for Mobilizing Online Action

Rowena L. Briones, Melissa Janoske, and Stephanie Madden

On August 23, 2007, Google designer Chris Messina first introduced the hashtag on Twitter as a means of keeping track of related content (Digital Marketing Philippines, n.d.). Since then, the symbol (#) has carried over to other social media platforms such as Instagram, Vine, and Facebook to allow users to easily participate in trending topics, monitor events, and/or provide contexts for posts. By using hashtags, social media users can filter through millions of posts to remain informed about whatever they are most interested and passionate about.

More recently, hashtags have been used by nonprofit organizations in particular as a means of motivating social media users to share content related to social issues, moving individuals toward actions such as donating, volunteering, and advocating for the cause. Because many nonprofits operate with limited monetary resources (Seltzer & Mitrook, 2007; Waters, Burnett, Lamm, & Lucas, 2009), spreading awareness of their cause and carrying out the organizational mission can be a challenge. Social media, by way of hashtags, can help these organizations communicate with publics in a more cost-effective way (Bortree & Dou, 2012).

Within the past five years, two social media campaigns in particular have garnered an incredible amount of attention. The first is the Kony 2012 campaign launched by Invisible Children, Inc. on March 5, 2012, whose viral video received more than 100 million views within six days (Wasserman, 2012). The second is the ALS Ice Bucket Challenge, which raised over $100 million within the span of just one month in the summer of 2014 (Diamond, 2014). Though both of these campaigns sparked many conversations and many shares, a more in-depth investigation can determine how Invisible Children and the ALS Association differed in terms of social media strategy and execution.

Therefore, the purpose of this chapter is to explore these two cases via a qualitative content analysis of social media content posted in response to these two campaigns. Data for this analysis include blog posts, Facebook posts, and tweets related to Kony 2012 and the Ice Bucket Challenge. The research conducted offers a glimpse of how these two nonprofit organizations used social media to foster more online engagement and interaction. Furthermore, this chapter provides insight on how hashtags could be used as a way to promote activism and spur online donations.

Nonprofits and Social Media

In the nonprofit sector, which in 2014 included more than 1.5 million 501(c) (3) organizations (Center on Nonprofits and Philanthropy, 2014), social media use is ubiquitous. According to a study conducted by the University of Massachusetts Dartmouth Center for Marketing Research, 97% of nonprofits use some form of social media (Barnes, 2010). However, research has shown that nonprofit organizations have been largely unsuccessful in building relationships with their audiences through interactive dialogue (Ingenhoff & Koelling, 2009; Kang & Norton, 2004; Waters et al., 2009), sharing primarily organization-centric information (Sharma, 2014) and focusing on information distribution rather than actual engagement (Bortree & Seltzer, 2009; Seltzer & Mitrook, 2007). In spite of these criticisms, one nonprofit organization that has effectively engaged in two-way communication with publics is the American Red Cross. In 40 in-depth interviews with American Red Cross employees who send or manage social media communication, Briones, Kuch, Liu, and Jin (2011) found that a focus on dialogue allowed the organization to build relationships focused on recruiting and retaining volunteers, providing faster disaster response services, and engaging the media.

In another study, Lovejoy and Saxton (2012) argued that nonprofit organizations are using Twitter more effectively to engage publics via dialogic and community-building practices than they have with traditional websites, but ultimately questioned whether dialogue should be viewed as the key form of social media-based organizational communication. In particular, Lovejoy and Saxton (2012) postulated that information may always be at the base of communication, meaning even organizations using social media well would send out more information than action-oriented messages. Rather than viewing dialogue as the pinnacle of communication, they argue it should instead be seen as simply another piece of the communication puzzle (Lovejoy & Saxton, 2012).

In terms of types of messages, Saxton and Waters (2014) found that call-to-action messages, which include a "clear goal of soliciting the public's help in lobbying, advocacy, or volunteering efforts" (p. 294), as well as donations and financial support, elicited the highest levels of engagement. Saxton and Waters (2014) concluded that more attention should be paid to messages that ask stakeholders to do something for the organization rather than say something at the organization. While social media's ability to serve as a cost-effective means of communication for nonprofit organizations has been studied, little research has focused on the effectiveness of social media for raising funds for an organization or cause. A review of this research is described in detail below.

Social Media and Fundraising

More recently, many nonprofits have used social media and other online spaces to help meet the needs of their fundraising efforts, as these technologies can serve a very useful and important function for organizations (Seo, Kim, & Yang, 2009). According to Kelly (1998), fundraising is defined as "the management of relationships between a charitable organization and its donor publics" (p. 8). Online fundraising in particular is a growing practice among nonprofit organizations; as the Blackbaud Charitable Giving Report (2013) states, there was a 13.5% increase in online fundraising during 2013 in the United States, with online giving accounting for 6.4% of all charitable giving in 2013. For many organizations, the online fundraising method is unique in that it allows for the mobilization and recruitment of potential donors who would otherwise be unreachable via other methods (Reddick & Ponomariov, 2013). A study conducted by Flannery, Harris, and Rhine (2009) on 24 major national nonprofit organizations found that online giving played a key factor in acquiring and retaining new donors. These new donors who give primarily via the Internet tend to be younger, more entrepreneurial, more socially conscientious, and more likely to give larger gifts than their offline counterparts (Flannery et al., 2009; Saxton & Wang, 2013; Wagner, 2002). However, Saxton and Wang (2013) found that social media tends to draw in donors who are more likely to give smaller donations as well. Therefore, online fundraising has the potential to recruit and retain a variety of donors from various populations who are willing to give a wide range of gifts to different organizations.

Another interesting aspect of the online giving phenomenon is its ability to use large social networks to reach prospective donors. Saxton and Wang (2013) describe this concept as crowdfunding, where organizations can reach geographically dispersed people around the globe who are willing to support the cause and spread the word using peer-to-peer fundraising methods (p. 853). This is especially important for individual donors, as online giving actions may dictate a person's online identity. As Randi Zuckerberg, former Director of Market Development and Spokeswoman of Facebook, noted,

> Through social media, people not only donate money, but even more importantly, their reputation and identity. Each time someone clicks "like" or joins a cause on Facebook, they are broadcasting that message to hundreds of their friends, and aligning themselves with a particular issue.
>
> (Vericat, 2010, p. 177)

Thus, individuals who feel more personally associated with or invested in a particular cause are more likely to contribute to charities linked directly to that cause (Reddick & Ponomariov, 2013), and are then more willing to share that personal connection on social media channels. Prospective donors are also more likely to contribute to causes that their close networks also support and about which they are concerned (van Leeuwen & Wiepking, 2013).

Hashtag Activism

Depending on the mission and purpose of a nonprofit organization, it may be necessary to engage in activism to create change on specific issues because "social media have engendered interactive, dynamic systems of organizational action and public reaction" (Saxton & Waters, 2014, p. 280). Digital activism, which encompasses hashtag activism, is a term that explains the usage of a wide variety of digital technology in activist campaigns, in which the ease, speed, and affordability of digital tools allow for a broader scope and reach of an activist network (Earl & Kimport, 2011; Joyce, 2010).

One way that social media allows activists to build dialogue around salient issues is through the use of hashtags—tags or identifiers that help to categorize conversations (Stache, 2014). For activists, hashtags work as a cue to "continually predicate renewed attention" (Warner, 2002, p. 61) for social justice messages. Hashtag activism can be beneficial for increasing awareness of advocacy efforts by allowing a range of activists, from individuals to billion-dollar corporations, to spread their message (Stache, 2014).

However, a potential pitfall of hashtag activism is that the hashtag itself can be co-opted and used beyond its original intention (Stache, 2014). For example, the #NotBuyingIt campaign, which was started by Representation.org, was intended for Twitter users to use the hashtag to call out sexist or gender stereotypes in the media. However, people have used the #NotBuyingIt campaign in conjunction with annoyance over Coca-Cola's marketing strategies and the political situation in Israel, meaning that it is now used to express any general frustration by online publics rather than its original intention (Stache, 2014). Misuse of activist campaign hashtags demonstrates that the

> hashtag is a good way to allow members of an advocacy or social justice group to show public support, but it may not be a great tool for educating those who are not aware of, or who do not care about, the original intention of the campaign.
>
> (Stache, 2014, p. 2)

Whether through the use of hashtags or other social media tactics, digital activism relies on the credibility and impact of the activist organization presenting the message. Trust is an important factor for nonprofit organizations, which "often have to build up trust in situations where they do not always have a trustworthiness advantage" (Greiling, 2007, p. 5). Given the ease with which organizations can send out their messages on social media, and the potential for virality and spreadability beyond typical audiences, skepticism may be increased regarding the motives of activist groups and how potential donations will be used.

Case Overviews

As previously mentioned, the two cases of hashtag activism studied in this chapter are the Kony 2012 campaign by Invisible Children (which raised $5 million in 48 hours) and the ALS Ice Bucket Challenge from the ALS Association (which raised over $100 million in one month). The histories of these cases are described in more detail below.

Kony 2012

On March 5, 2012, Invisible Children released a 30-minute documentary on YouTube called *Kony 2012*. The activist organization was focused on stopping the Lord's Resistance Army (LRA), a militant group headed by a man named Joseph Kony that is committing human rights abuses in Eastern and Central Africa. The video depicted then Invisible Children co-founder Jason Russell talking to his five-year-old son about the atrocities committed by Kony, spliced with images and discussions of Kony's takeover of certain parts of Africa. The video highlighted Invisible Children's work to stop him. The *Kony 2012* video received over 100 million views in just six days, making it at that time the most viral video in history (Wasserman, 2012). Unfortunately, almost immediately after the release of the video, Invisible Children dealt with backlash and questions about the legitimacy of the organization, the motivations of the founders, and their financial decisions. Coupled with Russell's social media-intensified public breakdown, Invisible Children faced a number of challenges in 2012. Perhaps the biggest challenge, however, was in not fulfilling their stated mission to capture Joseph Kony by the end of 2012. At the time of writing in late 2014, Joseph Kony was still in hiding, presumably somewhere in Africa, and still leading the LRA (McCoy, 2014).

Never fully recovering from the public scrutiny of the Kony 2012 campaign, in mid-December 2014, Invisible Children announced a massive overhaul of the organization, shutting down their mass media and awareness efforts, firing their executive board and most of their staff, and focusing solely on a select few programs in Africa and "doing the hard work in the trenches on Capitol Hill" (Invisible Children, 2014, para. 1). The letter on their website, signed simply "Invisible Children," also notes that they "believe in the integrity of this movement and that your commitment will endure with or without a trending hashtag" (Invisible Children, 2014, para. 1).

ALS Ice Bucket Challenge

An even more recent example of successful hashtag activism occurred when the ALS Association started the Ice Bucket Challenge on July 29, 2014. In just 30 days, the organization had raised $100.9 million dollars from over three million donors (ALS Association, 2014b). The Ice Bucket Challenge encouraged individuals to do one of two things: either to donate to the ALS Association, or to dump a bucket of ice water over their heads. People were also encouraged to tag friends, families, or anyone in the world to then make the decision about contributing to the cause. The campaign was intended to raise both money and awareness for the association. A wide variety of individuals, including celebrities like Jennifer Aniston and Leonardo DiCaprio, and business leaders like Mark Zuckerberg and Bill Gates, took the challenge, both by being covered in ice water and in donating to the cause. The challenge has been called the "first truly global video meme" (ReelSEO, 2014, para. 1) and "ALS ice bucket challenge" was the sixth most searched term on Google in 2014 (Google, 2014, para. 1).

As a result of the challenge, the ALS Association also saw a 30–100% increase in their other fundraising efforts, including registration for Walks to Defeat ALS (ALS Association, 2014c, para. 1). In order to determine what to do with the donated money, the association is currently holding meetings with key stakeholder groups to create a plan, although they note a strong push to increase and improve ALS-related research (ALS Association, 2014d, para. 1). In October 2014, they announced an initial $21.7 million expenditure from the Ice Bucket Challenge to support six programs, including grants to treatment centers, work with genome centers to understand the genetic aspects of ALS, and expansion of therapeutic approaches for treating ALS (ALS Association, 2014d, para. 1).

Research Questions

Based on the literature review and attributes of the two comparative cases, the following research questions are posed:

RQ1: How did the Kony 2012 and ALS Ice Bucket Challenge cases encourage online engagement via social media?

RQ2: How did the Kony 2012 and ALS Ice Bucket Challenge cases mobilize online giving via social media?

RQ3: What were the public and organizational perceptions of hashtag activism of Kony 2012 versus the ALS Ice Bucket Challenge?

Method

To answer these research questions, the research team conducted a qualitative content analysis of publicly available social media data related to the Kony 2012 and ALS Ice Bucket Challenge cases, including 194 blog posts (159 from Kony and 35 from ALS), 800 tweets (400 each for Kony and ALS), 107 Facebook comments from Kony, and 495 Facebook posts from ALS.

Sampling

A unique and systematic sampling process was used to collect the final data set for this study. The social media and organizational response of Kony 2012 were analyzed in a previous study (Briones, Madden, & Janoske, 2013) and will inform the results of the current study. The sampling frame used for the Kony 2012 case includes the initial release of the *Kony 2012* video (March 5, 2012) to the time of the release of Invisible Children's second video about Kony 2012 (April 9, 2012). The ALS Ice Bucket Challenge data were collected within the period from July 29, 2014 (the day before the challenge first started) to October 1, 2014 (the day ALS announced they were starting to distribute the money from the Ice Bucket Challenge contributions).

Blog Posts

For the Kony 2012 case, a total of 159 blog posts from March 5 to April 4, 2012 were analyzed, including 19 official blog posts from Invisible Children. Blog posts were obtained through a systematic search of the top 10 blogs on world politics and the top 10 blogs on U.S. politics according to the website Technorati. Examples of blogs analyzed included "Jezebel," "Mashable," "Boing Boing," and "The Atlantic." For the ALS Ice Bucket Challenge, a total of 35 blog posts were analyzed. When the Ice Bucket research was conducted, Technorati was no longer functioning as a ranking system for blogs, so a Google Blog Search was used. Terms searched were *Ice Bucket Challenge blog*, *ALS Ice Bucket Challenge blog*, and *ALS blog*.

Twitter

The social media search engine Topsy.com, the largest searchable index of Twitter data to date, was used to collect tweets on the two cases. The top 100 tweets based on Topsy's relevance filter were sampled from a number of search terms based on the specific dates previously mentioned, including *Kony*, *KONY*, *Kony 2012*, *KONY2012*, *#IceBucketChallenge*, *Ice Bucket Challenge*, *#ALSIceBucketChallenge*, and *ALS Ice Bucket Challenge*. Hashtags were not used for the Kony search terms due to the ubiquitous nature of the terms themselves, and the definitely less ubiquitous nature of hashtags in 2012.

Facebook

For the Kony 2012 case, 107 Facebook comments in direct response to the first *Kony 2012* video posted on March 5, 2012 were gathered. For the ALS Ice Bucket Challenge case, a total of 495 Facebook posts from the top two Facebook community pages, Ice Bucket Challenge (88,373 likes) and ICE Bucket Challenge (39,353 likes), as well as Facebook search results for *#icebucketchallenge* and *#ALSicebucketchallenge* were collected and analyzed.

Data Analysis

The proposed research questions were used as a guiding framework to assist with the data analysis process, which was employed via constant comparative method to establish themes that emerged from the data (Corbin & Strauss, 2008). Using data display techniques suggested by Miles and Huberman (1994), Excel spreadsheets and Microsoft Word documents were used collaboratively by the research team to record observations made from the data. The team then used a series of steps to code the data. First, each researcher independently coded the social media data collected. Then, the team met periodically to discuss how findings were initially coded, and subsequently continued to revise the codes through additional data analysis, making note of any new themes that emerged. Thus, through continuous discussion via in-person meetings and electronic correspondence, the research team used an inductive data analysis process that led to the final set of themes that will be reported below (Glaser & Strauss, 1967). However, the research team also employed a deductive approach in their data analysis by contextualizing the data within the literature examined, i.e., non-profits and social media, social media and fundraising, and hashtag activism (Miles & Huberman, 1994), leading to the final set of themes that seek to answer the proposed research questions, which will be described in detail below.

Results

RQ1: Online Engagement via Social Media

When it came to encouraging people to become involved with either the Kony 2012 campaign or the Ice Bucket Challenge, Invisible Children and ALS chose a wide variety of strategies. Themes to come from this were: *motivation and inspiration, education and awareness, satire or humor, emotional appeals, personal connections*, and *simplicity and urgency*.

Motivation and Inspiration

In their attempts to get people involved with their respective causes, both Invisible Children and the ALS Association focused on what was motivating and inspiring about their causes. *ThinkProgress* wrote about Invisible Children that their "strength lies in their ability to connect with folks outside the beltway about something that doesn't have a direct or immediate impact on American lives" (Margon, 2012, para. 6). This change in connection was seen as a positive, as the *Huffington Post* noted that "I mean, for once we are not talking about the new iPad" (Baghai, 2012, para. 3).

Twitter users also found ways to be both short and inspiring. User @stephen fry (2014) noted that it was "one for all, and all for #ALS." @huffingtonpost (2014a) drew attention by spotlighting that "this man has ALS, and his #icebucketchallenge will make you laugh, then cry." Similar things happened with Kony on Twitter, where user @zaynmalik (2012) said "just seen the youtube video and I am officially inspired!" Overall, people watched videos of others taking action for a cause they believed in, and were moved to respond like one Facebook commenter who noted: "Inspiring! Let us make a difference!" (Hand, 2012).

Education and Awareness

However, it was not simply enough to inspire those watching. The ALS Association and Invisible Children also needed to make sure people understood the issues being discussed, and to get others to help them in doing so. People encouraged others to learn about the issues, like an animal hospital whose workers took the Ice Bucket Challenge and posted to Facebook that they "took the time to read about ALS and challenge everyone reading this to do the same" (Wachusett Animal Hospital, 2014). Others encouraged their followers to read the story of the movement's founder or would provide a basic understanding of the disease themselves as part of their Ice Bucket posts. *Mediaite* blogged that "it's worth acknowledging that raising awareness is an important part of advocacy. And awareness is what IC does best" (Vamburkar, 2012, para. 4). Similarly, @alyssa_milano tweeted "#ALS facts and why the #icebucketchallenge is actually important in raising awareness."

Satire or Humor

As awareness was raised and more people understood their structure, it then became possible for individuals to poke fun at the campaigns. Sometimes this meant that animated or fictional characters, like the penguins from Dream-Works' *Penguins of Madagascar* movie, Kermit the Frog, and Homer Simpson, took the Ice Bucket Challenge. One Twitter user attempted to get the Stark family, from *Game of Thrones*, to take the Ice Bucket Challenge, but then said, "just kidding, they're dead" (@navalny, 2014). Other times, this poking fun meant that, as @mashable (2014) noted, "the #IceBucketChallenge is already a Halloween costume."

Sometimes, humor was used as another way to draw attention to the campaigns themselves or to other issues. @huffingtonpost (2014b) tweeted that "Paris Hilton uses the #icebucketchallenge to further awareness of her existence." Twitter user @miilkkk (2014) hinted at slacktivism issues with his tweet, in an overtly satirical, oft-repeated (and impossible to source to the original) parody of Jay Z lyrics: "if you tweetin' about Kony, I feel bad for you son; he snatched 99 children and your post saved none."

Emotional Appeals

Often an emotional impulse increased online engagement, as one Kony Facebook fan said, "I was touch[ed] by the film and I will share it to others [sic]" (Dorceus, 2012). *Forbes* blogged about this, saying that "this combination of engaging the head and the heart is integral in generating urgency around a change initiative" (Akhtar, 2014, para. 6). *Wired* made a similar note, succinctly stating that *Kony 2012* "hits like an emotional sledgehammer" (Ackerman, 2012, para. 5). Sometimes, getting stars like Kourtney Kardashian to be emotional resulted in increased Twitter popularity, like when she tweeted "in tears and I want to help make a difference. Make KONY famous" (@kourtneykardash, 2012). Non-celebrities are also affected, like @jasminevillegas (2014), tweeting "for those of you who think the #ALSicebucketchallenge is useless, this man has als. watch."

Personal Connections

Those emotional connections were also important in the building of personal connections and personal stories. The *Kevin MD* blog talked about how "the challenge connected people through the challenging process as well as the sharing of videos, in fact, many did the challenge with another person pouring or in a group with friends and colleagues" (Gualtieri, 2014, para. 10). *Ignite Social Media* noticed this as well, and talked about how "people don't have relationships with organizations, they have relationships with other people. Rather than trying to forge and replace those relationships, the ALS Association capitalized on existing friendships to go viral" (Stein, 2014, para. 4). People were willing to share those personal stories on social media as well, like a gentleman who posted on Facebook "in honor of my dad who suffered from ALS & went to heaven last year ... our whole staff got in on the #ALSIceBucketChallenge today" (Furtick, 2014). This may have also been a strategic decision on the part of the organizations, mused *Foreign Policy* blog, where

> moving from the LRA as a whole to Kony as an individual, I think made it more specific and individual. There's always a tension between getting people's attention without over-simplifying, but I think that it made sense for them to focus on Kony as an individual.
>
> (Fish, 2012, para. 8)

Simplicity and Urgency

Often, the most urgent messages were the simplest, like @IMkristenbell's (2014) tweet that "ive [sic] never tweeted anything as important as this DO NOT SLEEP THROUGH A REVOLUTION." This urgency was inherent in *Ignite Social Media*'s coverage of the Ice Bucket Challenge, "perhaps the most ingenious and overlooked component ... people are busy and if they don't have a reason to do something right now, they will often end up not doing it at all" (Stein, 2014, para. 8). This notion, combined with the fact that "the challenge had very simple rules, low cost and low risk" (Gualtieri, 2014, para. 10), made it very easy to complete.

In contrast, the *Kony 2012* video was seen as "undoubtedly simplified," and not always in a positive sense (Finck, 2012, para. 1). It was "designed for the Internet, where attention spans are notoriously short" (Finck, 2012, para. 1), and the simplicity means that "meddlesome details like where Kony actually is aren't important enough for Invisible Children to make sure its audience understands ... what is important is simple: Stop Kony" (Wilkerson, 2012).

RQ2: Online Giving via Social Media

Both Invisible Children and the ALS Association also worked to mobilize online giving efforts toward their causes by way of their social media engagement. Four themes emerged from the social media data that provides insight on specifically how that was employed: *emphasizing ease of giving, using key influencers, capitalizing on social networks,* and *maintaining accountability and transparency.*

Emphasizing Ease of Giving

In the same vein as the simplicity theme previously described, spreading the word about their causes via social media allowed both Invisible Children and the ALS

Association to emphasize how incredibly easy it was to donate to their organizations through those same channels. As angelino (2012) stated in a *DailyKos* blog post, "The KONY 2012 campaign gives people some simple options for taking action—contacting a cultural or political influencer, sharing the video, and yes, donating." The ease of donating to the Kony 2012 cause was shared on Twitter as well, mainly through requesting retweets as @StopKonySource (2012) did: "For the next hour, every RETWEET will be worth $0.08. RETWEET AND HELP DONATE TO THE INVISIBLE CHILDREN #StopKony."

The ALS Ice Bucket Challenge followed suit by using the viral nature of the challenge to encourage large numbers of people to donate. As stated by Torossian (2014, para. 4) in a *Business2Community* blog post:

> Many just dumped the ice, but millions also donated. ALS was already a household name, but now it's front of mind for many millions more households. And, in today's marketplace of ideas, NOW thinking is what matters most. More people are giving on impulse, and mobile or online giving has made it easier than ever to give in to that urge.

Using Key Influencers

Both Kony 2012 and the Ice Bucket Challenge harnessed the power of key influencers such as celebrities, music artists, and political figures to motivate individuals to take action. For Invisible Children, this was an intentional tactic, as "the filmmaker who made 'Kony 2012,' Jason Russell, met with 20 'culture-makers,' including Tim Tebow, Angelina Jolie, Ryan Seacrest and Taylor Swift, to lobby for their support of the film" (Flock, 2012, para. 4). According to a *Washington Post* blog article, "celebrities and Twit-lebrities got involved, with everyone from Justin Bieber to Oprah Winfrey encouraging their multitudinous followers to support Invisible Children" (Hesse, 2012, para. 1). Oprah continued her support via Twitter, as she tweeted, "Everybody who's tweeting me about #LRA I've helped. Gave Major dollars had Invisible Children on my show 2x. showing #STOPKONY Mar 18 #OWN" (@Oprah, 2012).

The Ice Bucket Challenge also had an unprecedented number of influencers accepting the challenge and inviting others to do the same. Oprah once again demonstrated her support, as a Facebook post from community page Ice Bucket Challenge (2014a) shared Oprah's video and claimed, "If Oprah is in ... it's worldwide!" Less than a month into the challenge, the same Facebook community asked, "Is it us or are all the celebs getting into this?" (Ice Bucket Challenge, 2014b). One item to note is that few of these key influencers fail to mention the actual act of donating. Even fewer mention how much will be donated, unlike musician @nikkisixx (2014), whose tweet offers these details: "WE ACCEPT Motley Crue's ALS Ice Bucket Challenge! Friday Night in Indy. $10,000 and a whole lotta ice water!"

Capitalizing on Social Networks

A number of organizations, as well as individuals, used their social networks to raise more money for the ALS Association. This was mostly done through an announcement of donating additional money for every like/share, as was done by Sky Zone Richmond (2014):

> we are committing to donate $0.50 for every Like and $1.00 for every Share on this post by midnight tomorrow night to continue raising awareness. Our donations will go straight to the www.CindyColemanALSfund.org to support our own hometown hero who helped raise so many of us in Richmond. We love you Cindy!

Other organizations got involved by way of motivating employees to get involved via social media, as was done by Berkshire Bank Foundation (2014) on Facebook:

> Berkshire Bank joined the cause to help knock out ALS. We've raised the stakes by challenging our employees to take part in the Ice Bucket Challenge. Berkshire Bank will be donating $50 for each of the first 50 employees that take part in the challenge. Check it out! #ALS #icebucketchallenge #AMEB.

Finally, some social media users used these campaigns to raise awareness and funds for other organizations outside of the ALS Association and Invisible Children. As *Jezebel* blogger Baker (2012) wrote: "If Kony 2012 inspired you to donate money to the region, check out these charities, all of which received four star ratings on Charity Navigator: AMREF USA, Doctors Without Borders, and Water.org" (para. 12).

Maintaining Accountability and Transparency

Finally, both Invisible Children and the ALS Association faced pressure to maintain transparency in terms of how donations were being used by the organizations. Invisible Children especially came under fire for their financial practices, as was mentioned in this *Foreign Policy* blog post: "There is intense criticism out there over Invisible Children's finances, including that it spends too much money on administration and filmmaking, while still touting its on the ground NGO-style projects" (Wilkerson, 2012, para. 19). Invisible Children (2012) immediately took action to respond to this criticism, and made many statements via their blog, such as this one: "We are committed, and always have been, to be 100% financially transparent and to communicate in plain language the mission of the organization so that everyone can make an informed decision about whether they want to support us."

The ALS Association was being monitored as well, as the organization continued to raise more and more funds. As @huffingtonpost (2014c) tweeted,

"Where is all that money going?" As was the case with Invisible Children, the ALS Association also took immediate action. As the *Wall Street Journal* blog reported:

> the group very quickly created an ice-bucket information site on its main website, with lots of details and press releases. It also deployed its social-media manager to help defuse false information about its operations on Facebook and other sites, since there were various rumors circulating around about the group's operations.
>
> (Silverman & Gellman, 2014)

RQ3: Public and Organizational Perceptions of Hashtag Activism

While Kony 2012 and the ALS Ice Bucket Challenge were both initially perceived as a success by both the public and the organizations, these perceptions ultimately diverged for Kony 2012 while remaining in greater harmony for the ALS Ice Bucket Challenge. Four themes emerged from the data that help to explain this divergence, and in the case of the ALS Association, convergence, of perceptions: *slacktivism*, *effective*, *public scrutiny*, and *handling success*.

Slacktivism

Both Kony 2012 and the Ice Bucket Challenge were perceived by many as examples of slacktivism, "in which people are more interested in bringing attention to themselves than to a cause while ostensibly participating" (Gualtieri, 2014, para. 6). In addition to the implied narcissism of participating in social-mediated causes, slacktivism is also viewed as a quickly changing fad. Ben Keesey, CEO of Invisible Children, responded to this aspect of perceived slacktivism by saying:

> I think I understand, a lot people are wondering, "Is this some kind of slick, fly by night, slacktivist thing?" when actually it's not at all. It's actually a really—it's connected to a really deep, very thoughtful, very intentional and strategic campaign.
>
> (Invisible Children, 2012)

Similarly, one Facebook user explained the Ice Bucket Challenge as "a game of Would-You-Rather involving the entire internet where, appallingly, most Americans would rather dump ice water on their head than donate to charity. It's trendy to pretend that we care, but eventually, those trends fade away" (Carlos, 2014).

Others, however, tried to reappropriate the term slacktivist to not embody the negative connotations associated with it:

> Say what you will about Invisible Children, but the KONY 2012 campaign's flaw is not in creating slacktivists. The term, in its essence, negates the potential of social media to create change. KONY 2012 explicitly states

that its goal is to make Joseph Kony famous, because 99% of the world doesn't (or didn't) know who he is—and it has been darn successful at doing just that.

(Fox, 2012, para. 5)

Effective

While recognizing that the premise of the Ice Bucket Challenge may be inane, and there is little chance an army of young Americans will catch Joseph Kony on social media, there was a recognition that these types of appeals are effective in terms of increasing awareness and funding. Dewey (2014, para. 3) wrote that

Let's be clear: The cycle is tiresome. It's stupid. It's primarily intended, by all accounts, to let the challenger (a) exhibit his altruism publicly and (b) show off how good he or she looks soaking wet. But it also … works. It works well, in fact.

Although critiquing the Kony 2012 campaign, Mao (2012) conceded that "We can complain about the gaps, but we also have to celebrate the fact that at least part of our story has been told. And told powerfully."

The Les Turner ALS Foundation (2014) also confirmed the effectiveness of the campaign by saying in a Facebook post:

Just in case there is any doubt, the viral #ALSicebucketchallenge campaign is making a huge impact to all ALS organizations around the world! It is not only raising awareness for ALS, but in raising much needed funds to find cure! We are happy to report that donations to the Les Turner ALS Foundation are up 3,696% this week! Thank you to all those who are participating, contributing and nominating others. Keep up the good work and please continue to share your videos on our wall!

Public Scrutiny

Although both campaigns were perceived as effective in accomplishing certain goals, this level of notoriety opened both organizations up to more scrutiny than ever before. As Gray (2014, para. 7) wrote in *Salon*,

The ALS Ice Bucket Challenge—a convergence of philanthropy, viral meme culture and hashtag activism that would have seemed unbelievable even a decade ago—by its very nature has opened itself up to a good deal more scrutiny than most other charity efforts ever face.

While the legitimacy of the organization and cause were not questioned, the means through which the challenge occurred received public scrutiny. For example, due to severe drought conditions in California at the time, as well as the inability of many people around the world to access clean water, people perceived dumping ice water on heads as wasteful. The ALS Association (2014a) responded directly to these criticisms in a Facebook post, writing that "Due to drought conditions in parts of the country, we are asking people to re-purpose their water when taking the challenge. Learn more under the 'Spread Awareness' section of this page on how you can help us to #StrikeOutALS." Additional criticism of the Ice Bucket Challenge came from perceived "funding cannibalism" (MacAskill, 2014), which refers to the idea that instead of raising money for their own cause, charities take money that could be donated to other causes instead, thus cannibalizing other causes. MacAskill (2014) goes on to explain that "Because people on average are limited in how much they're willing to donate to good causes, if someone donates $100 to the ALS Association, he or she will likely donate less to other charities." Therefore, success for the ALS Association is scrutinized as taking away support from other causes.

For Kony 2012, much of the public scrutiny surrounded the legitimacy of the organization and its mission. As Feldman (2012, para. 1) wrote,

> After almost a week of hearing about KONY 2012, the campaign is slowly but surely coming under a lot of warranted skepticism. Any activist video that starts by spending two minutes on the power of liking YouTube videos and Facebook statuses should raise a few eyebrows.

Handling Success

Success happened organically for the ALS Association, which had not planned for the success of the campaign. Similarly, for Invisible Children, the new noto-riety was something that the organization was not equipped to handle. For Invis-ible Children, the concentrated focus on Jason Russell backfired when he suffered from reactive psychosis and was found naked in the streets, which his wife attributed to the "sudden transition from relative anonymity to worldwide attention—both raves and ridicules, in a matter of days" (Tapscott, 2012, para. 1). Billing itself as an experiment in the power of social media, Baghai (2012) wrote that "we have to thank Invisible Children and Jason Russell for sacrificing their reputations for this great learning experience" (para. 2).

Rather than basking in the glow of a successful campaign, Invisible Children immediately had to go on the defensive and address the unanticipated negative backlash it had received. Within days, the organization launched a comprehen-sive website that addressed the primary criticisms being leveled against the organization, such as lack of financial transparency, inaccurate portrayal of the conflict, and the ultimate goal of the campaign. Margon (2012) wrote that "instead of continuing to debate the strengths and weakness of the Kony2012 video, or attack Invisible Children for their lack of financial transparency, let's figure out how to turn this momentum into a constructive opportunity that can result in smart policies that will have a positive, real-time impact in the affected areas of central Africa."

Because public scrutiny of the ALS Association came more in the form of questioning the purpose of dumping water over heads, as well as funding cannibalism, the organization handled its new financial windfall by highlighting the new opportunities for research that the organization could pursue. The ALS Association sent out a letter thanking those who donated and participated in the ALS Ice Bucket Challenge: "Because of the unprecedented level of awareness and support the Ice Bucket Challenge is generating, we now have the opportunity to consider more exciting and innovated projects than ever before" (Inquisitr, 2014, para. 3).

Discussion

Through analyzing publicly available social media in an attempt to answer the three research questions, this study has provided valuable insight into how both the Kony 2012 campaign from Invisible Children and the Ice Bucket Challenge from the ALS Association encourage online engagement, mobilize online giving, and build or influence public and organizational perspectives of hashtag activism (see Table 13.1 for a list of specific recommendations).

Hashtag activism, as discussed here, offers the opportunity for anyone and everyone to become involved with a cause (Stache, 2014), especially when that cause makes them think, connects with them on an emotional level, or is endorsed by a friend or celebrity. This increased awareness is important, but whether or not it clearly leads to actual offline action is still up for significant debate. These social media campaigns started with the two organizations and their respective messages, but quickly became less about actual dialogue with the organization and more focused on connections with personal networks. Some of these were call to action messages, with the organizations soliciting donations or shares or likes (Saxton & Waters, 2014), while other social media messages can be perceived as pure self-promotion unrelated to the cause (Liu, 2012).

One of the most noticeable distinctions between the two campaigns was the gap between public and organizational perceptions of Kony 2012, whereas the public and organizational perceptions of the ALS Ice Bucket Challenge proved to be in greater harmony. While both campaigns were perceived as effective in mobilizing online support, for Kony 2012, public perception of the campaign quickly turned to public scrutiny. This ended up putting Invisible Children in a position where the organization had to defend its choices and the very mission of the organization itself. While not altering its position, Invisible Children had to concede with the public perception that the organization was a fraud and was misleading naive, but well-intentioned, youth. The ALS Association, however, decided to go with a different approach. Although neither campaign completely avoided public scrutiny, the more successful each campaign became, the more skeptical social media users became of the organizations and what the donations were being used for. The ALS Association took the criticisms as an opportunity to articulate the chance for the organization to explore new options with regard to what to do with the new windfall. This was to be accomplished through active stakeholder engagement with what to do with the funds. In contrast, while articulating a perception of accountability and transparency, Invisible

Table 13.1 Hashtag Activism Recommendations

Recommendation	Explanation	Support from study
Take criticisms as opportunity	Instead of becoming defensive, organizations should exercise active stakeholder engagement, transparency, and accountability when faced with backlash from critics.	*Wall Street Journal* blog: "The [ALS] group very quickly created an ice-bucket information site on its main website, with lots of details and press releases. It also deployed its social-media manager to help defuse false information about its operations on Facebook and other sites, since there were various rumors circulating around about the group's operations."
Online engagement + offline engagement	Organizations should include strategies that incorporate an offline component that takes online action to a more tangible level.	*Daily Kos* blog: "The KONY 2012 campaign gives people some simple options for taking action – contacting a cultural or political influencer, sharing the video, and yes, donating."
Personal relevancy is key	Messages need to speak to target audiences in a way that makes them feel personally connected to the organization's issue.	*Ignite Social Media* blog: "Rather than trying to forge and replace those relationships, the ALS Association capitalized on existing friendships to go viral."
Have a clear call to action	Messages should indicate clear, realistic, simple step-by-step ways for supporters to become involved, whether it is online or offline.	*Washington Post* blog: "Let's be clear: The cycle is tiresome. It's stupid. It's primarily intended, by all accounts, to let the challenger (a) exhibit his altruism publicly and (b) show off how good he or she looks soaking wet. But it also … works. It works well, in fact."
Incorporate key influencers	Organizations should partner with key influencers (i.e., politicians, celebrities) that would resonate well with the target audience and motivate them to take further action.	*Washington Post* blog: "Celebrities and Twit-lebrities got involved, with everyone from Justin Bieber to Oprah Winfrey encouraging their multitudinous followers to support Invisible Children."

Children did not budge from its financial focus of awareness and advocacy, meaning that a majority of its funds went to administration and funding the videos that were the forefront of their awareness campaigns.

This idea of the financial focus was something that broadened with the ALS Association. Seemingly everyone, from celebrities to politicians to the girl next door, was donating, which pressured individuals to conform to the bandwagon and donate as well (Saxton & Wang, 2013). It should be noted that, as Saxton and Wang (2013) found in their study, these individuals also tended to give in smaller amounts, although as noted in the introduction, the ALS Association managed to raise well beyond their initial fundraising goals, demonstrating that truly, every little bit helped. As donations for the ALS Association continued to increase, the organization also increased their stakeholder engagement, asking for recommendations on how to best use the funds. Thus, the ALS Association demonstrated that strong online engagement, coupled with offline engagement, can lead to a positive response from publics, building organizational trust and reputation.

Additionally, those who are personally affected by a cause are more likely to donate (Reddick & Ponomariov, 2013). Here, simplicity and tangibility seemed to work well for the ALS Association and against Invisible Children. Approximately 30,000 Americans have ALS at any given time (ALS Association, 2010), meaning many Americans may know someone with ALS. Given the geographical distance, fewer Americans know someone connected to Kony, or who was a victim of his actions. People could understand, generally, how donations would be used to fund research for ALS (even if the researchers were not promising to find a cure). Invisible Children, however, simplified a complex geopolitical issue for a young, social media-based audience, and the main call to action (purchasing a $30 action kit) had a very tenuous, and heavily scrutinized, connection to the stated goal of capturing Joseph Kony. Someone watching an Ice Bucket Challenge video had at least two immediate, clear actions they could take (make their own video and/or donate money to ALS) to help those suffering; someone watching the *Kony 2012* video had few, if any, tangible actions to take (call a political official, purchase an action kit) that had a clear connection to those suffering. The tangibility, and instant gratification, of completing the Ice Bucket Challenge allowed for a catharsis that made the participant feel as if they did something. With this said, this analysis shows that fewer people are going to continue to participate if they do not believe they can make a clear, tangible impact, almost immediately. Nonprofit organizations considering this approach should make sure that their call-to-action messages are clear and simple, yet realistic and personally relevant.

A final interesting facet that emerged from these cases is the interaction with celebrities for both campaigns. Not everyone knew about the issues or the organizations involved with these two campaigns, but trusted leaders (i.e., politicians, musicians, celebrities) were talking about the issues, and participating in some way, which helped increase participation (Greiling, 2007). Fictional characters like Homer Simpson, celebrities like Kim Kardashian and Lady Gaga, sports figures like Cristiano Ronaldo and ESPN anchors, even, in the case of Edvard Munch, individuals long dead were resurrected in the name of activism. Similarly, some celebrities needed to defend themselves for acting or not acting in ways that the general public deemed permissible. For example, a number of people tweeted at Oprah after the release of *Kony 2012*, asking her to talk about the issue on her show. Her response was that she had already had the founders of Invisible Children on her show, multiple times, and had donated significant funds to the cause. However, because that event did not include the most viral video of its time, people were not aware that it had occurred, and were upset with her for not furthering the cause. The idea, then, that celebrities are necessary to draw attention to a cause may mean that all celebrities need to be prepared to contribute, or they will have an irate fan base to answer to when they are forced to defend their choice to not take action. Future research can further explore the true impact that these key influencers have when it comes to digital activist campaigns such as Kony 2012 and the Ice Bucket Challenge.

Conclusion

Comparing and contrasting social media-based activism through Invisible Children's *Kony 2012* video and the ALS Association's Ice Bucket Challenge allowed for a broad understanding of what is involved in developing a successful digital activism campaign. Relationship building, engagement, an ability to draw direct, clear lines between the issue and how an individual can help—all of these factors can allow an organization to build their cause up beyond the pitfalls of hashtag activism and public scrutiny. Rather than throwing ice cold(!) water on the idea of hashtag activism, nonprofit organizations should take the opportunity to learn from both the successes and failures of campaigns such as Kony 2012 and the Ice Bucket Challenge in order to more strategically harness moments of collective engagement around diverse, yet equally as important, causes. Table 13.1 summarizes core recommendations for hashtag activism.

References

Ackerman, S. (2012, March 7). Viral video hopes to spur arrest of war criminal [Web log post]. Retrieved from www.wired.com/dangerroom/2012/03/kony-2012.

Akhtar, V. L. (2014, September 18). Engaging a volunteer army: Lessons learned from the Ice Bucket Challenge [Web log post]. Retrieved from www.forbes.com/sites/johnkotter/2014/09/18/engaging-a-volunteer-army-lessons-learned-from-the-ice-bucket-challenge.

ALS Association. (2010). *Facts you should know.* Retrieved from www.alsa.org/about-als/facts-you-should-know.html.

ALS Association. (2014a, August 21). Thanks to all who are taking the #IceBucket Challenge! [Facebook post]. Retrieved from www.facebook.com/hashtag/icebucket challenge.

ALS Association. (2014b, August 29). The ALS Association expresses sincere gratitude to over three million donors. Retrieved from www.alsa.org/news/media/press-releases/ice-bucket-challenge-082914.html.

ALS Association. (2014c, September 22). Ice Bucket Challenge enthusiasm translates to support of ALS activities. Retrieved from www.alsa.org/news/archive/ice-bucket-challenge-092214.html.

ALS Association. (2014d, October 2). The ALS Association announces initial commitment of $21.7 million from Ice Bucket Challenge donations to expedite search for treatments and a cure for ALS. Retrieved from www.alsa.org/news/media/press-releases/ibc-initial-commitment.html.

alyssa_milano. (2014, August 17). #ALS facts and why the #icebucketchallenge is actually important in raising awareness [Twitter post]. Retrieved from https://twitter.com/Alyssa_Milano/status/501216032892014592.

angelino. (2012, March 8). Kony 2012: Viral hope or viral cynicism? [Web log post] Retrieved from www.dailykos.com/story/2012/03/08/1072287/-Viral-Hope-or-Viral-Cynicism-A-draft-masquerading-as-a-diary.

Baghai, I. (2012, March 12). Kony 2012 shows the power of youth and social media [Web log post]. Retrieved from www.huffingtonpost.com/iman-baghai/kony-2012-why-i-support-t_b_1339474.html?view=print&comm_ref=false.

Baker, K. (2012, March 7). Think twice before donating to Kony 2012, the charitable meme du jour [Web log post]. Retrieved from http://jezebel.com/5891269/think-twice-before-donating-to-kony-2012-the-meme-du-jour?popular=true.

Barnes, N. G. (2010). Social media usage now ubiquitous among US top charities, ahead of all other sectors. Retrieved from www.umassd.edu/media/umassdartmouth/cmr/studiesandresearch/charity2010.pdf.

Berkshire Bank Foundation. (2014, August 14). Berkshire Bank joined the cause to help knock out ALS [Facebook post]. Retrieved from www.facebook.com/hashtag/icebucketchallenge.

Blackbaud. (2013). Charitable giving report: How nonprofit fundraising performed in 2013. Retrieved from www.blackbaud.com/nonprofit-resources/charitablegiving#.VJRw2DAA.

Bortree, D., & Dou, X. (2012). The role of proximity in advocacy communication: A study of Twitter posts of Sierra Club groups. In S. Duhé (Ed.), New media and public relations (2nd ed., pp. 178–188). New York: Peter Lang Publishing, Inc.

Bortree, D. S., & Seltzer, T. (2009). Dialogic strategies and outcomes: An analysis of environmental advocacy groups' Facebook profiles. Public Relations Review, 35(3), 317–319.

Briones, R. L., Kuch, B., Liu, B. F., & Jin, Y. (2011). Keeping up with the digital age: How the American Red Cross uses social media to build relationships. Public Relations Review, 37(1), 37–43.

Briones, R., Madden, S., & Janoske, M. (2013). Kony 2012: Invisible Children and the challenges of social media campaigning and digital activism. Journal of Current Issues in Media & Telecommunications, 5(3), 205–234.

Carlos, E. (2014, August 18). The idea is to dump a bucket of ice water over your head… [Facebook post]. Retrieved from www.facebook.com/hashtag/ALSicebucketchallenge.

Center on Nonprofits and Philanthropy, Urban Institute, National Center for Charitable Statistics. (2014). Quick facts about nonprofits. Washington, DC. Retrieved from http://nccs.urban.org/statistics/quickfacts.cfm.

Corbin, J. M., & Strauss, A. C. (2008). Basics of qualitative research (3rd ed.). Thousand Oaks, CA: Sage.

Dewey, C. (2014, August 12). Stop hating on the ice bucket challenge: It's raised millions of dollars for charity [Web log post]. Retrieved from www.washingtonpost.com/news/the-intersect/wp/2014/08/12/stop-hating-on-the-ice-bucket-challenge-its-raised-millions-of-dollars-for-charity.

Diamond, D. (2014, August 29). The ALS Ice Bucket Challenge has raised $100 million— and counting. Forbes Magazine. Retrieved from www.forbes.com/sites/dandiamond/2014/08/29/the-als-ice-bucket-challenge-has-raised-100m-but-its-finally-cooling-off.

Digital Marketing Philippines. (n.d.). The history and power of hashtags in social media marketing (infographic). Retrieved from http://digitalmarketingphilippines.com/the-history-and-power-of-hashtags-in-social-media-marketing-infographic.

Dorceus, L. W. (2012, March 5). I was touch[ed] by the film [Facebook comment]. Retrieved from www.facebook.com/invisiblechildren.

Earl, J., & Kimport, K. (2011). Digitally enabled social change: Activism in the Internet age. Cambridge, MA: MIT Press.

Feldman, J. (2012, March 11). ABC's Jake Tapper on KONY 2012: Some of the information is not factually accurate [Web log post]. Retrieved from www.mediaite.com/tv/jake-tapper-on-kony-2012-some-of-the-information-is-not-factually-accurate.

Finck, A. (2012, March 16). *Foreign Policy*: Invisible Children responds [Web log post]. Retrieved from http://blog.invisiblechildren.com/2012/03/16/foreign-policy-invisible-children-responds.

Fish, I. S. (2012, March 12). Kristof on Kony [Web log post]. Retrieved from http://blog.foreignpolicy.com/posts/2012/03/12/kristof_on_kony.

Flannery, H., Harris, R., & Rhine, C. (2009). *2008 DonorCentrics Internet giving benchmarking analysis*. Charleston, SC: Target Analytics.

Flock, E. (2012, March 8). Kony 2012 campaign gets support of Obama, others [Web log post]. Retrieved from www.washingtonpost.com/blogs/blogpost/post/kony-2012-campaign-gets-support-of-obama-others/2012/03/08/gIQArnHkzR_blog.html.

Fox, Z. (2012, March 9). KONY 2012 may be flawed, but slacktivism isn't the enemy [Web log post]. Retrieved from http://mashable.com/2012/03/09/kony-slacktivism.

Furtick. (2014, August 21). In honor of my dad who suffered from ALS [Facebook post]. Retrieved from www.facebook.com/hashtag/alsicebucketchallenge.

Glaser, B. G., & Strauss, A. L. (1967). *The discovery of grounded theory*. Chicago: Aldine.

Google. (2014). Top charts: Searches. Retrieved from www.google.com/trends/topcharts#vm=cat&geo=US&date=2014&cid.

Gray, S. (2014, August 16). The truth about the "Ice Bucket Challenge" [Web log post]. Retrieved from www.salon.com/2014/08/16/the_truth_about_the_ice_bucket_challenge.

Greiling, D. (2007). Trust and performance management in non-profit organizations. *The Innovation Journal Public Sector Innovation Journal, 12*(3), 1–23.

Gualtieri, L. (2014, September 30). The ALS Ice Bucket Challenge: Analysis of why it went viral [Web log post]. Retrieved from www.kevinmd.com/blog/2014/09/als-ice-bucket-challenge-analysis-went-viral.html.

Hand, S. (2012, March 5). Inspiring! Let us make a difference! [Facebook comment]. Retrieved from www.facebook.com/invisiblechildren.

Hesse, M. (2012, March 9). Invisible Children's "Kony 2012" video goes viral: But what does this mean? [Web log post]. Retrieved from www.washingtonpost.com/lifestyle/style/invisible-childrens-kony-2012-video-goes-viral-but-what-does-this-mean/2012/03/09/gIQADMhF2R_story.html.

Huffingtonpost. (2014a, August 22). This man has ALS, and his #icebucketchallenge will make you laugh, then cry [Twitter post]. Retrieved from https://twitter.com/huffingtonpost/status/503066659754897409.

Huffingtonpost. (2014b, August 29). Paris Hilton uses the #icebucketchallenge to further awareness of her existence [Twitter post]. Retrieved from https://twitter.com/huffingtonpost/status/505457386090680321.

Huffingtonpost. (2014c, August 30) The ice bucket challenge has raised $88.5 million (and counting) for ALS. Where is all that money going? huff.to/1tHdyi8 [Twitter post]. Retrieved from https://twitter.com/HuffingtonPost/status/505946863984721920.

Ice Bucket Challenge. (2014a, August 21). If Oprah is in … it's worldwide! [Facebook post]. Retrieved from www.facebook.com/icebucketchallenges.

Ice Bucket Challenge. (2014b, August 20). Adam Sandler – is it us are all the celebs getting into this? [Facebook post]. Retrieved from www.facebook.com/icebucketchallenges.

IMkristenbell. (2012, March 6). ive never tweeted anything as important as this DO NOT SLEEP THROUGH A REVOLUTION [Twitter post]. Retrieved from https://twitter.com/imkristenbell/status/177121311527669760.

Ingenhoff, D., & Koelling, A. M. (2009). The potential of Web sites as a relationship building tool for charitable fundraising NPOs. *Public Relations Review*, 35(1), 66–73.

Inquisitr. (2014, October 1). ALS Ice Bucket Challenge is dying out but still bringing in donations: You won't believe the total [Web log post]. Retrieved from www.inquisitr.com/1513210/als-ice-bucket-challenge-is-dying-out-but-still-bringing-in-donations-you-wont-believe-the-total/#YF5ZGcIvBADjK9Qv.99.

Invisible Children. (2012). Questions & answers [Web log post]. Retrieved from http://s3.amazonaws.com/www.invisiblechildren.com/critiques.html.

Invisible Children. (2014, December 15). A message for all the past and present supporters of Invisible Children. Retrieved from http://invisiblechildren.com.

jasminevillegas. (2014, August 22) for those of you who think the #ALSicebucket challenge is useless, this man has als. Watch. [Twitter post]. Retrieved from http://twitter.com/JASMINEVILLEGAS/status/503762828214673408.

Joyce, M. (Ed.). (2010). *Digital activism decoded: The new mechanics of change*. New York, NY: International Debate Education Association.

Kang, S., & Norton, H. E. (2004). Nonprofit organizations' use of the World Wide Web: Are they sufficiently fulfilling organizational goals? *Public Relations Review*, 30(3), 279–284.

Kelly, K. S. (1998). *Effective fund-raising management*. Mahwah, NJ: Lawrence Erlbaum Associates.

Kourtneykardash. (2012, March 7). Just watched the KONY 2012 video. In tears and I want to help make a difference. Make KONY famous. [Twitter post]. Retrieved from https://twitter.com/kourtneykardash/status/177652280907141120.

Les Turner ALS Foundation. (2014, August 14). Just in case there is any doubt [Facebook post]. Retrieved from www.facebook.com/hashtag/alsicebucketchallenge.

Liu, B. F. (2012). Toward a better understanding of nonprofit communication management. *Journal of Communication Management*, 16(4), 388–404.

Lovejoy, K., & Saxton, G. D. (2012). Information, community, and action: How nonprofit organizations use social media. *Journal of Computer-Mediated Communication*, 17(3), 337–353.

MacAskill, W. (2014, August 14). The cold, hard truth about the ice bucket challenge [Web log post]. Retrieved from http://qz.com/249649/the-cold-hard-truth-about-the-ice-bucket-challenge.

Mao, N. (2012, March 21). Guest post: I've met Joseph Kony and Kony 2012 isn't that bad [Web log post]. Retrieved from http://blog.foreignpolicy.com/posts/2012/03/21/guest_post_ive_met_joseph_kony_and_kony_2012_isnt_that_bad.

Margon, S. (2012, March 8). A partial defense of Invisible Children's Kony 2012 campaign [Web log post]. Retrieved from http://thinkprogress.org/security/2012/03/08/440851/defense-kony-invisible-children.

mashable. (2014, August 22). Sigh. The #IceBucketChallenge is already a Halloween costume. [Twitter post]. Retrieved from https://twitter.com/mashable/status/502865949956247553.

McCoy, T. (2014, March 24). Hunt for Joseph Kony takes U.S. into one of world's most dangerous countries. *Washington Post*. Retrieved from www.washingtonpost.com/news/morning-mix/wp/2014/03/24/hunt-for-joseph-kony-takes-u-s-into-one-of-worlds-most-dangerous-countries.

miilkkk. (2012, March 10). if you tweetin' about Kony, I feel bad for you son; he snatched 99 children and your post saved none. [Twitter post]. Retrieved from https://twitter.com/miilkkk/status/178680273062465536.

Miles, M. B., & Huberman, A. M. (1994). *Qualitative data analysis* (2nd ed.). Thousand Oaks, CA: Sage.

navalny. (2014, August 22). I challenge Ned Stark, Catelyn Stark, and Robb Stark to do the ALS Ice Bucket Challenge. Just kidding, they're all dead. [Twitter post]. Retrieved from http://twitter.com/navalny/status/502876570500202496.

nikkisixx. (2014, August 20). WE ACCEPT Motley Crue's ALS Ice Bucket Challenge! Friday Night in Indy. $10,000 and a whole lotta ice water! [Twitter post]. Retrieved from http://twitter.com/NikkiSixx/status/502308814470000640.

Oprah. (2012, March 7). Everybody who's tweeting me about #LRA I've helped. Gave Major dollars had Invisible Children on my show 2x. showing #STOPKONY Mar 18 #OWN. [Twitter post]. Retrieved from https://twitter.com/oprah/status/177616438964658176.

Reddick, C. G., & Ponomariov, B. (2013). The effect of individuals' organization affiliation on their Internet donations. *Nonprofit & Voluntary Sector Quarterly*, *42*(6), 1197–1223.

ReelSEO. (2014, December 17). 2014 ALS Ice Bucket Challenge results: Biggest video meme EVER! Retrieved from www.reelseo.com/ice-bucket-challenge-video-meme.

Saxton, G. D., & Wang, L. (2013). The social network effect: The determinants of giving through social media. *Nonprofit & Voluntary Sector Quarterly*, *43*(5), 850–868.

Saxton, G. D., & Waters, R. D. (2014). What do stakeholders "like" on Facebook? Examining public reactions to nonprofit organizations' informational, promotional, and community-building messages. *Journal of Public Relations Research*, *26*(3), 280–299.

Seo, H., Kim, J. Y., & Yang, S.-U. (2009). Global activism and new media: A study of transnational NGOs' online public relations. *Public Relations Review*, *35*(2), 123–126.

Seltzer, T., & Mitrook, M. A. (2007). The dialogic potential of weblogs in relationship building. *Public Relations Review*, *33*(2), 227–229.

Sharma, R. (2014, March 13). How nonprofits use social media to engage with their communities. *Nonprofit Quarterly*. Retrieved from https://nonprofitquarterly.org/management/23837-how-nonprofits-use-social-media-to-engage-with-their-communities.html.

Silverman, R. E., & Gellman, L. (2014, September 16). ALS Association tries to avoid pitfalls after summer's social-media sensation [Web log post]. Retrieved from http://online.wsj.com/articles/ice-bucket-challenge-when-success-creates-problems-of-its-own-1410810931.

Sky Zone Richmond. (2014, August 12). We have accepted the #IceBucketChallenge to raise awareness [Facebook post]. Retrieved from www.facebook.com/hashtag/icebucketchallenge.

Stache, L. C. (2014). Advocacy and political potential at the convergence of hashtag activism and commerce. *Feminist Media Studies*. doi: 10.1080/14680777.2015.987429.

Stein, K. (2014, September 9). 5 reasons the ALS Ice Bucket Challenge went viral [Web log post]. Retrieved from www.ignitesocialmedia.com/uncategorized/5-reasons-als-ice-bucket-challenge-went-viral.

stephenfry. (2014, August 22). Benedict Cumberbatch goes for the #IceBucketChallenge [Twitter post]. Retrieved from https://twitter.com/stephenfry/status/502866284254863360.

StopKonySource. (2012, March 10). For the next hour, every RETWEET will be worth $0.08. RETWEET AND HELP DONATE TO THE INVISIBLE CHILDREN #StopKony [Twitter post]. Retrieved from https://twitter.com/StopKonySource/status/178607322665467905.

Tapscott, D. (2012, March 26). Kony 2012: Rethinking global problem solving [Web log post]. Retrieved from www.huffingtonpost.com/don-tapscott/kony-2012-rethinking-glob_b_1379371.html?view=print&comm_ref=false.

Torossian, R. (2014, September 23). ALS Ice Bucket Challenge, what happens next? [Web log post]. Retrieved from www.business2community.com/nonprofit-marketing/als-ice-bucket-challenge-happens-next-01015372#D7qlJIk3poTTJgTC.99.

Vamburkar, M. (2012, March 8). How Kony 2012 is raising awareness, but also raising questions. *Mediaite*. [Web log post]. Retrieved from www.mediaite.com/online/how-kony-2012-is-raising-awareness-but-also-raising-questions.

van Leeuwen, M. H. D., & Wiepking, P. (2013). National campaigns for charitable causes: A literature review. *Nonprofit & Voluntary Sector Quarterly, 42*(2), 219–240.

Vericat, J. (2010). Accidental activists: Using Facebook to drive change. *Journal of International Affairs, 64*(1), 177–180.

Wachusett Animal Hospital. (2014, August 18). Team WAHPR took the #ALSicebucket challenge [Facebook post]. Retrieved from www.facebook.com/hashtag/alsicebucket challenge.

Wagner, L. (2002). The "new" donor: creation of evolution? *International Journal of Nonprofit and Voluntary Sector Marketing, 7*(4), 343–352.

Warner, M. (2002). Publics and counterpublics. *Public Culture, 14*(1), 49–90.

Wasserman, T. (March 2012). *"Kony 2012" tops 100 million views, becomes the most viral video in history [STUDY]*. Retrieved from http://mashable.com/2012/03/12/kony-most-viral.

Waters, R. D., Burnett, E., Lamm, A., & Lucas, J. (2009). Engaging stakeholders through social networking: How nonprofit organizations are using Facebook. *Public Relations Review, 35*(2), 102–106.

Wilkerson, M. (2012, March 7). Guest post: Joseph Kony is not in Uganda (and other complicated things) [Web log post]. Retrieved from http://blog.foreignpolicy.com/posts/2012/03/07/guest_post_joseph_kony_is_not_in_uganda_and_other_complicated_things.

zaynmalik. (2012, March 8). make Kony famous! The Kony 2012 campaign … just seen the youtube video and i am officially inspired! [Twitter post]. Retrieved from https://twitter.com/zaynmalik/status/177831566695858176.

14 Social Media at a Regional Food Bank

The Case of Second Harvest

Greg Higgerson, Melissa Kear, Maria Shanley, and Dave Krepcho

In today's nonprofit world, personal relevance is king. People are bombarded with information throughout their waking hours at a rate never before seen. In order to cut through that, a nonprofit must have strategies that engage multiple communications channels, including social media.

Content must be carefully chosen through the perspective of what will be most important for social media followers to hear and see about the organization's mission, NOT what is most important to the organization. A balance of mission moments and donor recognition activities must be struck. Donor recognition is not unimportant, however. When followers see "who" the organization is thanking, and how genuinely they do so, it helps them to frame their own idea of whether the mission is a good fit for them personally.

It will never be enough for an organization to "dabble" in social media. It's not the kind of thing that can be visited in a staffer's "spare time," or just handed off to an intern, and hope to be effective. There needs to be a well-considered strategy that is implemented daily by dedicated staff and/or very high-level volunteers. For most organizations this will require investment in highly skilled staff.

Be Strategic with Messaging

Message discipline matters in social media. An organization should pick a small handful of overarching "essential themes" that they want people to associate with their work, and try to tie every post and image together with one of them. Again, these should be chosen based on potential interests of donors, volunteers. When the overall message gets spread too thin, people stop paying attention, and start paying attention to someone else's organization that appears to be more focused.

What is "hot'" today in social media absolutely will not be so in a year from now (or less). This is another reason to have savvy staff on top of social media management: to monitor trends and audience preferences. Who would have guessed two years ago that Facebook is now considered by younger people to be "for old people"? Adaptability will remain key in the future.

Organizations should actively reach out to members of the blog community that have a natural connection with their mission, and "court" them. Bloggers are one of the very best ways to bring new followers on board that the organization wouldn't have reached any other way.

The "free gravy train" days of social media are drawing to a close. A Facebook post used to reach anyone and everyone who follows your page, but that fell by the wayside a few years ago. Now, a post will only reach a wide audience of your followers if you pay for a boost of that message. Other social media have begun to follow Facebook's lead on that, and soon it will be necessary for any organization to "pay to play." This will require even more planning and investment.

We use Facebook, Twitter, Instagram, Google+, YouTube, LinkedIn, and Pinterest, but the ones we keep up with mostly are Facebook and Twitter. Social media is a tool to build a relationship with your followers; as a nonprofit, you create a foundation of trust and goodwill with the hope that your followers will be advocates for your mission—be that a donation, volunteer time, or a voice.

Know Your Audience and Be Flexible, Nimble, Creative

People from all walks of life like to be a part of something that makes a real difference. There is no shortage of people to reach out to, you simply have to know where to look. Social media is not a static being, it is dynamic and always changing, growing, and innovating. Are you looking for millennials? Baby boomers? Donors? Volunteers? These are all questions we have to ask ourselves as a nonprofit organization, and the social media platform is no different. One day, a social media channel is booming with millennials, and then their baby boomer parents join, and the millennials are shifting to another platform. It is important to keep up with where your audience is, and know the culture of that social media platform to best communicate with them.

Most nonprofits have a very slim budget that keeps them from hiring a whole team of marketers who can crawl multiple social media sites and interact on them all day. With a small team, it is important not to stretch yourself too thin across too many social media channels. It is critical to do your research, find where your donors/volunteers/advocates are, and focus on them on only a couple strong social media channels. Doing this allows you to produce quality, well-focused content.

In the end, the foundation of successful social media is experimentation. What works on one social media channel may not work on another; what works with one audience, may not work with another. Sometimes it takes trying new things and speaking the same message five different ways to find the correct voice needed to communicate effectively with your audience. Expect and accept change, become fluid, but have a solid message. Not every post will be successful, not every picture will affect your audience as you hoped, but each of those are a lesson that can be molded into something new, and hopefully successful in meeting your goal of more donors, volunteers, and advocates for your cause.

Second Harvest jumped on the social media bandwagon six years ago. We started off with Facebook, Twitter, Flickr, and YouTube. Since then we have added LinkedIn, Google+, and Instagram. Part of our success is due to a plan in place for postings on the channels that really benefit us, Twitter and Facebook.

On Facebook, women aged 35–44 make up the majority of our fans. We post at least two times a day during the week and schedule during some weekends. We do a great job of balancing out our content during the week by having themes for specific days. What do we post on Facebook? We thank volunteer groups, thank our financial donors with photos of their check presentations, show photos of foods in our warehouse, promote events that support the food bank, and share stories in the news that talk about hunger.

We also make sure to go through and leave comments when anyone posts on our page or asks a question on one of our posts. We also make sure to tag companies or groups in the community when we thank them. We've noticed an increase in Facebook activity from businesses or groups that volunteer or donate funds to the food bank. We can never thank people enough for helping us, and for us Facebook is another channel where we can go to thank them.

The only time we request funds on Facebook is the last month of the year. Our posts match the graphics of our banners and paid media that we have out in the community. We have plans to buy ads this year on Facebook to try to generate some funds. With just our posts, Facebook brought in around $5,000 last year.

#GivingTuesday

We participated in #GivingTuesday the past two years and raised over $20,000 both years. In 2013, we came up with a plan for #GivingTuesday and raised $28,000 online in one day. The campaign was successful because it involved many communication channels. We had amazing TV coverage from the local news station WESH2 News, a very visual social media campaign (Thunderclap, Twitter, Facebook, blogs, our social media ambassadors), WESH's social media power, and an email campaign. All these forces working together and the 24-hour deadline drove people to donate. Our social media ambassadors included some of the top local food and mom bloggers in Central Florida. We used Facebook, Twitter, LinkedIn, and Instagram to push out our very visual #GivingTuesday graphics leading up to the day, December 2. In 2014, we raised $34,000 online with the same strategy plus a $20,000 match, totaling $54,000 in one day.

Keep on Blogging

We post a blog at least once a week. We drive traffic to our blog through our social media channels and online newsletter. Employees from our programs, operations, community kitchen, and development teams are asked to contribute on a monthly basis. Because of this we are able to generate great content that normally one person could not do on their own. The Second Harvest blog is a central online location where donors and supporters can get the latest news from Second Harvest. Whenever possible, tell a story; people are interested in other people. Statistics and numbers are only one part of your message; however, people will pay more attention and be more likely to remember a short story of a person helped. The following are extracts from blog posts.

Stories of Hope and Courage: Hector's Story

When I met Hector, he was feeling hopeless. A vet of the Air Force, Hector worked in the civil service industry for over 25 years, until a back injury started to deteriorate his health. Known for his kind heart and eagerness to help others, Hector provided support to both his parents and siblings, until recently, when his condition worsened, and affected his ability to continue working.

Deciding to go through the lengthy process of applying for disability, Hector reached a point where he realized that he needed to apply for food assistance. Restricted with work, money was tight, which meant Hector would have to make hard decisions about necessities like paying for utilities and medication, and affording food. Luckily, with assistance from a Benefits Connection Specialist from Second Harvest Food Bank of Central Florida, Hector was approved for SNAP benefits, which meant tough situations at home could be alleviated, and he wouldn't have to worry so much about having enough to eat.

Hector was truly grateful for the help he had received. Once he was approved, he admitted that he had been close to losing hope. Hector had begun to feel like a burden on his parents, but now he was in a place where things were looking up.

I cannot articulate the depth of the joyful euphoria I witnessed in his eyes as he told me he'd been approved and how glad he'd been to be able to do his grocery shopping. I am just so grateful to be a part of this "circle of hope." Hope returned to a broken heart is truly priceless.

Opportunity for More Food

As you know, we still have our work cut out for us to close the food insecurity gap. Public policy plays a big role in helping to feed people. We're working with Feeding America and members across the United States to lend our collective voices to an important opportunity being considered in Congress. We've shared the request below with our food donors and partner agencies asking them to participate as well. Right now, we have an important opportunity to advance our mission by showing Congress that their constituents care about ending child hunger.

The Child Nutrition Reauthorization is moving forward in Congress, and we need your help to support it. We encourage you to send a letter to congress.

Encourage Congress to make new investments in child nutrition programs, particularly during out of school times—after school, holidays, weekends, and summer—when our network steps up to fill the gaps. Simply click here to send your letter.

We have a rare opportunity before us to advance our mission and we hope you'll send a message to congress to help support it.

Thank you!

Community Comes Together for Class 7 Graduation

This past week, we graduated Class 7 of our Culinary Training Program. The Darden Community Kitchen continues to provide life-changing opportunities to people who may need that second chance in life. In fact, we have placed 100% of our graduates into jobs at graduation.

This past graduation was lucky enough to have three great guest speakers. Congressman Daniel Webster joined us as a special guest and shared that reading every day can make a huge difference in both knowledge and outlook on life, while, Pam Nabors, CEO of Career Source delivered the commencement message and emphasized the almost unlimited opportunities that await our graduates in Central Florida's booming food service industry.

One of the most touching speeches came from former graduate Maria Andersen, who shared her personal testimony, and described how her experience in our Culinary Training Program led to great job opportunities, and inspired her to continue her education even further by enrolling into college for an advanced level of training.

With your help, Second Harvest is continuing to *"feed the line"* of people who need the daily nourishment for the strength to get through the day, and *"shorten the line"* through this culinary program. Once graduates are out on their own and earning a living they can provide the *"food for tomorrow"* for their families through their newfound career.

If you have not had the chance to see our culinary program in action, please do not hesitate to contact us. It would be our pleasure to provide a tour and an up-front-and-close look at our operation.

Whether you volunteer at the food bank, donate food, or are a financial donor, we thank you! If Second Harvest Food Bank is new to you, we have a variety of ways for you to join the fight against hunger in Central Florida, so please contact us.

Thank you, here's to Class #8!

Examples of Second Harvest Social Media

Twitter: http://twitter.com/2harvestCFL
Facebook: www.facebook.com/pages/Second-Harvest-Food-Bank-of-Central-Florida/28394917492
YouTube: www.youtube.com/user/foodbankcentralfl
Flickr: www.flickr.com/photos/shfbcf

15 Branded "Man"

Myth of "Free" Services and the Captured Individual

Arthur J. Sementelli

Some popular thought posits that a creative destruction event has occurred, allowing for the possibility of a nonhierarchical market economy understood as a digital turn (Westera, 2013). This claim includes a perceived shift toward the provision of "free" information, services, and products arguing that it has limited or eliminated classic modes of exchange for economic and non-economic goods. This chapter instead challenges such assertions, particularly through the lens of social media. Rather than the creation of some nonhierarchical, non-economic free exchange system, this moment of "creative destruction" has instead opened a space for an unconscious or quasi-conscious system akin to barter to emerge. In this space, privacy and behavior become the items that define economic value for monopolies and other powerful institutions. It becomes both commercially viable and economically desirable to create virtual panopticons allowing for the constant surveillance of behavior (both consumer and non-consumer) to manage and marketize this new "currency" more effectively. The rules and rituals of these market panopticons (Bentham, 1995; Foucault, 1977), where people are under continual surveillance, in turn create a number of issues for the public sector that has not yet adapted to this moment of creative destruction.

It has already been established that the public sector currently cannot harness privacy, wisdom (Edwards, 2002; Zavattaro & Sementelli, 2014), and consumer behavior as tools for exchange. Public institutions are ill-equipped to deal with such shifts and often are left behind when faced with new modes of exchange. This creates opportunities for further privatization, outsourcing, and contracting as means to address these new modes. These practices, over time, become more consistent with current norms of consumer behavior. People consequently become more "comfortable" with these new practices while earlier modes of exchange simultaneously become more onerous (e.g., the application of taxes and fees) when used to provide public goods and services. Potentially, these events can create a crisis of legitimacy and further opportunities for a hollow state. As governments are charged with representing their constituents, the question emerges regarding whether or not government or the public sector more generally can and should foster or impede these processes.

Yet without regulatory guidance and inaction, we are left with the emergence of a "branded man." Branded, in this case, has a double meaning. First, it refers to the marks made with a hot iron, typically used to show ownership of livestock. The second meaning refers to the incorporation of a commercial trademark, label, etc., into one's day-to-day life. Of course, the selection of one brand over another can lead to a third notion of branding as a mark of stigmatization. Like its predecessors "economic man," one-dimensional man (Marcuse, 1964), and "administrative man" (Denhardt & Perkins, 1976), branded man represents a shift in the way individuals interact with organizations and institutions. It can expand discussions of rent-seeking behavior (Dreyer & Kouzmin, 2009; Krueger, 1974) along with the emergence of digital panopticons, where exchange value rapidly becomes tied to access to information as a mode of currency, and where "privacy" merely increases the value of this new currency through its increased scarcity or simply through novelty itself.

The goal of this chapter is to articulate this emergence of "branded man," grounding it within the existing literature, and contextualizing it within current socioeconomic institutions. Furthermore, it extends the Kouzmin, Sankaran, & Hase (2004) argument for "harvesting" people in the economic sense albeit within the context of the digital turn, which opens multiple opportunities for new structures to enhance biopower throughout societies (Foucault, 1980) while simultaneously creating opportunities to further hollow out the administrative state (Milward & Provan, 2000).

One Dimension

The notion of a person heavily influenced by economies is not new. Marcuse (1964) offered the concept of a one-dimensional man. Central to his discussion, industrial society creates false "needs." These needs then tie people into existing institutions, including those for consumption. Interestingly enough, Marcuse (1964) pointed to the role that mass media and advertising have in the process of creating these needs and raised concerns about them. One might argue that contemporary media and advertising have become dominant means of exchange in this now "digital" society.

It is possible to argue further that in contemporary society things are no longer even consumed as much as they are *consummated* (Baudrillard, 1998, p. 99). This refers to the possibility or desire that something (often intangible) can have its *reference* consumed or at least used as part of one's identity. In this sense, someone is not buying an item, but instead is buying what the item represents, in essence its "brand." For example, someone might buy a purse, while another might buy a Louis Vuitton bag. The purse would be the item, and the brand represented by the item is "Louis Vuitton." Similarly, people might buy a car, while another chooses to buy a Mercedes Benz, again consummating a behavior instilled by media. A third example might be the purchase of a phone or computer by one person, or an iPhone or iMac by another. In each case, we have substantively similar items, with varying degrees of value imbued by media in this "new" economy.

These sorts of behaviors extend beyond the sort of one-dimensional perspective offered by Marcuse (1964). Aptitude for critical thought and opposition are not just withering, they are actively being socialized out of behavior.

These processes of normalization become part of everyday life and people become rote "consumers"—thereby controlled rather effectively by the manipulation of signs and symbols to determine which, if any, are the prevailing references that need to be consumed at any given time. Such behavior extends beyond notions of consuming a good. Consuming an idea rather than a good preserves and maintains the sign or reference, allowing it to be periodically recycled, repackaged, repurposed, and reused (Baudrillard, 1998).

This sort of integrated, observed, and cultivated consumer behavior has a variety of effects. For example, it *can* more deeply integrate differentiated groups into society (Eggers, 2004; West, 2004), better stabilize institutions, and undermine the possibility for dramatic changes even in the face of social and economic crises (Westera, 2013). In addition, this emergent behavior can create conformity, for otherwise nonintegrated members including outsiders, minorities, and the intelligentsia are beholden to the same sort of consumer behaviors as many of the "in groups." We also find this contemporary consumer society, with its often rote consumption (or consummation) of brands, bridges, tolerates, and encompasses more historically marginalized groups than other modes of social control, creating an environment of market-driven "tolerance" (Wolff, Moore, & Marcuse, 1969) if not acceptance around such consumer behavior.

The relative costs of these brands and associated consumer behaviors can vary enough to allow odd combinations to arise including homeless people with iPhones, impoverished renters with Mercedes or other luxury branded cars, and even a "Bass Cat Jaguar" boat being towed by a 1987 Toyota pickup (conspicuous consumption). In contemporary society these behaviors manifest while consumers simultaneously share their acquisitions on Facebook, Instagram, and Twitter. In each case, the brand selection and consumption identifies a point of inclusion, a bridge to the mainstream, a path to tolerance that thereby makes a consumer "less marginalized" symbolically creating options for mainstream interaction and behavior if not inclusion.

Social Media Is Tracking Me

People argue social media fosters a sense of connectedness (Bertot & Jaeger, 2010), allowing for the construction of two-way dialogic relationships (Grunig & Grunig, 1991), yet at the core, it is a vehicle to display conspicuous consumption of "branded" items, services, and even thoughts. More often than not, we find that the integration of social media into other elements of one's online life connects social and consumer behavior, allowing for a new repository of information to be analyzed, developed, and shaped to refine a digital panopticon (Zavattaro & Sementelli, 2014) employed to mold social, political, and consumer behavior into something deemed acceptable if not desirable to some group of power elites.

What is interesting about the emergence of social media in particular comes from the relative acceptance of the loss of privacy. People willingly trade access to their consumer behavior for the opportunity to connect online via Facebook,

Twitter, and other apps using their phones and computers made by Apple, Google, and Microsoft. In addition, many organizations employ overt mechanisms used to "improve" marketing and service choices (Netflix, Amazon) for consumers. In many cases, these intrusions are pitched as tools to better customize a user experience to make it more enjoyable (Marshall, 2007), relevant (Richter, 2012), or valuable rather than as a breach of privacy.

Depending upon the consistency and variety of data points, their offerings can become much more consistent, often making the product or service more appealing to consumers. The more people have appealing experiences, the greater the potential to fall into the "one-dimensional" scenario articulated by Marcuse (1964). Yet, these processes for providing consistent, appealing brands and experiences undermine the possibility for any sort of "great refusal" à la Marcuse (1964) as the rigging of the game, the offering of inclusion (and acceptance) creates a tender trap, where wants (but not needs) can be temporarily satisfied with the consumption (or consummation) of the brand *du jour*.

This consumer behavior ends up presenting as normalized, conforming behavior (Foucault, 1977; Sementelli & Herzog, 2000), which Marx might identify as a new opiate of the masses. Even the most trite marketing schemes link consumption and happiness (McDonald's, I'm *loving* it), where the consumption of a branded item then leads to a happy result (i.e., love). In practice, when this is paired with expertise in food sciences, for example, we find that people can become conditioned to consume the product or brand (Gearhardt, Grilo, DiLeone, Brownell, & Potenza, 2011), thus reinforcing the socialized behaviors with biological (neural and behavioral reinforcement).

As the economy is irrevocably linked to other sectors, we find it particularly useful to examine some of the adaptations employed in public and nonprofit organizations. In public affairs and administration in particular, consumer-focused tools including social media tend to fall short of the goal of meaningful, two-way engagement (Brainard & Derrick-Mills, 2011; Brainard & McNutt, 2010; Hand & Ching, 2011). Social media continues to expand usage across sectors despite such limitations, with cities, police stations, and other public agencies adopting, for example, Facebook pages often without meaningful content or services.[1] This is not unique to the public sector, as businesses habitually market to groups outside their target markets sometimes making consumers more confused than anything else.

"Consumer" behavior across sectors has a number of consequences. As this "economy" expands we find that some understand civic as a form of capital (Oxendine et al., 2007) or as a resource (Shipps, 2003), then officials might *use or consume* citizens for civic action, employing them as a mechanism or tool to achieve some sort of directed end—as manipulated public relations tools (Zavattaro, 2010). This is marketing and consumption at its finest. Behaviors are shaped and branded as "collaboration." In this sense, "collaboration" (understood as marketing and consumption) happens as part of a larger political, social, or economic spectacle (Edelman, 1988). In the public sector in particular, the commodity of consent is often shaped, influenced, and sometimes manipulated by media (Herman & Chomsky, 2002).

Interestingly enough we find that across sectors, the emergence of digital panopticons have become more the norm than exception. With the advent of one-way consumptive communication (Brainard & Derrick-Mills, 2011; Brainard & McNutt, 2010; Hand & Ching, 2011; Mergel, 2013), we discover these digital panopticons become more frequently socialized into day-to-day lives, more accepted, and less questioned. Rather than undermining the ills of "hierarchical" and "capitalist" systems identified by Hummel (2008) and Farazmand (1999) respectively in favor of populace, we find that the systems of control become more powerful, pronounced, and pervasive.

We discover as well that these tools have become little more than "billboards" (West, 2004), and less about things like collaboration or co-creation (DeSanctis & Poole, 1994; Orlikowski, 2000). Hearkening back to the science fiction movie *They Live* (Carpenter, 1988), these media platforms direct people to "obey," to "consume," and to *sleep* (meaning not question authority, etc.). Though crude and oddly cast, the basic concepts presented in the film resonate even more today than they did in the late 1980s when it first came out. Many are left making ersatz choices about goods, services, and even political parties, *feeling* anonymous (Zavattaro & Sementelli, 2014) but all while being tracked.

A Pound of Digital Flesh?

The interesting part of this digital "moment" is the manner in which commerce is conducted. In fairly recent history, consumers moved from bartering items and services for items and services, to trading money for items and services, then to trading the pixelated representations of money for items and services (Bitcoin, for example, as well as earlier commonly seen practices where online gamers purchase "in game" items via eBay and other outlets to enhance their experiences). This "moment" of creative destruction posed by some recent scholars simply closes the loop, moving the means of exchange back to bartering, albeit this time the currency is the individual themselves, their preferences, and their privacy. The value is obtained by "harvesting" these digital representations (Kouzmin et al., 2004) by collecting otherwise unavailable consumer information through "likes," shared pages, viewing tendencies, and responsiveness to advertisements.

This jump warrants a moment for explanation. The individual being "harvested" in this case does not necessarily encompass their physical being. Instead the focus on this means of exchange is the social being, the sort of Lacanian (Fink, 1995, 1996) constructed aspects of the self that are made up of and reflect the social interactions with others. Unlike trading labor or one's physical being for a good or service, often the consumer does not feel any pain associated with the exchange. Rather, we find that it is their circle of friends, family, and acquaintances that are exposed to marketing imagery, "opportunities" to participate in these existing exchanges, and ultimately to trade access to their digital or social "selves" for whatever good or service is being presented. In some ways this is more subtle than barter, more sinister than servitude. It is a nearly physically painless experience (unless your identity is stolen, or a virus is contracted), so the spread of this new mode of exchange becomes nearly viral as people envision getting something for nothing.

In practice, we find that the information being traded has a value that is far from nothing (Ghosh & Roth, 2013; Posner, 1981). It is the fabric of interactions that make up the social and digital world for many. In essence, people are trading the long-term residues of themselves, the elements of their existence that will in many cases outlive and outlast their physical forms for some good or service. We might even discover that the comparative "value" of these trades become staggered based on the difficulty to get said digital information along with the number of previous interactions undertaken, with a sort of value-based auction (Ghosh & Roth, 2013) becoming the norm rather than the exception.

Such a decision would make one's privacy or, more specifically, their private information the most valuable commodity in the digital realm. It is at this point where the public sector has the potential to impede or foster these branding processes. Structurally, we have any number of laws that reflect issues of freedom of information ranging from a variety of open record laws to sunshine legislation. In practice, the laws have led to issues of identity theft using public records (Meyers, 2007) along with some questions about how much can and should be made public.

In many cases, the practical issue of accessibility tends to override discussions of privacy. Citizens want to access web platforms at their convenience. They want to access their accounts online, to pay their utilities, and in some cases to "like" their city on Facebook, Instagram, and other social media sites. Compounding these conflicting issues of privacy and access, the rapid diffusion of technology, through Wi-Fi, smartphones and the like, allow for constant access along with constant monitoring. A few years ago, the program "Foursquare" allowed people to check into locations as a game. However, if you reflect on this game for a moment or two, you discover that it is both tracking and announcing your location, though arguably as a tool to promote the restaurant or venue where you happen to check in.

Some might be okay with announcing their location randomly to the public, but there are also people among us who might be troubled by such a revelation. Such overt sharing of patterns of behavior can set individuals up for a variety of exploitative situations. Covert gathering of behavior led to cruise line employees robbing the homes of passengers while they were on vacation (Phillips, 2010). One might only imagine the possibilities when such patterns are announced more publicly and "sold" as part of promoting a better experience. In such cases, the pseudo environment (Burke, 2008; Bybee, 1999) of the web can directly impact the "real" world.

Illusions, Privacy, and People

It is well documented that digital domains offer the illusion of privacy (Rashi, 1998). This illusion of privacy emerges from a *feeling* of safety and security (Tu, 2005). This false feeling of comfort can lead to a belief they are anonymous or secure, affording people the opportunity to engage in socially unacceptable behaviors including cyber bullying, flaming (Alonzo & Aiken, 2004; Lee, 2005), and cyber stalking (Silvia, 2014). Moreover, the media itself fosters the perception, often erroneously, that people are having a "private" conversation via chat, social media, etc. In practical terms, we find that a number of "private" communications are more frequently becoming public. In the case of actor Nicolas Cage, who recently lost his smartphone, he became concerned about the contents being made public (ANI, 2014). Simultaneously, some employers perform Facebook searches as part of their screening process (Jacobson, 2014).

Without undertaking much effort, most savvy users can easily identify and access browsing histories, reveal passwords, and uncover digital tracks. Computer professionals regularly access data including histories and cookies even when they have been "deleted." The concept of "privacy" in the workplace has for the most part been revealed as myth. In broader contexts, this ersatz privacy and security that engenders participation, sharing, and information revelation is both simulacra (Baudrillard, 2000) and tool for the "new" economy. Much like with the movement to gated communities (Sementelli, 2012) this shift, or digital turn, creates yet another expression of panopticism (Bentham, 1995) allowing for socioeconomic factors, influencers, and elites to inspire docility and passivity, all while steering behaviors (Foucault, 1977).

We are left with a situation where people are encouraged to avoid self-monitoring. Knowing that you're being observed falls away. People forget they are being watched, and forgetting panoptic presence can erode rational thought and action (Zavattaro & Sementelli, 2014). The combination of being watched, documented, and in some cases highly targeted by marketing reveals multiple opportunities to erode economically "rational" consumer behavior in favor of the sort of impulse buying desired and fostered by marketing professionals.

Gathering the Masses for Harvest

Beyond simply targeting potential customers and consumers, we find a concerted effort has been made to collect consumers as well. Tsuyaba (2009) along with Bettman, Luce, & Payne (1998) have illustrated that consumer decision making has been of critical importance. Since they tend not to have well-defined preferences and limited capacity to process, such preferences can be shaped if not constructed to drive consumption. Such strategies allow for the possibility of value capture (Bowman & Ambrosini, 2010) along with sister ideas of value creation and destruction. In this context, value is created or captured through opportunities created by this digital turn. As the notion of value is linked to information and relationships, there tends to be an immediate and ongoing information asymmetry that favors the seller in many cases.

The information asymmetry combined with an understanding of the patterns of behavior collected via social media and digital outlets provides the tools necessary not simply to market to consumers, but to effectively identify and brand them (as "loyal," "marginal," and other) and reinforce their behavior by collecting them as part of the company's brand or experience through reward programs (advertising swag, shirts, etc.) for conducive behaviors (free downloads if you like us on Facebook).

Consumer Capture

Moreover, beyond just encouraging people to "share" their information through the application of information asymmetry and inducements, there are some concerted efforts to capture groups of individuals and their information across sectors (Besley & Prat, 2006; Ferejohn, 1986; Slooten, 2011). This problem of capture has become quite pervasive. Scientists in particular have become interested in the influence of industry-sponsored research especially for environmentally sensitive policy issues (i.e., whaling). Practices including companies substantively modifying reports, omissions and withdrawals of findings, as well as other practices (Slooten, 2011) have led to a phenomenon called "closed science," raising issues of motive, trust, and value.

The capture of government agencies, particularly regulatory ones, is not a new phenomenon. Spiller (1990) conceptualized the argument using multiple agency theory. Melody (1997), in contrast, focused on the telecom industry to focus on issues of reform and independence. Carpenter (2004) advances these arguments further in the context of pharmaceutical regulation, illustrating how arrangements can favor well-organized wealthy interests with long-term ties to an industry or field. This is not limited to the United States; the issue of industry capture, favoritism, and the like were an emphasis in a World Bank report (Smith, 2000). Further reinforcing the scope of the problem, consider also Makkai and Braithwaite's (1992) study of nursing home inspections in Australia, highlighting the revolving door problem in practical terms and allowing for the proposition that this is a global phenomenon.

One might easily make the case that industry has made a habit of capturing regulatory agencies and their personnel for years. In this "new economy" after this digital turn, industries have simply extended these practices to include customers, consumers, and clients. Rather than creating the sort of nonhierarchical open economy suggested by some, we find in practice that economic effort has become more hierarchical, more tied to institutions, and has both the capacity and focus to shape consumer behavior to create value. As always, the creation of value is a focus of markets (Bowman & Ambrosini, 2010). In particular, emphasizing value capture through relationships among stakeholders. Value, of course, is seen through a resource-based lens (Bowman & Ambrosini, 2010), and their argument implies the need for optimal institutionalized relationships to maintain, develop, and otherwise cultivate value over time. Such a perspective ties efforts to a long-term strategic focus rather than a short-term tactical focus.

Tying the creation of value to long-term strategy, then, allows us to piece together the strategies discussed above using market language, beliefs, and symbols. Long-term, institutionalized market relationships optimized for the creation of economic value enter into structured long-term relationships with suppliers, investors, clients, consumers, and regulators. In many ways, this insti-tutional behavior is quite similar to the sort of vertical integration used during the creation of the great monopolies of the 1800s. Though in this case, the control extends further to include the consumer side of the equation and not just the production side. By capturing the supply and investment side of the economy, by influencing regulation and regulatory rules and procedures, and by shaping consumer perceptions of what is both valuable and desirable, we now have the capability to have "captured consumers" identified here as "branded man."

Branded Man

I first started noticing the emergence of branded man decades ago. There was a fervent, albeit small group of computer "nerds" in college who were absolutely wedded to the purchase of Apple products. They were seen as being aesthetic-ally superior to their PC counterparts. They were engineered to ensure that no part of the computer would be user replaceable, and there was arguably refined focus on building in a culture of functional obsolescence, requiring "enthusiasts" to purchase the next great thing (which ironically was called a NeXt). Fast forward a few decades, and there are still Apple people and PC people. Now there are also "android" people, along with any number of non-technologically oriented "brands."

People are habitually conditioned to see value in the Louis Vuitton brand, in the Dooney & Bourke brand, and of course Versace. Those of us a bit older have been conditioned to see the value in brands such as Mercedes Benz, Davidoff, Rolex, and even Kitchen Aid. This habituation creates the potential for value. It in effect "stores" value in the brand for consumption later. Children might not know that Kitchen Aid historically makes a sturdy mixer or that Mercedes Benz can make a good car, but they are socialized, exposed, and shaped to "buy into" the value of such brands. We are witnessing the beginning, not the apex, of an industry harvest of this stored consumptive value. Furthermore, as this value has become associated with the brand itself, rather than a particular item, one might be drawn not to the Davidoff cologne or the cigars but instead the leather goods, eyewear, coffee, cognac, and even pens and watches!

People cannot "consume" a brand. People can only consume *products* of the brand. They can, however, adorn themselves with the logos, etc., that the prod-ucts come in or are related to "branding" that person. As such, the value of the person becomes intertwined socially with the value of the brand or its associated product, thereby fusing the person with the brand. The person's value becomes a function of the collection and arrangement of these brands. The person at an extreme becomes a socially constructed amalgam of brands (like a race-car driver). This makes it rather easy to determine the relative value of the person as a consumer. The brand identifiers help industry to identify and determine which price point each person is at, ultimately determining their value as separ-able assets to a company, group, or industry.

At this time, it is important to note that though the meaning of value is relative, the captured individual, the emergence of branded man locks the consumer side of the economic equation, closing the system, while making it sustainable in the long term, albeit without the need for rational decision making, conscious choice, or awareness—as long as there is a continued *willingness to pay* (Wathieu, 2004). This *willingness* to pay helps determine what value means to firms and other private (and sometimes public) organizations. Wathieu (2004), in particular, subscribed to the theorem of interior maximums. In such a frame, willingness to pay (a proxy for value) is maximized at moderate frequency of consumption that is *habitual* in nature. What is interesting about this is that moderating consumption and habituating it is more complex than one might realize. According to Wathieu (2004), the "willingness to pay function" is not linear, but instead identifies points of sensitization and response recovery.

In practice, this means the creation of a "branded man" is more challenging. Consumers must remain in a sort of "zone of indifference" (Barnard, 1938) where their response to the act of consumption is maintained, habituated, and reinforced without "overdoing" the practice. Overdoing it can then lead to observable negative consequences potentially resulting in a withdrawal from consumer behavior. Over time, if managed to limit people from "overdoing it," these practices can become sedimented (Wittgenstein, 1972) allowing for the "branded man" as a form of life to continue and grow in numbers.

Over time, branded man can become identified within and accepted as habitus (Bourdieu, 1977). Once this habitus manifests, one might find that the zone of indifference might broaden, and desensitize individuals further to the consumptive behavior they are undertaking. Though it is not likely to alter the shape of the willingness to pay function, it can dilute the impact of sensitization. We are left in a society where statements such as the following become part of the common political discourse:

> It's to tell the traveling public: Get on board. Do your business around the country. Fly and enjoy America's great destination spots. Get down to Disney World in Florida. Take your families and enjoy life, the way we want it to be enjoyed.
>
> (G. W. Bush, September 27, 2001)

> This great nation will never be intimidated. People are going about their daily lives, working and shopping and playing, worshiping at churches and synagogues and mosques, going to movies and to baseball games...
>
> (G. W. Bush, November 8, 2001)

One can almost envision a youthful Kevin Bacon in full military regalia working through the streets saying "remain calm, all is well" (*Animal House*, Landis, 1978), and in this case, it actually helps to stave off a riot. There is an implicit agreement that emerges. Governmental entities prevent or moderate any shocks that might move a person out of their personal zone of indifference, and people continue to consume, to move through life and identify with the brand *du jour*, all while checking in, posting to Facebook to Instagram, and tweeting.

Conclusions: Complicity

In the case of "branded man" there are no public–private differences. Some could argue there are instead public–private partnerships, though not in the way we commonly understand them. The partnership is identified as such: the public sector helps to maintain and create docile bodies while the private sector shapes and "grooms" these bodies to become habituated consumers, thereby identifying more deeply over time with some brand or symbol. As firms morph, change, and reimagine themselves, the "brands" become portable, and are transferred to their new entities (Comcast becomes Xfinity, GTE becomes Verizon, etc.). Yet the cache of consumer dispositions, reactions, and preferences tend to be a bit stickier in practice.

This stickiness ends up being the point where the Internet, social media, and digital constructs emerge. Under the guise of free (understood as non-paid) services, consumers are led to believe they can get something for nothing. Software, services, and even tangible goods can all be gained without the exchange of money. Simply record what you're viewing on television, like us on Facebook, tell a few friends about our products and services, or just let us put these small ads in the corner of your PC, phone, or media player. "Free" in these cases means no cash transaction. It does not mean "free" in the sense there is no cost. Industry in cooperation with the public sector extracts value systematically through someone's willingness to "share" personal information, perceptions, and/or their brand loyalty.

The "new commerce" of the digital era relies on modes of exchange much like any other era. It remains hierarchical, insulated, and institutionalized, often more so than "cash" markets. As the mode of exchange changes from dollars to personal information, preferences, and access to friends and family, value becomes a function of the difficulty of the challenges met to gain your personal information, preferences, and patterns of behavior. In this sense, privacy itself is traded away for its commercial value, and existing governmental structures remain complicit in the process while being unable to capitalize on the phenomena to maintain or develop public goods and services in a period of resource constraints.

What is needed in this "21st century" public administration is an awareness, refinement, focus, and prioritization of how to understand these "new" modes of exchange. Public administration must rethink how it handles Freedom of Information Act requests, open records, and other long-standing approaches to governance. To protect what is left of privacy, public administration and government more generally must rethink its practices, procedures, and policies within this new lens of value. Otherwise, "free" information from open records searches will continue to try to capture consumer behaviors, and create more "branded" men.

In closing, one need only consider current practices. Moving from one house to another, even locally, triggers a stream of fliers, phone calls, and advertisements to appear. These arguably crude modes of engagement still rely heavily on the digital world to identify factors like (1) who is a new homeowner, (2) what services will they likely need, (3) what brands do they currently use, and

(4) what new services and goods can we expose them to in the hopes of capturing their consumer behavior? On the surface, these practices seem harmless. It seems almost trivial to consider this when war, famine, and unemployment is rampant. However, if "branded man" is truly the cornerstone of a "new" economy, then people and government should be concerned.

Note

1 In this case I am referring to situations where people can "like" a community but cannot actually do anything like pay a bill or initiate a service.

References

Alonzo, M., & Aiken, M. (2004). Flaming in electronic communication. *Decision Support Systems, 36*(3), 205–213.

ANI. (2014, April). Nicolas Cage worried about personal texts going public after losing cell phone. Retrieved from http://timesofindia.indiatimes.com/entertainment/english/hollywood/news-interviews/Nicolas-Cage-worried-about-personal-texts-going-public-after-losing-cell-phone/articleshow/33746071.cms.

Barnard, C. (1938). *The functions of the executive.* Cambridge, MA: Harvard University Press.

Baudrillard, J. (1998). *The consumer society: Myths & structures.* Thousand Oaks, CA: Sage Publications.

Baudrillard, J. (2000). *Simulacra and simulation.* Ann Arbor, MI: University of Michigan Press.

Bentham, J. (1995). *The panopticon writings* (Miran Bozovic, Ed.). London: Verso.

Bertot, J. C., & Jaeger, P. T. (2010). Using ICTs to create a culture of transparency: E-government and social media as openness and anti-corruption tools for societies. *Government Information Quarterly, 27*(3), 264–271.

Besley, T., & Prat, A. (2006). Handcuffs for the grabbing hand? Media capture and government accountability *The American Economic Review, 96*(3), 720–736.

Bettman, J., Luce, F., & Payne, J. (1998). Constructive consumer choice processes. *Journal of Consumer Research, 25*(3), 187–217.

Bourdieu, P. (1977). *Outline of a theory of practice.* Cambridge: Cambridge University Press.

Bowman, C., & Ambrosini, V. (2010). How value is created, captured and destroyed *European Business Review, 22*(5), 479–495.

Brainard, L. A., & Derrick-Mills, T. (2011). Electronic commons, community policing and communication: On-line police–citizen discussion groups in Washington, D.C. *Administrative Theory & Praxis, 33*(3), 383–410.

Brainard, L. A., & McNutt, J. G. (2010). Virtual government–citizen relations: Informational, transactional or collaborative? *Administration & Society, 42*(7), 836–858.

Burke, J. (2008). Primetime spin: Media bias and belief confirming information. *Journal of Economics and Management Strategy, 17*(3), 633–655.

Bybee, C. (1999). Can democracy survive in the post-factual age? A return to the Lippmann–Dewey debate about the politics of news. *Journalism and Communication Monographs, 1*(1), 29–62.

Carpenter, D. (2004). Protection without capture: Product approval by a politically responsive, learning regulator. *American Political Science Review, 98*(4), 613–631.

Carpenter, J. (Director), & Franco, L. J. (Producer). (1988). *They live* [Motion picture]. United States: Universal Pictures.

Denhardt, R., & Perkins, J. (1976). The coming death of administrative man. *Public Administration Review, 36*(4), 379–384.

DeSanctis, G., & Poole, M. S. (1994). Capturing the complexity in advanced technology use: Adaptive Structuration Theory. *Organization Science, 5*(2), 121–147.

Dreyer, W., & Kouzmin, A. (2009). The commodification of tertiary education within a knowledge economy. *Journal of Economic and Social Policy, 13*(1), 1–17.

Edelman, M. (1988). *Constructing the political spectacle*. Chicago, IL: University of Chicago Press.

Edwards, M. (2002). Public sector governance: Future issues for Australia. *Australian Journal of Public Administration, 6*(2), 51–61.

Eggers, W. D. (2004). *Government 2.0: Using technology to improve education, cut red tape, reduce gridlock, and enhance democracy*. Lanham, MD: Rowman & Littlefield.

Farazmand, A. (1999). Globalization and public administration. *Public Administration Review, 59*(6), 509–522.

Ferejohn, J. (1986). Incumbent performance and electoral control. *Public Choice, 50*(1), 5–25.

Fink, B. (1995). *The Lacanian subject: Between language and jouissance*. Princeton, NJ: Princeton University Press.

Fink, B. (1996). *Jacques Lacan: Ecrits*. New York: W. W. Norton Company.

Foucault, M. (1977). *Discipline and punish: The birth of the prison*. New York: Pantheon.

Foucault, M. (1980). *The history of sexuality: Vol. 1. An introduction*. New York: Vintage Books.

Gearhardt, A. N., Grilo, C. M., DiLeone, R. J., Brownell, K. D., & Potenza, M. N. (2011). Can food be addictive? Public health and policy implications. *Addiction, 106*(7), 1208–1212.

Ghosh, A., & Roth, A. (2013). Selling privacy at auction. *Games and Economic Behavior*. http//dx.doi.org/10.1016/j.geb.2013.06.013.

Grunig, J. E., & Grunig, L. A. (1991). Conceptual differences in public relations and marketing: The case of health-care organizations. *Public Relations Review, 17*(3), 257–278.

Hand, L. C., & Ching, B. (2011). You have one friend request: An exploration of power and citizen engagement in local governments' use of social media. *Administrative Theory & Praxis, 33*(3), 362–382.

Herman, E., & Chomsky, N. (2002). *Manufacturing consent: The political economy of the mass media*. New York: Pantheon Books.

Hummel, R. (2008). *The bureaucratic experience: The postmodern challenge*. Armonk, NY: M. E. Sharpe.

Jacobson, R. (2014, January 13). Facebook snooping on job candidates may backfire for employers. *Scientific American* Online. Retrieved from www.scientificamerican.com/article/facebook-snooping-on-job.

Kouzmin, A., Sankaran, S., & Hase, S. (2004). Harvesting people: Toward the political economy of a knowledge society. *International Journal of Knowledge, Culture and Change Management, 4*, 341–348.

Krueger, A. (1974). The political economy of the rent-seeking society. *American Economic Review, 64*(3), 291–303.

Landis, J. (Director). (1978). *Animal house* [Motion picture]. Hollywood, CA: Universal Studios.

Lee, H. (2005). Behavioral strategies for dealing with flaming in an online forum. *The Sociological Quarterly, 46*(2), 385–403.

Makkai, T., & Braithwaite, J. (1992). In and out of the revolving door: Making sense of regulatory capture. *Journal of Public Policy, 12*, 61–78.

Marcuse, H. (1964). *One dimensional man.* Boston, MA: Beacon Press.

Marshall, G. (2007). Commanded to enjoy: The waning of traditional authority and its implications for public administration. *Administrative Theory and Praxis, 29*(1), 102–114.

Melody, W. (1997). On the meaning and importance of "independence" in telecom reform. *Telecommunications Policy, 21*(3), 195–199.

Mergel, I. (2013). Social media adoption and resulting tactics in the U.S. federal government. *Government Information Quarterly, 30*(2), 123–130.

Meyers, L. (2007, February 5) Online public records facilitate id theft. NBC News. www. nbcnews.com/id/16813496/ns/nbc_nightly_news_with_brian_williams-nbc_news_investigates/t/online-public-records-facilitate-id-theft/#.U3DXsyhLqfE.

Milward, B., & Provan, K. (2000). Governing the hollow state. *Journal of Public Administration Research and Theory, 10*(2), 359–380.

Orlikowski, W. J. (2000). Using technology and constituting structures: A practice lens for studying technology in organizations. *Organization Science, 11*(4), 404–428.

Oxendine, A., Sullivan, J., Borgida, E., Riedel, E., Jackson, M., & Dial, J. (2007). The importance of political context for understanding civic engagement: A longitudinal analysis. *Political Behavior, 29*(1), 31–67.

Phillips, R. (June 11, 2010). Woman accused of using cruise line job for burglaries. CNN. com. Retrieved May 7, 2014, from www.cnn.com/2010/TRAVEL/06/11/vacationers. burglarized.

Posner, R. (1981). The economics of privacy. *American Economic Review, 71*(2), 405–409.

Rashi, G. (1998). From the editors: The illusion of privacy and competition for attention. *Journal of Interactive Marketing, 12*(3), 2–4.

Richter, N. (2012, September 25). 3 ways to use technographics to deliver a relevant customer experience. *Marketing News & Expert Advice.* www.clickz.com/clickz/column/2207728/3-ways-to-use-technographics-to-deliver-a-relevant-customer-experience.

Sementelli, A. (2012). Panopticism, elites, and the deinstitutionalization of the civic. In A. Kakabadse & N. Kakabadse (Eds.), *Global elites: The opaque nature of transnational policy determination* (pp. 74–86). London: Palgrave.

Sementelli, A., & Herzog, R. (2000). Framing discourse in budgetary processes: Warrants for normalization and conformity. *Administrative Theory and Praxis, 22*(1), 105–116.

Shipps, D. (2003). Pulling together: Civic capacity and urban school reform. *American Educational Research Journal, 40*(4), 841–878.

Silvia, G. (2014, January 21). Facebook cyberstalking: The dark side of social media. Fox News, LA. Retrieved from: www.myfoxla.com/story/24044124/facebook-cyberstalking-the-dark-side-of-social-media#ixzz312pw6cwt.

Slooten, E. (2011). Industry capture of marine science: What price independence? *Aquatic Conservation Marine and Freshwater Ecosystems, 21*(2), 109–111.

Smith, W. (2000). Regulating utilities: Thinking about location questions. World Bank Summer Workshop on Market Institutions, July.

Spiller, P. (1990). Politicians, interest groups, and regulators: A multiple-principals agency theory of regulation, or let them be bribed. *Journal of Law & Economics, 33*(1), 65–101.

Tsuyaba, I. (2009). Realization of SCM and CRM by using RFID-captured consumer behavior information. *Journal of Networks, 4*(2), 92–99.

Tu, C. (2005). The relationships between social presence and online privacy. *The Internet and Higher Education, 5*(4), 293–318.

Wathieu, L. (2004). Consumer habituation. *Management Science, 50*(5), 587–596.

West, D. M. (2004). E-government and the transformation of service delivery and citizen attitudes. *Public Administration Review, 64*(1), 15–27.

Westera, W. (2013). *The digital turn: How the Internet transforms our existence.* Bloomington, IN: AuthorHouse.

Wittgenstein, L. (1972). *On certainty.* New York: Harper & Row.

Wolff, R., Moore, B., & Marcuse, H. (1969). *A critique of pure tolerance.* Boston, MA: Beacon Press.

Zavattaro, S. (2010). Municipalities as public relations and marketing firms. *Administrative Theory & Praxis, 32*(2), 191–211.

Zavattaro, S., & Sementelli, A. (2014). A critical examination of social media adoption in government: Introducing omnipresence. *Government Information Quarterly.*

16 The Risks of Social Media

Full Transparency, Partial Transparency, and Empowering Transparency

Thomas A. Bryer

Real or not real? This is the question Peeta Mellark in *The Hunger Games* trilogy asks in the third book to ascertain whether his memory is accurate or the drugged re-socialization perpetrated by Capitol officials has supplanted the truth. Real or not real? This is a good question to ask while reading the excerpt below from a recent public event transcript at a technology company:

> There is [an area] of public life where we want and expect transparency, and that's democracy. We're lucky to have been born and raised in a democracy, but one that is always undergoing improvements. When I was a kid, to combat back-room political deals, for example, citizens insisted upon Sunshine Laws. These laws give citizens access to meetings, to transcripts. They could attend public hearings and petition for documents. And yet still, so long after the founding of this democracy, every day, our elected leaders still find themselves embroiled in some scandal or another, usually involving them doing something they shouldn't be doing. Something secretive, illegal, against the will and best interest of the public. No wonder public trust for Congress is at 11 percent.
>
> [Introduction of member of Congress]
> I'm as concerned as you are about the need for citizens to know what their elected leaders are doing. I mean, it is your right, is it not? It's your right to know how they spend their days. Who they're meeting with. Who they're talking to. What they're doing on the taxpayer's dime. Until now, it's been an ad hoc, system of accountability. Senators and representatives, mayors and councilpersons, have occasionally released their schedules, and have allowed citizens varying degrees of access. But still we wonder, Why are they meeting with that former-senator-turned lobbyist? And how did that congressman get that $150,000 the FBI found hidden in his fridge? How did that other senator arrange and carry out trysts with a series of women while his wife was undergoing cancer treatment?
>
> We've all wanted and expected transparency from our elected leaders, but the technology wasn't there to make it fully possible. But now it is. [I]t's very easy to provide the world at large full access to your day, to see what you see, hear what you hear and what you say. I intend to show how

democracy can and should be entirely open, entirely transparent. Starting today, I will be wearing [a necklace with a camera embedded within]. My every meeting, movement, my every word, will be available to all my constituents and to the world. [Every moment will be broadcast live.]

Real or not real? It *could* be real. As such, it does not matter much that the excerpt comes from a novel (Dave Eggers' *The Circle*, 2013, pp. 205–208). Indeed, the whole of Eggers' dystopian novel centers on the core idea that for transparency to work, sharing everything is essential. Sharing *everything* is essential. If an individual has an illness and does not share news of that illness with *everyone* through social media, then the perhaps few people who share the illness are missing an opportunity to bond and for medical experts to detect previously unobserved patterns. Treatments and cures can be delayed and potentially never found due to secrets kept by some or many people. Like an illness, if a government official has a meeting with someone but does not disclose it, the meeting can lead to corruption and ethical lapses. Transparency—complete transparency—is the preventive and antidote. It is the truth serum.

It could be real. If enough people say it is real, it is real. Perception is worth more in understanding truth than objective fact. Reality or truth is not the realm of the expert; it is the realm of mass opinion. Of course, mass opinion can shift pretty rapidly based on the forces in government, corporate, or media organizations that actively manipulate the masses. Truth then is context-specific, with context defined not just by people and place but by time. Alternative truths may not be discussed as a majority of people adopt a uniform or majority opinion outlook, restricting the ability for citizens of an alternative outlook to speak their mind. This phenomenon is called a spiral of silence.

Reflecting on the tendency for human beings to take shortcuts in decision making and the lack of trust in each other's political wisdom specifically, I summarize this state of affairs as follows:

> [A]s citizens, in our collective ignorance and mutual distrust, we tend to follow each other, thus creating the equivalent of lemmings running off a cliff en masse because no one knew enough to think or act differently than the popular opinion of the moment indicated.
>
> (Bryer, 2014, p. 16)

Ultimately, the drug that clouds Peeta Mellark's memory is the drug of mass socialization on social media. Real or not real?

In this chapter, I offer an indictment of the social technologies that are increasingly being used by government to communicate to, if not with, citizens. Their use is grounded in the same idea expressed by Eggers: transparency, full and complete, is essential for a strong society. However, the indictment is more nuanced. First, I offer an indictment of the full transparency model—no secrets anywhere, espoused by the member of Congress in Eggers' novel. Second, I offer an indictment of social media use that is less than full. In other words, full transparency is useless if not contextualized with some grand narrative or bridging expertise. Partial transparency provides too much opportunity for corruption; secrets kept amidst the promise of openness. In closing, I suggest the only acceptable use of social media in government: a use that includes investment in the education and development of the citizenry. Information is power, except when it overwhelms. This is where we begin.

Indictments of Full Transparency

We begin with a thought experiment in the form of a story. Citizen Jim (CJ) is a passionate man. Like many Americans, he maintains the certainty of his convictions regardless of available facts or understanding of such facts. He is thrilled that governments, from federal to local, are finally releasing all data about themselves and about the societies they govern. Now, he thinks, he can prove the waste in government, the lack of family values, and the criminal intent of immigrants.

He begins his quest for damning data by researching the salaries of government employees. They are searchable in a public database maintained by the state government. Convinced that university professors are overpaid, he validates his fears when he sees that new "assistant" professors make an average of $65,000 for nine months! The salaries go up from there, with some showing big increases during a time when the economy was in the dumps. Proudly, CJ pulls these data and blasts on social media and letters to newspaper editors that professors are clearly overpaid.

Concerned that elected officials will pick up on this theme, university officials offer a public response. They say the salaries are justified, as the university is employing people who have studied a variety of scientific, social, and economic issues for many, many years; we are paying for the best minds, often from around the world. This response, however, only makes CJ more upset. Why do we need the "best minds" when all the information we need is available with a few clicks of the mouse?

Let us pause our story for a moment. Clearly, this is a strawman, but strawmen are common in divided societies. Indeed, they are perhaps more common in divided society than the complex human character that is real (but I refer the reader to the introduction for some thoughts on what is more real—mass opinion or some other form of "objective" fact). There are three issues here. First, full transparency reduces the value of expertise. Second, full transparency may omit context, thus increasing the percentage of poorly informed or dangerously misinformed citizens. Third, full transparency has the potential to simply overwhelm even the most well-informed individual.

When there is full transparency, the notion of subject matter expert is diminished to the extent "expertise" is democratized with low-cost access to information. Let us imagine a dialogue between CJ and a (overpaid) professor on this point:

PROFESSOR: You now have access to all of my salary information. Why do you think I am overpaid?

CJ: It is obvious. You teach, what, 2 days per week for a few hours each day.
PROFESSOR: Could you teach my class?
CJ: Yes, no problem. Give me a few hours to study the topic with some Google searches. Really, any of your "students" can do the same.
PROFESSOR: Do you know what else I do with my days and nights?
CJ: I bet you do not spend time in your office. I'll give you some credit, though. You probably meet with students and help them with their Google searches. Maybe you write some books but none that I have seen.

Again, this is a strawman presentation but one that is grounded at least to some extent in mass opinion. Whether the expert is a professor with years of experience teaching students the finer points of complex science or philosophy, or a regulator working for a government agency with years of generalist and specialist training, the expertise is challenged. It is not just challenged by citizens who have legitimate oppositional and experiential expertise, such as watermen opposed to scientist-regulators overseeing crab harvests in the Chesapeake Bay (Ernst, 2003). Instead, the challenge comes from "armchair scientists" who have neither lived experience nor expertise based on years of reading, reflection, and discussion. The battle lines are thus drawn, and traditional and experiential experts alike may reject the opinions of the masses given the lack of hard knocks or book-based pedigree (see, for example, Harter, 1997).

When expertise is diffused through full transparency, the expertise of mass opinion can spread rapidly. Rumors abound like birds chirping one in response to another, following and echoing, creating beautiful music … only the music is tweets from a keyboard and their popularity is based on the number of likes and retweets. Rumors can be particularly rampant and difficult to control on microblogging services such as Twitter (Finn, Metaxas, & Mustafaraj, 2014), difficult to break through to find credible information (Sikdar, Kang, O'Donovan, Höllerer, & Adali, 2012), and challenging to find critical credible information in the case of time-sensitive events (Castillo, Mendoza, & Poblete, 2012).

As rumors spread, they do so increasingly detached from the original context that may have propagated them. This can be damaging to governance, governments, and elected officials who are caught in the deluge of tweeters unable to break through. The mayor of Vilnius, Lithuania, Remigijus Šimašius, summed up social media this way:

> My answer was that I don't think it's possible now [to win an election because of Facebook], but it's possible to lose one on Facebook. If you are on Facebook and make a mistake, mistakes are more visible and spread more often, so you have to react quite quickly, because it may turn into a huge communication disaster—it's made even easier than on other channels.
>
> (East, 2015)

Indeed, the sheer quantity of information available through full transparency—some of high quality, some of lesser quality—can overwhelm and further disempower citizens. Not understanding context or how to interpret information, or how to extract the high quality from the low quality, may set citizens up to fail. Full transparency is not a model fit to a civic and intellectual culture that is mostly passive.

Indictments of Partial Transparency

Whereas full transparency is challenged by risks of unprepared citizens engaging with an overwhelming and acontextual amount of data, partial transparency in which only select information is shared in an open manner is challenged by the risk of bias, corruption, and incivility. These challenges exist under the guise of transparency and thus are even more troublesome, as they may go unnoticed.

Partial transparency includes sharing select information, sharing information in a manner that is inaccessible to a lay public, and otherwise restricting access to information. It also allows for anonymity on both the citizen and government side of the table, where a citizen can choose to not self-identify, and government officials can choose to "hide" behind a common handle or username.

In these cases, citizens may not contribute in a high-quality manner to the conversation if they are not able to understand the information being shared. For instance, public comments submitted through the federal web portal, regulations.gov, were found to be emotionally based, off topic, and generally not beneficial for the regulatory decision process (Bryer, 2013). Citizens who are permitted to be anonymous may have freedom to express themselves without fear of personal censor or risk, but such freedom may breed incivility (Borah, 2013; Gervais, 2014).

Overall, partial transparency is a glass-half-full means to say partial secrecy. With any secrecy, and particularly when citizens do not know what is kept secret and why, active distrust can spread. When the choice is to share some things or share all things (full transparency, with fully accessible language), the answer should always be to share all things. However, to avoid the risks of full transparency as stated previously, there needs to be a focus on citizen education.

Empowering Transparency

Transparency fails when citizens feel empowered given their access to vast amounts of information but when the objective (not mass opinion) reality is that power granted is mere illusion. Actual power with full or partial transparency rests with those individuals and organizations which have the time and tools necessary to read, interpret, and publicly report ideas based on the information available. In other words, the people, though feeling powerful, can be manipulated by those who have a specific policy or programmatic agenda—this is particularly true in the case of complex policy matters such as climate change (Lahsen, 2005).

To achieve objective empowerment in which citizens can access, understand, interpret, and make decisions based upon information requires that any social media initiatives include an embedded platform for citizen education.

For instance, information that is shared via social media or on web portals like regulations.gov should be written in fifth grade English, with graphics, and interactive links and contact information for more information and to ask (and get answers to) questions.

I recall a personal episode not related to social media but to transparency and empowerment; as an unintended landlord in the midst of the housing crisis (Bryer, 2012), I had a question about how a Maryland law should be interpreted regarding the use of an unlicensed individual to clean and make repairs to a house after a tenant departs. My first instinct was to call the state agency charged with enforcing said law; the response I received was that I should consult a lawyer to get an interpretation. This is clearly not empowering and is quite harmful for citizens who cannot afford such legal advice.

Indeed, the lack of empowerment experienced through overwhelming full transparency or biased partial transparency can be debilitating for our democratic institutions. As I have previously argued,

> it is perhaps not surprising that we have little civility in our politics, whether grassroots or professional—citizens are locked in a self-fulfilling, self-reinforcing, vicious cycle of disempowerment, demobilization, distrust, and limited opportunity for meaningful engagement. Lashing out, in an adversarial, uncivil way, may be a last recourse, a desperate attempt on the part of citizens to have attention paid, which only perpetuates the perception that citizens are not of the caliber to represent their own interests and collective well-being. It is a self-fulfilling, self-reinforcing vicious cycle.
> (Bryer, 2014, pp. 17–18)

To provide access to information and "expert" interpretation of said information requires substantial resource commitments. The ideal is more akin to the enabling bureaucracy (Adler & Borys, 1996), in which the individual is given the tools and knowledge about the tools to diagnose and solve a problem, and is thus not dependent on an outsider (except for dialogue and deliberation). As I argued in previous writing (Bryer, 2013), if we fail to invest fully, we ought to call the democratization and transparency exercise for the facade it is, and be open about the expert, elite-driven governance that dominates in our society.

References

Adler, P., & Borys, B. (1996). Two types of bureaucracy: Enabling and coercive. *Administrative Science Quarterly, 41*(1), 61–89.

Borah, P. (2013). Interactions of news frames and incivility in the political blogosphere: Examining perceptual outcomes. *Political Communications, 30*(3), 456–473.

Bryer, T. A. (2012). Identity crisis: Searching for personal responsibility, justice and community in the real estate market crash. *Public Integrity, 14*(3), 299–311.

Bryer, T. A. (2013). Public participation in regulatory decision-making: Cases from Regulations.gov. *Public Performance and Management Review, 37*(2), 263–279.

Bryer, T. A. (2014). *Higher education beyond job creation: Universities, citizenship, and community*. Lanham, MD: Lexington Books.

Castillo, C., Mendoza, M., & Poblete, B. (2012). Predicting information credibility in time-sensitive social media. *Internet Research, 23*(5), 560–588.

East, G. (2015). Vilnius mayor: Using social media is like picking up a phone or replying to emails. Retrieved May 21, 2015 from http://en.delfi.lt/lithuania/politics/vilnius-mayor-using-social-media-is-like-picking-up-a-phone-or-replying-to-emails.d?id=67997976.

Eggers, D. (2013). *The circle*. New York, NY: Alfred A. Knopf.

Ernst, H. R. (2003). *Chesapeake Bay blues: Science, politics, and the struggle to save the bay*. Lanham, MD: Rowman & Littlefield.

Finn, S., Metaxas, P. T., & Mustafaraj, E. (2014). Investigating rumor propagation with TwitterTrails. Retrieved May 21, 2015, from http://arxiv.org/abs/1411.3550.

Gervais, B. T. (2014). Incivility online: Affective and behavioral reactions to uncivil political posts in a web-based experiment. *Journal of Information Technology & Politics.* 10.1080/19331681.2014.997416.

Harter, P. J. (1997). Fear of commitment: An affliction of adolescents. *Duke Law Journal, 46*(6), 1389–1428.

Lahsen, M. (2005). Technocracy, democracy, and U.S. climate politics: The need for demarcations. *Science, Technology & Human Values, 30*(1), 137–169.

Sikdar, S., Kang, B., O'Donovan, J., Höllerer, T. H., & Adali, S. (2012). Cutting through the noise: Defining ground truth in information credibility on Twitter. *Human, 2*(3), 151–167.

Part IV

Social Media in Government

Future Directions

Conclusion and Next Steps for Research and Practice

Thomas A. Bryer

Social media tools can have a potentially transformational effect on government and nonprofit organizations. Within the pages of this book, we see many examples of this potential, whether they are in police operations, emergency management, community building and pride, or brand identity.

With every case of success, though, we see limitations and risks. For instance, Brainard found that the Washington, DC Police Department is not achieving its goals in using social media; individuals may be losing their identity within the social and branded environments; citizens may be manipulated in the development of mass opinion; individuals may further be overwhelmed in their capacity for accessing and meaningfully interpreting data shared through social and other online tools. Beyond that, we must address a host of legal and ethical issues to ensure records compliance and to prevent the appearance of bias, censor, preference, or discrimination.

Transformation was promised with e-government as well but largely failed to live up to the dream of technocratic and democratic visionaries. The same and other scholar and practitioner visionaries are perhaps a little more gun-shy with social media. As Zavattaro noted in the Introduction, there may be a perception that public administration scholarship has a bias in identifying the shortcomings in practice of using social media in government. We certainly see that in a number of published articles on the subject, where scholars have been slow to embrace the passion of early e-government advocates.

This hesitation may be for good reason. The technology is more complicated, is continually evolving, and is creating unique stakeholder–government engagements that have not previously been possible if even contemplated. It is better to temper expectations while searching for those transformational practices to emerge, informed by theory and implemented through the vigor of passionate practitioners—of the caliber we saw write for this book.

In the balance of this conclusion, I offer an agenda, built on the chapters presented but going beyond them. A separate agenda is suggested both for scholars and for practitioners; the agendas may overlap but may also follow unique paths as we strive to unlock what could be the transformational potential of social media in government.

A Scholarly Agenda

There are three paths the scholarly community ought to take to advance research on the use of social media in government and nonprofit sectors. First, there needs to be concerted effort to assemble more case studies of existing and emergent practice. These include point in time studies that look deeply at the relationships within government and between government and various stakeholders within the social media context, and they also include longitudinal studies that follow the emergence and evolution (or devolution) of social media implementation within a particular jurisdiction or agency. Brainard's study reported in this book is a good example of this kind of analysis. These case studies can identify practices across cultures and environments that are successful in cultivating strengthened relations between governments, nonprofits, and their stakeholders.

Second, there needs to be more empirical studies that assess both motivations for adopting social media tools within government and nonprofit organizations, as well as outcomes associated with the adoption. There is a group of Ph.D. students at the University of Central Florida, studying public affairs, who are addressing this need in their individual dissertation research. Danny Seigler defended his dissertation in spring 2015; his focus was on social media adoption within local government agencies. His data consisted of a nationally disseminated survey to officials in three functional agencies. These are the kinds of studies we need to promote and further develop. As the group of "social mediators" (as the UCF Ph.D. students are called) demonstrates, the topic is well fit for innovative dissertation research.

Part of this agenda must focus as well on refining ranking and rating systems for governments within the United States and around the world for their "achievements" in e-government, including social media. One of the social mediators, Pamela Medina (now on the faculty at University of Colorado Denver) and I have considered this issue and found in preliminary analysis that the popular ranking systems are exclusively input- and output-based. They assess governments on their capacity for interaction using social media; they do not assess actual engagements or outcomes achieved due to those engagements. This is a line of research that needs to be further developed. The emerging dissertation plans of Sarah Stoeckel and Wanzhu Shi will provide support of this much-needed agenda.

Third, there needs more theoretical development, including normative theories of how social tools can and ought to be used within the public sphere, as well as critical theories that consider the power imbalances that are created in a full or partially developed transparent environment. Despite the democratization of expertise, members of the academy will remain as having a special obligation to consider these issues and to communicate clearly with practitioners about both the opportunities and real dangers of using social media technologies for public purposes.

A Practitioner Agenda

Practitioners have their own special obligation to explore and experiment with emergent technologies. Scholars can advise but are is the people on the ground who will know on a daily basis what works, when, how, and often why. Experimentation, however, cannot be done on the cheap. Government and nonprofit agencies must strategically invest, incurring the costs of producing social processes using these technologies while mitigating costs to the institution of democracy itself.

In experimenting with new approaches, professionals should seek to partner with scholars, such as those who have written chapters for this book, to document the efforts. This will enable the development of the kinds of case study research that are necessary from the scholarly perspective. As we see in these chapters, there is already much experimentation happening; most, however, is happening under the radar and known only within the local communities or agencies in which it is being conducted. Partnership with university communities can help shine a light on new efforts and ideas, so that the broader community of governments and nonprofits can learn from what is happening on the ground—both the successes and mistakes. Indeed, when it comes to social media experimentation, we should adopt the notion from Dave Eggers's novel, *The Circle* (reported in Chapter 16), that sharing *everything* is essential.

Conclusion

Technologies are changing rapidly. Facebook and Twitter are the popular tools of 2015, and they may remain so for another year or two at most. Even if the brand of Facebook remains, the tool is likely to look considerably different in the not too distant future, or it might be supplanted by a social technology that is only now a tiny spark in the imagination of a high school student in the middle of the United States or elsewhere around the world. This book provides a state of the art in theory and practice for social media use in government, as well as nonprofit, organizations. The art will take new forms and shapes; as we have demonstrated the ability for integrating scholarly and practitioner voices within this book, so must we forge the same relations in developing, studying, and reporting on the next waves of social media development and implementation. We look forward to the journey.

About the Editors

Staci M. Zavattaro, Ph.D., is Associate Professor of Public Administration at the University of Central Florida. Her book, *Cities for Sale: Municipalities as Public Relations and Marketing Firms*, was released by SUNY Press in 2013. Her work appears in journals including *Urban Studies*, *Tourism Management*, *Government Information Quarterly*, *Place Branding and Public Diplomacy*, *Journal of Place Management and Development*, *Administrative Theory & Praxis*, and *Administration & Society*. Her research interests include administrative theory, place marketing, and organizational communication. Palgrave Macmillan published her book titled *Place Branding Through Phases of the Image*.

Thomas A. Bryer, Ph.D., is Associate Professor in the School of Public Administration, Director of the Public Administration track of the PhD in Public Affairs program, and Director of the Center for Public and Nonprofit Management at the University of Central Florida. He teaches primarily in the interdisciplinary Public Affairs doctoral program in the College of Health and Public Affairs. His research focuses on citizen participation, volunteerism, and collaboration across sectors. Professor Bryer has won multiple awards for his research, teaching, and service, has published in the top journals of his discipline, and is the author or editor of two additional books: *Higher Education beyond Job Creation: Universities, Citizenship, and Community* (2014, Lexington Books), and *National Service and Volunteerism: Achieving Impact in Our Communities* (2015, Lexington Books). In 2015, he received a Fulbright award for the study of citizen engagement in Lithuania, which he will implement over the course of three years beginning in fall 2015 at Kaunas University of Technology, and he was named a Visiting Professor at the Institute for Public Policy and Professional Practice at Edge Hill University (United Kingdom).

About the Contributors

Karabi C. Bezboruah, Ph.D., is a faculty member of the University of Texas at Arlington where she teaches courses in public administration and policy. Her research interests are in public and nonprofit management, and organizational behavior.

Lori A. Brainard, Ph.D., is Associate Professor at the Trachtenberg School of Public Policy and Public Administration at George Washington DC. Her research focuses on communications, in particular how citizens, government agencies, and nonprofit/grass-roots organizations use technologies to engage in public life.

Rowena L. Briones, Ph.D., is an Assistant Professor of Public Relations at the Richard T. Robertson School of Media & Culture. Her research agenda explores how social media and technology impact public relations and health communication in terms of campaign development and relationship building, particularly in the areas of sexual health, crisis communication, and risk communication. She has an extensive research record, with publications in top journals in the fields of public relations and health communication including *The Journal of Public Relations Research*, *Public Relations Review*, *PRism*, *Health Communication*, and *Journal of Health Communication*. She is currently an Affiliate Faculty Member of the Robertson School's Center for Media+Health, as well as the VCU's Institute for Women's Health, where she is a member of the Intimate Partner Violence/Sexual Assault Research Development Workgroup.

Lindsay Crudele is a digital communications strategist who served across two mayoral administrations as the City of Boston's first director of social media; she founded a pioneering, award-winning digital engagement program that helped transform the relationship between citizens and their government, through everyday engagement and historic crisis communication. She lives in Boston.

Martinella M. Dryburgh, Ph.D., is Director of the Posey Leadership Institute at Austin College in Sherman, Texas. Her research interests are focused on leadership and ethics in the digital age.

Nicole M. Rishel Elias, Ph.D., is an Assistant Professor in the Department of Public Management at John Jay College of Criminal Justice, CUNY and Research Fellow at the U.S. Equal Employment Opportunity Commission Office. Her research explores public representation and participation, and technology and governance with a particular focus on sex, gender, and race. She is the co-founder of Women in the Public Sector at John Jay College. Dr. Elias regularly works with practitioners at the federal level, and she served as the Lead Faculty Advisor to the U.S. Office of Personnel Management on the 2015 government-wide Inclusive Diversity Strategic Plan.

Peter S. Federman is a recent graduate of the Masters of Public Administration—Public Policy program at John Jay College of Criminal Justice, CUNY. During his MPA program, Mr. Federman presented at national and regional conferences and severed as a research assistant for two years. In 2015 he was awarded an ASPA Founder's Fellowship along with several academic honors from John Jay College, including the Institute for Criminal Justice Ethics Award, Graduate Research Scholarship, Young Scholars Award, and Carl Schreiber Memorial Award. In fall 2015, Mr. Federman will begin his Ph.D. in the Public Administration program at the University of Kansas where he was awarded the Chester A. Newland Fellowship.

Patricia C. Franks, Ph.D., CA, CRM, IGP, is the author of *Records and Information Management* and was team lead for ANSI/ARMA Standard *Implications of Web-based Collaborative Technologies in Records Management* and the technical report, *Using Social Media in Organizations*. She is co-editor of the *Encyclopedia of Archival Science*. As a member of the InterPARES Trust research team she leads two projects: *Social Media & Trust in Government* and *Retention and Disposition in a Cloud Environment*.

Suzanne L. Frew (The Frew Group) is an independent consultant in strategic communications, emergency management, and community resilience. Ms. Frew brings over 20 years of experience in planning, field operations, capacity building, and training and exercise. She has supported public and private sector and nongovernmental agency clients throughout the mainland U.S. and island jurisdictions, Canada, Asia Pacific, and Southeast Asia. She is passionate about implementing cross-cultural, innovative solutions for inclusive community outreach and multi-sector engagement for risk reduction.

Alisha Griswold is a nationally recognized preparedness trainer and disaster technologist. She is Founder and Chair of the Emerging Technology Caucus for the International Association of Emergency Managers, a technical adviser to the Homeland Security Center of Excellence, a member of the Virtual Social Media Working Group, a subsidiary of DHS Science and Technology, and trainer on behalf of the National Disaster Preparedness Training Center. Ms. Griswold is currently employed by the Port of Seattle where she creates custom crisis training and drills for a variety of disciplines and regional affiliates. She is a vocal proponent for inclusive preparedness strategies, evidence-based practices, and transparency in government.

Greg Higgerson, CFRE, is Vice President, Development at Second Harvest Food Bank of Central Florida. During his 19 years at Second Harvest, he has directed an ever-growing fundraising and marketing effort that has raised more than $65 million to help provide food for Central Florida's struggling individuals and families. Greg is a past President of the Central Florida Chapter of the Association of Fundraising Professionals (AFP), and was selected as Central Florida's "Outstanding Fundraising Professional' by that organization in 2008.

Melissa Janoske, Ph.D., is an Assistant Professor in the Journalism department at the University of Memphis, where she teaches public relations and crisis communication. Dr. Janoske has published research on both crisis and social media more generally, including expert recommendations for best practices in crisis communication, social media activism, and online communities and social networking. She earned her Ph.D. at the University of Maryland, where her dissertation was funded by the National Consortium for the Study of Terrorism and Responses to Terrorism (START), a Department of Homeland Security Center of Excellence. She earned her BS and MS from Radford University in Virginia. Dr. Janoske has also been a full-time instructor at Lynchburg College in Virginia, and is an active member of the Public Relations Society of America.

Warren Kagarise is the City of Issaquah's communications coordinator and is responsible for the city's engagement through traditional and digital media tools, including the city's website, social media platforms, and e-newsletter. In 2014, 3CMA (City–County Communications and Marketing Association) recognized the Communications team with a first-place Savvy Award for Most Creative Activity with Least Dollars Spent for a community-building Super Bowl celebration, and a national Award of Excellence for the city's Instagram account. Before joining the city, Warren worked as a journalist at the *Issaquah Press*, the community's newspaper of record. In 2011, he was honored by the Washington Newspaper Publishers Association as News Writer of the Year, the highest honor for a community journalist statewide. Warren, a University of Florida graduate, also worked as a journalist and public relations professional in his home state of Florida before relocating to Washington State.

Melissa Kear has been in the social media and online marketing field for more than seven years. Currently, she is the Online Marketing Coordinator for Second Harvest Food Bank of Central Florida and manages all of their social channels, creates content for distribution, and provides other creative services such as digital media production and design, and photography at the food bank.

Dave Krepcho joined the Second Harvest Food Bank of Central Florida in July 2004 as President and CEO. Dave earned his BA from Columbus College of Art & Design in Columbus, Ohio. In 1992, Dave became the Executive Director of the Miami Food Bank. Dave went on to work for Feeding America in Chicago, the nation's largest hunger relief organization. He served as the Vice President of Business Development, responsible for all product donations and relationships with the national food industry. Dave was also responsible for developing national programs designed to obtain more food for the 205 member food banks across the United States. During his time with Feeding America, Dave led a team that acquired 450 million pounds of donated food annually.

Stephanie Madden is currently a doctoral candidate at the University of Maryland studying the intersection of activism, nonprofit communication, risk/crisis communication, and social media. Prior to starting her Ph.D., she was a full-time communication researcher at the National Consortium for the Study of Terrorism and Responses to Terrorism (START), a Department of Homeland Security Center of Excellence. She earned her M.A. in Communication from the University of Maryland, and her B.A. in Communication Studies from Vanderbilt University.

Cayce Myers, Ph.D., LL.M., J.D. is an Assistant Professor at Virginia Tech in the Department of Communication. Dr. Myers's research focuses on public relations and the law, particularly the area of federal agency regulation of online promotional content. He received his Ph.D. in mass communication from the University of Georgia Grady College of Journalism and Mass Communication, his LL.M. in media law from the University of Georgia School of Law, and his J.D. from Mercer University Walter F. George School of Law.

Ray Parr currently serves as a Personnel Psychologist with the U.S. Office of Personnel Management in the Office of Diversity and Inclusion, which leads and manages the government-wide diversity and inclusion (D&I) effort. His research and publications have focused on the impact diverse interpersonal relationships can have on individuals' attitudes and beliefs. He has a B.S. in Psychology and Applied Statistics from Sonoma State University, M.S. in Industrial Organizational Psychology from San Francisco State University, and Business Psychology Certificate from London Metropolitan University.

Arthur J. Sementelli, Ph.D., is an Associate Professor and Ph.D. program coordinator for the School of Public Administration, Florida Atlantic University. He is the Associate Editor of *Administrative Theory and Praxis* and the Managing Editor of the *International Journal of Organization Theory and Behavior*. His research interests include environmental and resource management, public sector economics, critical theory, and organization studies.

Maria Shanley currently works at Second Harvest Food Bank of Central Florida as Digital Marketing Manager. She oversees the website, online fundraising, social media outlets, blog posts, and email communications. Her task is to get Second Harvest Food Bank news out to you through all possible web channels. Maria has over 10 years of experience working with Convio/Blackbaud online tools. She graduated from the University of Central Florida with a

Marketing degree. Prior to working at Second Harvest, Maria worked at PBS/NPR affiliate WMFE, another nonprofit in the Orlando area.

Stephanie H. Slater became the Boynton Beach Police Department's Public Information Officer in April 2007, following seven years as a crime reporter for the *Palm Beach Post* and *Boca Raton News*. A New York native, Slater is a graduate of the S.I. Newhouse School of Public Communications at Syracuse University, where she majored in print journalism. She serves as president of the National Public Information Officers Association, and is former secretary of the Florida Law Enforcement Public Information Officers Association. She is a frequent guest speaker about law enforcement's use of social media, has contributed to several books about government's use of social media, and served on a panel that helped develop a model social media policy for the International Association of Chiefs of Police.

Alan Steinberg is a Postdoctoral Fellow in the Department of Political Science at Sam Houston State University. His research agenda centers on how advances in technology are changing the face of political engagement, focusing on space and science technology, emergency and disaster management, and voting behavior. His current research explores how social media tools allow for new and enhanced avenues for civic participation and leadership.

Clayton Wukich, Ph.D., is an Assistant Professor in the Department of Political Science at Sam Houston State University. His research interests include intergovernmental relations and collaborative governance, particularly within the policy domain of disaster and emergency management. His research focuses on how public sector and nonprofit organizations use information and communication technology to increase public participation and interagency coordination.

Index

Page numbers in *italics* denote tables, those in **bold** denote figures.